Perspectives on Children's Testimony

S.J. Ceci   D.F. Ross   M.P. Toglia
Editors

Perspectives on Children's Testimony

Springer-Verlag
New York   Berlin   Heidelberg
London   Paris   Tokyo

Stephen J. Ceci
Department of Human Development
  and Family Studies
Cornell University
Ithaca, New York 14853-4401, U.S.A.

David F. Ross
Department of Human Development
  and Family Studies
Cornell University
Ithaca, New York 14853-4401, U.S.A.

Michael P. Toglia
Department of Psychology
State University of New York–
  Cortland
Cortland, New York 13045, U.S.A.

With 6 Figures

Library of Congress Cataloging-in-Publication Data
Perspectives on children's testimony / Stephen J. Ceci, David F. Ross,
  Michael P, Toglia, editors.
  p.   cm.
  Bibliography: p.
  Includes indexes.
  ISBN 0-387-96864-4
   1. Children as witnesses—United States.   2. Psychology, Forensic.
I. Ceci, Stephen J.   II. Ross, David F., 1959– .   III. Toglia,
Michael P.
KF9672.P47   1988
345.73′066′08805—dc19
[347.30566088054]   88-26567

Printed on acid-free paper

Typeset by Asco Trade Typesetting Ltd., Hong Kong.
Printed and bound by Edwards Brothers, Inc., Ann Arbor, Michigan.
Printed in the United States of America.

9 8 7 6 5 4 3 2 1

ISBN 0-387-96864-4 Springer-Verlag New York Berlin Heidelberg
ISBN 3-540-96864-4 Springer-Verlag Berlin Heidelberg New York

Preface

This volume is the second in a series that deals with child witnesses. Our first volume, *Children's Eyewitness Memory* (1987), was primarily concerned with issues surrounding the veracity and durability of children's recollections. It grew out of an APA symposium we organized in 1985, to coincide with an important trend in the American legal system, namely, increasing numbers of young children being called on to offer testimony in juvenile and criminal proceedings. At that time, we had little empirical knowledge about what factors influence children's recollections, especially as they relate to the law. Since then, there has been a steady accretion of knowledge on this topic—some of it sparked by that volume. The current volume, *Perspectives on Children's Testimony*, focuses on adults' attributions about child witnesses. It is an outgrowth of a symposium we organized for the biennial meeting of the Society for Research in Child Development in 1987. Among the many lacunae in our knowledge about child witnesses is how they are perceived by jurors. At present, little research has been directed to this issue. We hope that this volume makes a modest beginning toward filling this gap.

Perspectives on Children's Testimony contains current empirical research on factors that affect adults' (e.g., jurors', judges', and attorneys') perceptions of the child witness. These factors include characteristics of the child witnesses themselves, such as their age and speech style, as well as adults' beliefs concerning children's memory capabilities, including whether or not the child's testimony is "scripted" (i.e., whether it is a prepared script of their testimony or their own words). The book is designed to provide researchers, criminal justice workers, attorneys, judges, psychiatrists, and psychologists with knowledge about adult beliefs regarding child witnesses and how these beliefs may influence verdicts. A variety of new techniques are employed in assessing adult views of the child witness. This volume includes several special features. In addition to the contributions on adult perception, the volume includes one chapter that treats in-depth the techniques for interviewing child victims of sexual abuse and two other chapters that provide invited commentaries, one by a legal specialist affiliated with the American Bar Association and the other by an experimental social psychologist who specializes in psycholegal issues. Both commentators have prepared critical/theoretical integrations of the empirical chapters; one provides interesting insights into the impact of current research on the child witness on sexual abuse prosecutions and the other suggests how these findings can be incorporated into a larger sociopsychological framework. Also of interest are two chapters devoted to an examination of children's perceptions and knowledge of the American legal system. These features help make this volume a resource for those who work with children and the law.

It has become a convention to acknowledge in the Preface the shortcomings of a volume while boasting of its strengths. The present volume's main shortcoming has to do with the applicability of the findings to juvenile and criminal justice proceedings. When we invited the contributors to write chapters, we asked that they describe their most recent empirical research on this topic without stipulating that the research be "applied." This was no oversight. We firmly believe that science and policy are intellectually separate enterprises and ought not be wed by fiat. Our volume is eclectic in this regard; some chapters are quite relevant to current legal practices and others less so. For example, several of the jury simulations reported here employ adults chosen from the community who resemble actual jurors demographically. And the mock trials are based on actual trial transcripts, with actual attorneys and judges playing their respective roles. Other chapters, however, employ far less realism, using student jurors, abbreviated (written) transcripts rather than video or live, and so forth. Is one approach better than the other? Well, one is far closer to application than the other. But that is not the sole, or even main, criterion for making this judgment, nor should it be. As scientists, we believe knowledge is an incremental process that slowly builds over time. A headlong rush to become ecologically valid and "applied" can result in a predominance of studies that focus on aspects of cases that are most congenial to applied research paradigms but ignore the more difficult basic mechanisms that need to be illuminated to permit a complete understanding.

Thus, we are not disappointed that some of these chapters contain descriptions of basic sociopsychological and cognitive mechanisms that underpin adults' attitudes about children; in fact, we are heartened by their inclusion. But they need to be recognized for what they are—namely, the beginning of a scientific struggle to gain a complete understanding. Once the basic mechanisms are known, the next generation of research can capitalize on these insights as a starting point for the next round of studies, until finally the end product is of practical relevance. This reflects our "logical positivist" interpretation of how science builds toward an understanding of a phenomenon. And if our own experience is anything to go on, this is what will happen in the aftermath of this volume, because it is precisely what we witnessed in our first volume. At that time commentators with a strong applied orientation were concerned that much of the research literature lacked ecological validity. Now two years later, we see a plethora of studies that are characterized by their ecological validity. It is exciting to witness this building process, and these new studies appear to be quite relevant for practitioners. But the first steps in this process (the conduct of basic research) cannot be ignored, and often it is best studied within the constraints of a laboratory context.

Attorneys who are involved with child victim-witnesses know how harrowing and difficult such an experience can be. In addition to the fears surrounding the examination and cross-examination of child witnesses (e.g., fear of revictimizing the child), there is an overriding concern about judges' and jurors' reactions to the child's performance. We found very little that would help one predict how adults viewed child witnesses. Although there is still much we need to know before our understanding is complete, we are beginning to fathom the mind and attitudes of adults toward children. The picture is a complex one, as the reader will soon see.

Ithaca, NY

Stephen J. Ceci
David F. Ross
Michael P. Toglia

Contents

Contributors

JOSEPHINE A. BULKLEY, American
Bar Association, 5304
Wapakoneta Road, Bethesda,
MD 20816, USA

STEPHEN J. CECI, Department of
Human Development and Family
Studies, Martha Van Rensselaer
Hall, Cornell University, Ithaca,
NY 14853-4401, USA

DAVID DUNNING, Department of
Psychology, Cornell University,
Uris Hall, Ithaca, NY 14853, USA

GAIL S. GOODMAN, Department of
Psychology, State University of
New York–Buffalo, Buffalo, NY
14226, USA

MICHAEL R. LEIPPE, Department of
Psychology, Adelphi University,
Garden City, NY 11530, USA

MURRAY LEVINE, Department of
Psychology, SUNY–Buffalo,
Buffalo, NY 14226, USA

GEORGIA N. NIGRO, Department of
Psychology, Bates College,
Lewiston, ME 04246, USA

DAVID C. RASKIN, Department of
Psychology, University of Utah,
Salt Lake City, UT 84112, USA

DAVID F. ROSS, Department of
Human Development and Family
Studies, Martha Van Rensselaer
Hall, Cornell University, Ithaca,
NY 14853-4401, USA

KAREN J. SAYWITZ, Department of
Psychiatry, Harbor/U.C.L.A.,
1000 West Carson Street,
Torrance, CA 90509, USA

MICHAEL P. TOGLIA, Department of
Psychology, State University of
New York–Cortland, Cortland,
NY 13045, USA

AMYE WARREN-LEUBECKER,
Department of Psychology, 350
Holt Hall, University of
Tennessee–Chattanooga,
Chattanooga, TN 37403, USA

GARY L. WELLS, Department of
Psychology, Iowa State
University, Ames, IA 50011,
USA

* Senior authors.

1
Determinants of the Child Victim's Perceived Credibility

GAIL S. GOODMAN, BETTE L. BOTTOMS, BARBARA B. HERSCOVICI, and PHILLIP SHAVER

It is heartbreaking to realize that children fall victim to crime. We like to think of childhood as a time of innocence, trust, and protection. Yet children are not immune from assault. To protect children from the dangers of such crimes as child abuse, murder, sexual exploitation, and kidnapping, legal action is often required. If legal action results in a trial, a child may be required to take the stand (Goodman, Jones et al., 1988).

When a child testifies, whether or not justice is done may depend largely on jurors' perceptions of the child's credibility. Although the credibility of any victim/witness may be questioned, there are reasons to expect that children's credibility will be of particular concern. Jurors may believe that children's memory is relatively poor and that they are easily coached. Alternatively, jurors may assume children are inherently honest and too naive to make false reports. Regardless of the specific position taken, such "theories" about the abilities of children are likely to affect their perceived credibility. The question of how jurors' theories about children's abilities affect the perceived credibility of a particular child witness is explored in this chapter. As a starting point, we assume that most jurors hold at least two kinds of theories and that these influence their perceptions of children's credibility as witnesses (see also Goodman, Golding, & Haith, 1984). One theory is that children are generally as honest as adults, if not more honest—a theory that might predispose jurors to believe child witnesses. The second theory is that young children's cognitive abilities are less developed than those of adults, which might be expected to lead jurors to question children's testimony under many conditions.

We propose, however, that the second theory does not necessarily lead to a devaluing of children's statements. Rather, it can lead jurors to believe

The research described in this chapter was funded in part by a grant to Gail S. Goodman from the National Center on Child Abuse and Neglect. We are grateful to Thomas Dunn, Arapahoe County District Attorney's Office, Denver, Co, and Kenneth Gordon, private practice, Denver, Co, for serving as the attorneys in Experiment 1.

children at some times and to disbelieve them at other times. Whether a child's credibility is weakened or strengthened by jurors' adherence to the second theory depends on how jurors' views of children interact with the details of a particular case. Moreover, at some age—probably late in childhood or during adolescence—the cognitive abilities children need to testify accurately about most events start to converge with the relevant cognitive abilities of adults. At this point, barring specific reasons to suspect dishonesty, the presumption that children are more honest than adults may lead to perceptions of heightened credibility for children.

To support these claims, we review current work on jurors' perceptions of child witnesses. We then describe two recent experiments on determinants of jurors' perceptions of child victim/witnesses. In one experiment, we investigated jurors' abilities to evaluate the accuracy of children's testimony. That is, we examined whether jurors can distinguish between accurate and inaccurate testimony given by a child. In the second experiment, we examined jurors' theories about child versus adult victim/witnesses. Both experiments focused on the credibility of child victim/witnesses, but in relation to two very different kinds of trials, one concerned with malpractice and the other with sexual assault.

Research on Jurors' Perceptions of Child Witnesses

Until recently, few studies were concerned with jurors' perceptions of child witnesses. This area of research is now expanding rapidly; unfortunately, the findings from current studies are not entirely consistent.

A number of studies indicate that child witnesses are viewed as less credible than adult witnesses. Goodman, Golding, Helgeson, Haith, and Michelli (1987; see also Goodman & Michelli, 1981; Goodman et al., 1984) conducted three experiments in which mock jurors read about or heard the testimony of a six-, ten-, or thirty-year-old bystander eyewitness. Regardless of whether the testimony was presented in written form or on videotape, whether the subjects were undergraduate students or adults from the Denver community, or whether the trial concerned vehicular homicide or murder, mock jurors rated the six-year-olds as less credible witnesses than the thirty-year-olds. The credibility of the ten-year-olds fell between that of the other two age groups. Surprisingly, however, there were no significant effects of eyewitness age on mock jurors' judgments of guilt in any of the three studies.

Similarly, Leippe and Romanczyk (1987) report that bystander witness credibility increases with age from childhood to adulthood. Descriptions of a robbery-murder case were read by college students. The age of the key eyewitness was six, ten, or thirty years. The amount of incriminating evidence was also varied. The results duplicate those of Goodman et al.

(1987). Specifically, Leippe and Romanczyk found that the thirty-year-old eyewitness was viewed as more credible than the six-year-old. The ten-year-old's credibility fell between that of the other two witnesses. No significant main effect of eyewitness age on guilt ratings was found.

Interestingly, however, the amount of incriminating evidence affected the jurors' ratings of the defendant's guilt. When the incriminating evidence was weak or moderate, age differences were not found to affect verdicts, perhaps because a substantial majority of jurors voted "not guilty" based on lack of evidence. When the incriminating evidence was strong, the age of the eyewitness mattered. Under these conditions, the thirty-year-old's testimony resulted in 100 percent of the jurors rating the defendant as guilty, while the six- and ten-year-olds' testimonies resulted in only 58 percent of the jurors (for both ages) rating the defendant as guilty.

In a second experiment, Leippe and Romanczyk (1987) varied the age as well as the consistency of witness testimony. College students read a description of a mugging followed by murder. The sole eyewitness was a six-, ten-, or thirty-year-old onlooker. The onlooker later provided testimony that was either consistent or inconsistent over time. Leippe and Romanczyk found that testimonial consistency did not significantly affect the credibility of the ten- and thirty-year-old eyewitnesses but did significantly affect the credibility of the six-year-old. The consistent six-year-old was judged to be more credible than the inconsistent 6-year-old.

In contrast to the findings of Goodman et al. and Leippe and Romanczyk that children are viewed as less credible than adults, several other researchers report that children are seen as no less credible and may, in fact, be seen as more credible than adults. Ross, Miller, and Moran (1987) asked college students to watch a videotape of a simulated trial. The trial concerned a narcotics case in which a woman had been arrested for possession of cocaine. The key eyewitness, who was described as being either eight, twenty-one, or seventy-four years of age, testified for the prosecution that the cocaine had been in the woman's house for some time. The mock jurors rated witnesses on a variety of dimensions (e.g., accuracy, confidence, credibility, and truthfulness). No significant age effect on witness credibility was found: The eight-year-old was rated just as credible as the two adults. The eight-year-old was viewed as more accurate, intelligent, forceful, competent, consistent, and truthful than the twenty-one-year-old. The ratings for the seventy-four- and eight-year-old witnesses did not differ.

A few points concerning the Ross et al. study should be made. First, the particular case they used may have affected their findings. Jurors may have believed that the twenty-one-year-old was somehow involved in the drug deal whereas the eight- and seventy-four-year-olds were not. This interpretation of their findings fits well with our contention that children's credibility will vary as a function of case factors. Second, it is possible that the individuals who played the role of the key eyewitness were not representative of their age groups. This would explain the counterintuitive finding that the eight-year-old was judged as more intelligent, forceful, and competent than the twenty-one-year-old. Again, this possibility points to the many factors that can determine a child's perceived credibility in an actual case.

Johnson (1986) attempted to replicate the study by Goodman et al. (1984). Unlike these researchers, however, he presented the trial scenario on audiotape and varied the amount of contradictory evidence presented. Instead of the witnesses' credibility increasing with age, age had no effect. Like Ross et al., Johnson found that the child witness was actually judged to be somewhat more truthful and unbiased than the adult witness. Nigro, Buckley, Hill, and Nelson (this volume) also used the scenario developed by Goodman et al. to investigate jurors' impressions of child versus adult witnesses. The key eyewitness was described as either eight or twenty-five years old. Nigro et al. also varied the powerfulness of the witness's speech style. Subject-jurors rated the eight-year-old who used a powerful speech style as the most credible witness.

How can we explain the inconsistencies across these several studies? One possibility has to do with jurors' theories of children's honesty and cognitive abilities. In the Ross et al. and Nigro et al. studies, the youngest witness was eight years old. Perhaps jurors believe that children of this age are similar to adults in the cognitive abilities and relevant experience required to provide accurate testimony in the cases described. This possibility would explain why Goodman et al. and Leippe and Romanczyk tended not to find age differences between the credibility of ten- and thirty-year-old eyewitnesses. The belief that older children are reliable witnesses appeared in the literature as early as 1910, when Gross, a German judge, stated that a "healthy half grown boy" is the best possible witness for simple events (as cited by Whipple, 1912). The belief that older children are likely to have accurate memories for simple events, combined with the belief that children are basically honest, may have led to the findings of Ross et al. and Nigro et al.

Another possible explanation for the inconsistent findings across studies is implied by Leippe and Romanczyk's results. The amount of incriminating evidence may alter jurors' perceptions of a child's credibility. Thus, Johnson's inability to replicate the Goodman et al. study may be a result of differences in the amount of corroborating information presented. In any case, the fact that Johnson's subjects viewed the child witness as more truthful and unbiased than the adult witness points again to the belief that children are particularly honest witnesses.

In this chapter, we focus on the first possibility—that is, that jurors' theories about children's cognitive abilities and relevant experience can lead to different evaluations of their credibility. To develop this argument, we present findings from two recent experiments.

main idea

Juror's Ability to Discriminate between Accurate and Inaccurate Testimony

Recent research indicates that children, by at least the age of four years, can be quite accurate in reporting the main actions witnessed or experienced in real-life events (e.g., Goodman & Aman, 1987; Goodman, Aman, & Hirschman, 1987; Goodman & Reed, 1986; Marin, Holmes, Guth, & Kovac, 1979). Young children are also surprisingly resistant to suggestive questions concerning actions associated with abuse, such as being hit or having one's clothes removed (Goodman, Hirschman, & Rudy, 1987; Rudy, 1986). Yet, if jurors cannot distinguish accurate from inaccurate testimony, the child's accuracy is of little consequence. In fact, Wigmore (1909) argued that the crucial issue for psychological research on eyewitness testimony is not witness accuracy but the factfinder's ability to reach the truth (see also Melton & Thompson, 1987). With two exceptions (Leippe & Romanczyk, 1987; Wells, Turtle, & Luus, this volume), research on this matter has been limited to jurors' ability to distinguish accurate from inaccurate testimony given by adult bystander witnesses.

In a recent review of the literature on jurors' ability to reach the truth, Wells (1985) concluded that "there is no evidence supporting the view that people are good at evaluating the accuracy of eyewitness testimony under various conditions" (p. 60). This conclusion was based on a number of studies indicating that jurors cannot distinguish between accurate and inaccurate adult witnesses.

Two different experimental procedures have been used to investigate this issue. One involves asking subject-jurors to read descriptions of published research studies and predict the results. For example, Brigham and Bothwell (1983) asked randomly selected registered voters to read a scenario from a study by Leippe, Wells, and Ostrom (1978) dealing with a calculator theft and a scenario from a study by Brigham, Maass, Snyder, and Spaulding (1982) dealing with a customer's activities in a convenience store. In both studies (Leippe et al. and Brigham et al.), witnesses had attempted to identify the confederate from photo lineups. Brigham and Bothwell found that 70 to 91 percent of the registered voters overestimated witnesses' ability to identify the confederates.

Leippe and Romanczyk (1987) conducted a similar study, but one that investigated adult predictions of children's testimony. College students read about a brief (15-second) argument between an experimenter and an intruder, a scenario taken from a study by Marin et al. (1979). In that study, the argument was witnessed by individuals from one of four age groups—kindergartners and first graders, third and fourth graders, seventh and eighth graders, and college students. Contrary to the findings of Brigham and Bothwell, Leippe and Romanczyk report that subjects underestimated the accuracy of the witnesses. Of particular concern were subjects' estimates of accuracy as a function of eyewitness age. Leippe and Romanczyk's subjects did not believe there would be age differences in accuracy on a photo identification of the intruder but did believe there would be age differences in the accuracy of answering questions about the intruder and the event. In fact, Marin et al. did not find significant age differences on either measure.

The second experimental procedure used to investigate jurors' abilities to estimate the accuracy of eyewitness testimony has been championed by Wells (Lindsay, Wells, & Rumpel, 1981; Wells, Ferguson, & Lindsay, 1981; Wells & Leippe, 1981; Wells, Lindsay, & Ferguson, 1979; Wells, Lindsay, & Tousignant, 1980). This procedure has greater ecological validity than the first, in that mock jurors actually see witnesses testify about an event. For example, Wells, Lindsay, and Ferguson (1979) staged a theft that was witnessed by college students. The students were asked to identify the culprit from a photo lineup and were then cross-examined in front of mock jurors. The mock jurors were unable to distinguish accurate from inaccurate witnesses.

In other studies of this sort, Wells and his colleagues found that, regardless of accuracy, jurors are much more likely to believe confident than nonconfident witnesses (Lindsay et al., 1981; Wells & Leippe, 1981; Wells et al., 1979; Wells et al., 1980). For example, when viewing conditions for witnesses were varied so that some witnesses had a good opportunity to see the culprit while others did not, subject-jurors still placed great emphasis on the witnesses' confidence in assessing their statements; confident witnesses were believed to the same extent regardless of viewing conditions (Lindsay et al., 1981).

In this volume, Wells et al. report a study of mock jurors' abilities to estimate the accuracy of child versus adult witnesses. Adults and eight- and twelve-year-old children viewed a brief videotape of a kidnapping. The next day each witness was subjected to direct- and cross-examination by two researchers. Videotapes of these interviews were then shown to college students. Wells et al. found that jurors were fairly accurate in estimating the witnesses' accuracy except in one case: they underestimated the eight-year-olds' suggestibility.

In summary, research on jurors' ability to discriminate between accurate and inaccurate testimony indicates that subject-jurors often overestimate the accuracy of adult eyewitness testimony, placing too much emphasis on the confidence of witnesses. They may also overestimate children's ability to resist suggestion. In contrast, at least on some tasks (e.g., answering questions about a witnessed event), the abilities of child witnesses may be underestimated. It is important to note, however, that the few studies dealing with predictions of children's accuracy (Leippe & Romanczyk, 1987; Wells et al., this volume) examined bystander witnesses. Children who testify in court, however, are more likely to be victim/witnesses. Jurors' ability to predict the accuracy of a child's statements may differ depending on whether the child experienced an event or merely observed it. In the following section we describe the first study conducted on jurors' ability to distinguish between accurate and inaccurate testimony provided by child victim/witnesses.

Experiment 1: "Do You Remember the Last Time You Went to the Doctor?"

In this study, we were concerned with subject-jurors' impressions of the accuracy of testimony given by young children who had experienced a stressful event, receiving an inoculation at a medical clinic. The study included three phases. In Phase 1, children were surreptitiously videotaped while receiving shots from a nurse as part of their regular medical care. The subjects ranged in age from three to six years and came from families of relatively low socioeconomic status. Three to four or seven to nine days later, the children's memory for the event was tested. The results of the initial phase have been reported elsewhere (Goodman, Aman, & Hirschman, 1987) and are described here only briefly. The children were very accurate in recalling what happened, although their reports were often sketchy. Age differences were found in the ability to answer objective and suggestive questions accurately. Finally, children's ability to recognize the nurse in a six-person photo lineup was relatively poor, especially for the three-year-olds, whose performance fell to chance levels following a seven- to nine-day delay period. The children's parents, however, were just as unsuccessful in identifying the nurse.

The second phase was conducted at a university law school and involved direct- and cross-examination of five of the children nine to twelve months after their visit to the medical clinic. The children were screened to ensure that they had not returned to the clinic and had not received another shot. The long delay period was chosen to mimic the time that often passes between initial interviews by police or other authorities and testimony in actual trials. A prosecutor and a defense attorney from the community, both of whom had worked with real child witnesses, volunteered to direct- and cross-examine the children. For purposes of the study, the two men alternated roles as prosecutor and defense attorney.

Each parent–child dyad was individually brought to a moot courtroom at the law school. Upon arrival, the child was told that a set of questions would be asked about what happened the last time he or she got a shot. The child was then given a second memory test identical to the one given months before. This memory test helped to remind the child of the event in question. No feedback concerning the correctness of the child's responses was provided.

The "prosecutor" then entered the moot courtroom, greeted the family, and explained to the child what would happen. Specifically, he said that the

TABLE 1.1 Sample direct- and cross-examination questions (Experiment 1).

Direct-Examination Questions

What happened the last time you went to the doctor's office?
Was the person who gave you the shot a man or a woman?
Had you ever seen that person before that day?
I'm going to show you some photographs. Is the person who gave you the shot in these photographs?
Did you take your clothes off?
Did she make you swallow anything?
Did she hit you?
Did the person use one of these things on you that day? (attorney holds up a stethoscope)

Cross-Examination Questions

Have you ever seen the Easter bunny?
When was the last time the tooth fairy was at your house?
What did the nurse look like?
What did the doctor look like?*
Was there a refrigerator in the room?
How many chairs were in the room?
The truth is, you don't really remember who it was who gave you the shot, do you?*
What were you wearing that day?

* Suggestive questions.

child would be seated at the witness stand and be interviewed by himself and another attorney. He also explained that the child should tell the truth in response to all questions and indicated that it was fine to say "I don't know" if the child could not answer a question.

The child then took a seat at the witness stand, while her or his parents sat in the audience. The child was first asked a set of direct-examination questions by the prosecutor. As part of the direct examination, a six-person photo lineup that included the nurse was shown to the child and the child was asked if the nurse was pictured in it. The man playing the role of the defense attorney then asked a series of cross-examination questions. The cross-examination began with questions concerning the child's ability to distinguish fantasy from reality. For example, the child was asked if he or she had ever seen the Easter bunny. The child was then questioned more generally about the inoculation episode, and an average of six misleading questions (range four to six) were included.

While the attorneys were given some freedom to ask for clarification from the child and to follow the child's lead, the questioning generally conformed to a preestablished script that had been agreed on at an earlier meeting. It included some of the same questions that had appeared in the initial and delayed memory tests, in addition to a number of new questions. Sample questions from the script are presented in Table 1.1. At the completion of questioning, the child was thanked and given a toy. Phase 2 was videotaped in its entirety.

The children's responses were scored in terms of their accuracy in (1) answering the questions and (2) identifying the nurse. The children's overall scores in answering the questions ranged from about 50 to 70 percent correct. On the photo identification task, one of the five children accurately identified the nurse, who was pictured in photograph 1; one incorrectly chose the person pictured in photograph 5; two were unable to identify anyone; and one indicated some awareness of the correct nurse (i.e., said she had seen that nurse "at another doctor's office"). For purposes of analysis, the latter three children were grouped into an intermediate category.

Phase 3 consisted of showing the videotapes of the children answering the direct- and cross-examination questions to 100 college students who served as mock jurors. Twenty individuals (twelve females and eight males) were randomly assigned to view each of the videotapes.

Before viewing the videotape, each individual was asked to read a one-page description of a case involving a civil suit. The description stated that the child's parents had brought a medical malpractice suit against a nurse for giving their child an unauthorized shot that resulted in significant physical injuries. The nurse claimed that she had not given the child a shot and the child was confusing that visit to the clinic with a visit to a different clinic during which the child had received a shot. The nurse also claimed that the injuries to the child were sustained as a result of an undisputed fall, which had occurred within a day or two of the child's visit to the medical clinic.

Within each group, the subject-jurors were randomly assigned to one of two "defendant" conditions. Specifically, half of the jurors were told that the accused nurse was pictured in photograph 1 of the photo lineup; the other half were told that the accused nurse was pictured in photograph 5. In fact, the correct nurse was always pictured in photograph 1. The defendant condition was introduced to corroborate or refute the child's testimony. In an actual trial, a defendant would be seated before the jury, and whether or not the child could identify that person would be of critical importance.

Jurors were then shown the videotape of one of the children. Following that, each juror was asked to complete a questionnaire concerning the child's accuracy in answering questions about the nurse's physical appearance, the room, the actions that took place, and the timing of the event; the child's suggestibility, truthfulness, consistency, confidence, intelligence, attractiveness, and ability to distinguish fantasy from reality; the child's ability to correctly identify the nurse; the effects of stress on the child's accuracy; and how capable, compared with an adult, the child was of providing accurate testimony and how likely it was that the child had actually received a shot at the clinic. Finally, the jurors were asked to make a global rating of the child's credibility as a witness and a judgment about the defendant's innocence or guilt.

Preliminary analyses of the jurors' ratings revealed few sex differences or differences associated with defendant condition (nurse 1 vs. nurse 5). The following findings were collapsed across these factors.

The first question of interest was whether the jurors could distinguish between accurate and inaccurate testimony. To examine this question, correlations were computed between the children's actual accuracy scores and the jurors' perceived credibility scores as assessed on the global credibility question. These correlations revealed that the jurors were unable to discriminate between accurate and inaccurate testimony. Specifically, the correlation between the children's actual accuracy in answering the objective and the misleading questions and the jurors' ratings of the children's overall credibility was only $-.12$. The correlation between the children's actual ability to identify the nurse and jurors' ratings of overall credibility was $-.14$.

Although the jurors' impressions of the children's credibility were not reliably influenced by the children's accuracy, they were influenced by their age. The correlation between the jurors' overall credibility ratings and the child witness's age was .32 ($p < .001$). (All significance tests were two-tailed.) As it turned out, because of the children who happened to be included in the study, their accuracy in answering the questions and their age were actually *inversely* related ($r = -.26$, n.s. with $n = 5$). Thus, the jurors seemed to be assuming that the older children were more accurate witnesses when in fact they were not. On the photo identification task, the children's age and their accuracy were also negatively related ($r = -.85$, $p < .05$ with $n = 5$). Nevertheless, as was pointed out earlier, jurors were unable to discriminate between accurate and inaccurate performance on this task. (In addition, accuracy on the photo identification task was essentially uncorrelated with accuracy in answering the questions; $r = -.13$.)

To summarize, jurors' impressions of credibility were virtually independent of children's actual accuracy but were positively correlated with witness age. In addition, it is worth noting that, on average, the children's perceived credibility was low. The perceived credibility ratings ranged from "very uncredible" to "somewhat credible"; the most accurate child— a four-year-old who correctly identified the nurse and answered 70 percent of the questions correctly—was rated as "very uncredible."

To further explore determinants of jurors' impressions, their responses to individual questions were entered into a principal components analysis followed by varimax rotation. Five factors emerged, corresponding to the jurors' estimates of (1) the children's accuracy and confidence in answering the questions, (2) the children's suggestibility, consistency, and truthfulness, (3) the children's accuracy in identifying the nurse from the photo lineup, (4) the children's ability to provide accurate testimony (compared with an adult), as well as the effects of stress on their memory, and (5) the children's attractiveness.

TABLE 1.2 Correlations between child's age and perceived credibility measures (Experiment 1).

Perceived accuracy/confidence	.35**
Perceived suggestibility	−.04
Perceived consistency	.03
Perceived truthfulness	.23*
Perceived identification accuracy	.01
Perceived accuracy compared to that of an adult	.21*
Perceived effects of stress	.08
Perceived attractiveness	.11

*$p < .05$, two-tailed.
**$p < .01$, two-tailed.

Coefficient alphas were calculated to determine whether the factors formed coherent multi-item scales. Only the questions concerning the children's accuracy and confidence in answering the questions did so (alpha = .86). This scale is referred to as the perceived accuracy/confidence scale. The remaining items were analyzed separately rather than in scale form.

Table 1.2 presents the correlation between the perceived accuracy/confidence scale and the age of the child witness, as well as correlations between the remaining items and the age of the witness. As can be seen, the perceived accuracy/confidence scale was significantly related to age, as were the items concerning the child's truthfulness and her or his capability of providing accurate testimony compared with that of an adult.

Wells et al. (1979) have found that an adult witness's confidence has a powerful effect on perceived credibility. Correlations between ratings of the child's confidence, on the one hand, and the child's perceived overall credibility and the guilt ratings, on the other, were therefore examined. Taken alone, the child's perceived confidence correlated significantly with the child's perceived credibility ($r = .40$, $p < .01$) and with the jurors' impressions of the defendant's guilt ($r = .23$, $p < .05$). In reality, however, the children's perceived confidence and their accuracy in answering the attorneys' questions were not reliably related ($r = .09$), nor were children's perceived confidence and accuracy in identifying the nurse ($r = −.04$). Thus, it seems that jurors' impressions of confidence biased their ratings of witness credibility and defendant guilt.

It was also of interest to determine how the children's age and perceived credibility related to the subject-jurors' determinations of guilt or innocence. No significant relation between age and guilt was found ($r = .05$). Stepwise multiple regression analyses were conducted in which the child's age, the perceived accuracy/confidence scale, the child's actual accuracy in answering questions and identifying the nurse, the child's ability to answer the fantasy versus reality questions, and the remaining items from the jurors' questionnaire were entered in an attempt to predict the jurors' impressions of the defendant's innocence or guilt. The only significant predictor was the jurors' score on the perceived accuracy/confidence scale (beta = .42, $t = 4.57$, $p < .001$). Thus, as other studies (e.g., Goodman et al., 1984) have found, witness age alone did not directly affect judgments of a defendant's guilt.

The findings of this study indicated that subject-jurors were unable to discriminate between accurate and inaccurate testimony presented by child victim/witnesses. A significant part of the subject-jurors' judgments were, instead, based on the child's age, although age was not the sole determinant. The child's perceived accuracy and confidence also substantially contributed to jurors' determinations of a child's credibility. The age of the children did not directly determine how guilty or innocent the defendant was perceived to be.

The Effects of Age on Jurors' Perceptions of Children's Credibility in a Sexual Assault Case

Experiment 1 indicates that jurors are biased to assume that older children are more credible witnesses than younger children. But is this always the case? Our thesis is that children are viewed as less credible than adults to the extent that jurors believe children lack the cognitive skills or relevant experience needed to testify accurately. In some cases, however, the lack of cognitive skills or relevant experience may actually make children appear to be particularly credible. A case in point concerns sexual assault.

Little research exists on jurors' reactions to child sexual assault victims (but see Duggan, Aubrey, Doherty, Isquith, Levine, & Scheiner, this volume), even though children appear to be more likely to testify in this type of trial than in any other (Whitcomb, Shapiro, & Stellwagen, 1985). Children are particularly likely to testify in this kind of trial because of the prevalence of sexual assault against children (Finkelhor, 1979, 1984; Russell, 1983) and because the child victim is likely to be the only witness. Moreover, since child sexual assault typically involves fondling rather than rape, physical evidence is often unavailable. Thus, to prosecute such cases, the child may be required to take the stand.

Although little research exists on jurors' reactions to child sexual assault victims, psychologists have actively pursued research on jurors' reactions to adult rape victims. We review this research next, drawing inferences about how the factors investigated in adult studies might relate to cases involving children. We then present the findings of our own study of age differences in the credibility of sexual assault victims.

The rape literature indicates that a number of factors may influence jurors' perceptions of rape victims—prior sexual history, consent by the victim, provocativeness of the victim, relationship to the defendant, empathy toward the defendant or victim, and sex of the juror (Brownmiller, 1975; Dietz & Byrnes, 1981; Field, 1978, 1979; Field & Bienen, 1980; Luginbuhl & Mullin, 1981; for review, see Borgida & Brekke, 1985; and Wrightsman, 1987). The findings from adult studies are not always consistent, but they have implications for how child sexual assault victims may be perceived in court.

Research indicates that the more sexual experience a victim has had, the more she is blamed and the more her credibility suffers (Burt & Albin, 1981; L'Armand & Pepitone, 1982). It seems likely that, because children will be assumed to be less sexually experienced than adults, jurors may attribute less blame to them than to adults.

A common defense tactic in rape cases is to argue that the sexual relations did occur but the woman had consented to intercourse (Wrightsman, 1987). If the woman consented, the act is not rape. Children, however, are legally incapable of consenting to sexual acts. Since the "consent defense" is technically inapplicable to children, it would not be as likely to undermine children's credibility. Therefore, a child who reports sexual experiences may be seen as more credible than an adult.

Children also seem less likely to have their credibility questioned on the basis of being intentionally provocative. Children's naivety about sexual matters might preclude them from being intentionally provocative.

A child's relationship to a defendant cannot be used to attack a child's credibility. Jurors might feel that a woman's credibility is more questionable if she is claiming rape by a husband or boyfriend. With children, the relationship between the child and the defendant is more likely to be viewed as irrelevant. Sexual relations with a child are illegal regardless of the child's relation to the defendant.

In sum, previous research indicates that there are a number of reasons to expect children to be seen as more credible witnesses than adults in sexual assault cases. In addition, children's presumed lack of cognitive abilities may play a crucial role. Young children may be seen as lacking knowledge of sexual acts and, therefore, as unable to invent a story about sexual assault. Moreover, young children may be seen as incapable of planning revenge, again because of a lack of cognitive sophistication.

On the other hand, there may be reasons, based on children's cognitive abilities, for not believing them. Young children may be seen as highly suggestible, easily confused, or having poor memories. One purpose of our second study was to examine these possibilities.

Another purpose was to investigate sex differences in subject-jurors' reactions to sexual assault victims as a function of victim age. One of the most studied topics in the rape literature is sex differences in reactions to rape victims. Although no consistent sex differences have been found in judgments of defendant guilt (Kaplin & Miller, 1978; Lenehan & O'Neill, 1981), they have been found for factors related to victim and defendant credibility. Women identify more with rape victims than men do, and men identify more with defendants than women do (Borgida & Brekke, 1985; Kahn et al., 1977; Krulewitz & Nash, 1979). Men also attribute greater responsibility to the victim's character and actions than women do (Calhoun, Selby, & Warring, 1976; Luginbuhl & Mullin, 1981). It is possible that these biases extend to children. Furthermore, to the extent that women have been socialized to be more empathic than men toward children, women may show greater empathy to child victims and thus be more likely to believe them. Even so, to the extent that adults in general are more empathic toward children than toward adults, they may feel, regardless of their own gender, that a child's allegations of sexual assault are more believable than such allegations by an adult.

Experiment 2: The Sexual Assault Victim

One hundred twenty-one students enrolled in lower-level psychology courses at the University of Denver participated in the experiment. Thirty-four of these students were male; eight-seven were female. The participants ranged in age from eighteen to forty-five years, with a mean age of twenty-one years.

All of the participants read a one-page scenario describing details of an alleged sexual assault case. The case was similar in important ways to some actual cases of sexual assault. In the scenario, a female student claimed to have been sexually assaulted in her twenty-eight-year-old male teacher's office after school. In brief, the victim claimed that she had missed her usual ride home after class and had waited for her mother to come pick her up. Before her mother arrived, the victim was asked by the defendant to come into his office to discuss class grades. Once in his office, the victim claimed she was forced to engage in oral sex with him. Additional information about the case was presented in the form of testimony from the following five witnesses: the victim, the victim's mother, the defendant, a fellow teacher, and a school administrator. Of particular importance was testimony from the victim's mother and the teacher-defendant. The victim's mother claimed that when she picked her daughter up from school, the daughter appeared upset. After a week of repeated questioning, the daughter told her mother about the assault. The defendant testified that he remained at school later than usual that afternoon because of extra work. He recalled speaking briefly with the victim before she went out to wait for her ride. The defense rested on two assertions: that the victim had gotten the idea for the accusation from her mother's suggestive questioning and that the victim had been motivated to pursue the accusations by a desire for revenge over poor grades.

The variable of primary interest was the victim's age. She was described as being either six, fourteen, or twenty-two years old. Participants were randomly assigned to one of these age conditions, with the exception that approximately one-third of the males and one-third of the females were included in each condition.

After reading the scenario, participants were requested to judge the guilt or innocence of the defendant and to indicate their degree of confidence. The combination of these ratings resulted in a six-point scale that ranged from 1 (not guilty/very confident) to 6 (guilty/very confident). The subject-jurors were also asked to rate the credibility of each witness on a six-point scale from 1 (not at all believable) to 6 (extremely believable). In addition, forty-nine of the subjects were required to provide a brief statement about the reasons underlying their guilt and credibility judgments.

The findings revealed that the victim's credibility varied reliably as a function of age. When each subject-juror's credibility ratings were entered into 3 (victim age) × 2 (subject-juror sex) × 5 (witness) analyses of variance, with witness being the only factor to vary within subjects, a significant age × witness interaction emerged, $F(8, 452) = 2.54$, $p < .05$. The interaction was examined in detail through analysis of simple effects, followed by planned comparisons. The simple effect of age for the victim was significant, $F(2, 117) = 3.58$, $p < .05$. Planned comparisons revealed that the twenty-two-year-old ($M = 3.68$) was judged to be significantly *less* credible than the six-year-old [$M = 4.50$, $F(1, 117) = 7.20$, $p < .01$]. The credibility of the fourteen-year-old ($M = 4.08$) did not differ reliably from that of the six- or twenty-two-year-old. The credibility of the other witnesses did not differ significantly as a function of victim age, with the exception of the defendant. The defendant was seen as more credible when the case involved a twenty-two-year-old ($M = 3.10$) than when the case involved a six-year-old [$M = 2.52$, $F(1, 118) = 4.27$, $p < .05$]. The defendant's credibility did not differ reliably when the case involved a twenty-two- versus a fourteen-year-old victim ($M = 3.28$), but the defendant was seen as more credible when the case involved a fourteen-year-old rather than a six-year-old [$F(1, 118) = 7.42$, $p < .01$]. No significant sex of subject effects were found.

Participants' judgments of the defendant's degree of guilt also varied in relation to victim age. Specifically, the defendant was judged to be less guilty when the victim was a twenty-two-year-old [$M = 3.14$, $F(1, 109) = 13.23$, $p < .01$] or a fourteen-year-old [$M = 3.63$, $F(1, 109) = 4.94$, $p < .05$] than when the victim was a six-year-old ($M = 4.40$). The degree of defendant guilt did not differ reliably between the twenty-two- and fourteen-year-old conditions. Again, no significant sex of subject effects were found.

When the guilty versus not guilty judgments were analyzed, a similar picture emerged. No significant sex differences were found. Nevertheless, it is interesting to examine the means for the different age conditions as a function of subject sex (see Table 1.3). A high proportion of females and males thought the defendant was guilty when a six-year-old was the victim. A low proportion of the males believed that the defendant was guilty when a twenty-two-year-old was the victim. The lack of significance for the sex × age condition interaction may have been a result of the relatively small number of males (approximately eleven) included in each cell and the dichotomous nature of the data (guilty vs. not guilty).

TABLE 1.3 Proportion of participants voting "guilty" as a function of victim age and participant sex (Experiment 2).

	Victim Age		
	6 years	14 years	22 years
Males	.67	.55	.18
Females	.71	.61	.41

TABLE 1.4 Correlations between degree of guilt and witness credibility (Experiment 2).

	Victim Age		
	6 years	14 years	22 years
Defendant	−.77**	−.46*	−.53*
Victim	.80**	.73**	.78**

*$p < .01$, two-tailed.
**$p < .001$, two-tailed.

Correlations between witness credibility ratings and degree of guilt were computed to examine whether judgments of witness credibility and guilt ratings were related. In each of the three age conditions, significant correlations between degree of guilt and credibility ratings for the defendant and the victim were found (see Table 1.4). Thus, subject-jurors who believed the victim were more likely to find the defendant guilty.

As mentioned, forty-nine of the participants were asked to describe the basis for their credibility and guilt judgments. We were particularly concerned with examining rationales for judgments made about the victim. Were judgments of the victim's credibility influenced by jurors' theories about her cognitive abilities?

To address this question, we examined the subject-jurors' comments about the victim. On initial inspection, five categories of responses emerged: cognitive abilities, honesty, characteristics expected of sexual assault victims, blaming the victim, and miscellaneous. Comments about cognitive abilities included such statements as "I don't think a child of six would have the knowledge about assault to be able to make it up, unless it truly happened," "She seemed clear about what happened," "Her mother may have suggested it to her," and "I don't think her reasoning would be that advanced to plot out the sexual incident and her motive being a poor grade" (sic). Comments about honesty included the following: "Little girls wouldn't lie about some man sticking a penis in her mouth," "Usually children tell the truth," and "I don't think a 14-year-old would make up a story that accusational (sic) if she were just upset over grades." Comments

TABLE 1.5 Frequency of comments made about the victim/witness as a function of age (Experiment 2)

Type of Comment	Victim Age			χ^2	p
	6 years	14 years	22 years		
Total Cognitive	26	11	3	20.46	.001
Positive	22	2	0	37.00	.001
Negative	4	9	3	3.88	ns
Total Honesty	9	7	13	1.93	ns
Positive	9	7	8	.25	ns
Negative	0	0	5	—	—
Expected Characteristics	6	6	8	.40	ns
Positive	3	1	6	—	—
Negative	3	5	2	—	—
Blaming the Victim	0	1	1	—	—
Positive	0	0	0	—	—
Negative	0	1	1	—	—
Miscellaneous	6	4	4	—	—

Note: Chi-square values could not be computed in several cases.
ns = not significant.

about expected characteristics included the following: "She was afraid to tell anybody about the incident, which is normal," and ". . . I find it hard to believe she took a whole week to tell her mother." Comments that seemed to blamed the victim were few but consisted of such statements as "She could have avoided this type of assault." Miscellaneous comments included general statements such as "The story sounds real" and "The reasons why [she] was angry could have been any number of things."

Within each category, subcategories were created for positive and negative comments. Positive comments were defined as those that would enhance a witness's credibility. Negative comments were defined as those that lowered a witness's credibility. For example, a positive instance of the cognitive abilities category was, "She would probably not know enough about anatomy to lie about her teacher." A negative instance of the cognitive abilities category was, "The girl was 14 and at a very awkward age— entirely possible to create the story." Two raters independently scored the protocols; the proportion of agreement was .78.

As can be seen in Table 1.5, subject-jurors' comments differed depending on the age of the victim. Chi-square analyses indicated that subject-jurors made more comments about the younger than about the older victims' cognitive abilities. In particular, they made many more positive comments about the young victim. Also of note is the finding that subject-jurors seemed to question the twenty-two-year-old's honesty more than that of the fourteen- and six-year-old children. These findings lend support to our thesis that children's presumed honesty and lack of cognitive abilities at times enhance their credibility.

Conclusion

The two studies described here indicate that children's credibility is influenced by a variety of factors. Of particular importance are jurors' impressions of a witness's cognitive ability and honesty. In some cases, such as those investigated in prior research (e.g., Goodman et al., 1984) and in Experiment 1 here, young children's presumed lack of cognitive sophistication seems to result in lowered credibility. Two common denominators of these studies are that (1) the witness's credibility seemed to rely mainly on jurors' perceptions of the accuracy of memory and (2) young children (i.e., below seven years of age) served as witnesses. When, for example, the witness is an older child (e.g., Ross et al., 1987; Wells et al., this volume), he or she may be seen as quite capable of providing accurate statements.

In other cases, children's lack of cognitive ability may actually enhance their credibility. In Experiment 2, for example, subject-jurors seemed to believe that children lacked the ability to invent a sexual assault or plan revenge. Because the teacher was familiar and the victim's testimony concerned a salient, central event, memory was less likely to be a crucial issue. In addition to cognitive ability, the witness's honesty was of concern. Here again children were perceived to be more honest than adults. Thus, jurors' impressions of a child's credibility seem to vary depending on how their theories about children interact with important factors in a particular case. This renders the inconsistencies in existing research less surprising.

Future research should concentrate on jurors' ability to detect the accuracy or inaccuracy of children's testimony. In Experiment 1, there was no relation between the child witness's accuracy and jurors' perceptions of that accuracy. This question was examined with respect to a single situation, however, and for only five child witnesses. Perhaps jurors can better estimate a child's accuracy in other situations. The findings of Wells et al. (this volume) that mock jurors can validly judge the accuracy of testimony provided by older children and adult bystander witnesses indicate that there may, indeed, be some situations in which jurors can distinguish between accurate and inaccurate testimony.

Future research should also focus on issues of ecological validity. Psychologists have a nagging tendency to study the testimony of bystander witnesses to fairly brief, neutral events. A similar emphasis appears in the budding literature on jurors' perceptions of child witnesses (e.g., Goodman et al., 1984, 1987; Ross et al., 1987; Wells et al., this volume; but see Duggan et al., this volume). Because children are particularly likely to testify as victim/witnesses, this focus is of limited value. In the research reported in this chapter, we examined jurors' perceptions of child victim/witnesses. Experiment 2 provided interesting information about jurors' theories concerning a hypothetical sexual assault victim, but the study was based on a written scenario of a trial. More ecologically valid research on this subject is still needed. It is encouraging to us, however, that the results reported by Duggan et al. (this volume)—based on a study in many ways more ecologically valid than Experiment 2—are consistent with our findings. Duggan et al. found that, in a simulated child sexual assault trial, a nine-year-old child was viewed as a more credible victim/witness than a thirteen-year-old.

One issue concerning ecological validity may be particularly difficult to overcome, however. The decisions made by mock jurors in laboratory studies do not affect actual child victims or defendants. It may be more difficult to place one's faith in a child's testimony when this could result in an adult serving many years in prison. In actual cases, concerns about children's suggestibility, for example, may be given more weight in deciding a defendant's guilt than is indicated in laboratory studies. Thus, regardless of the findings of our research, in an actual case the fear of convicting an innocent person may make jurors more likely to question a child's word and vote "not guilty" when a child takes the stand.

References

Borgida, E., & Brekke, N. (1985). Psycholegal research on rape trials. In A. Burgess (ed.). *Research handbook on rape and sexual assault.* New York: Garland.

Brigham, J.C., & Bothwell, R.K. (1983). The ability of prospective jurors to estimate the accuracy of eyewitness identifications. *Law and Human Behavior, 7,* 19–29.

Brigham, J.C., Maass, A., Snyder, L.D., & Spaulding, K. (1982). The accuracy of eyewitness identifications in a field setting. *Journal of Personality and Social Psychology, 42,* 673–681.

Brownmiller, S. (1975). *Against our will: Men, women and rape.* New York: Simon & Schuster.

Burt, M.R., & Albin, R.S. (1981). Rape myths, rape definitions, and probability of conviction. *Journal of Applied Social Psychology, 11,* 212–230.

Calhoun, L.G., Selby, J.W., & Warring, L.J. (1976). Social perception of the victim's causal role in rape: An explanatory examination of four factors. *Human Relations, 29,* 517–526.

Deitz, S.R., & Byrnes, L.E. (1981). Attribution of responsibility for sexual assault: The influence of observer empathy and defendant occupation and attractiveness. *Journal of Psychology, 108,* 17–29.

Duggan, L.M., III, Aubrey, M., Doherty, E., Isquith, P., Levine, M., & Scheiner, J. (in this volume). The credibility of children as witnesses in a simulated child sex abuse trial.

Field, H. (1978). Juror background characteristics and attitudes toward rape: Correlates of jurors' decisions in rape trials. *Law and Human Behavior, 2,* 73–93.

Field, H. (1979). Rape trials and jurors' decisions: A psycholegal analysis of the effects of victim, defendant, and case characteristics. *Law and Human Behavior, 3,* 261–284.

Field, H., & Bienen, L. (1980). *Jurors and rape: A study in psychology and law.* Lexington, MA: Heath.

Finklehor, D. (1979). *Sexually victimized children.* New York: Free Press.

Finklehor, D. (1984). *Child sexual abuse: New theory and research.* New York: Free Press.

Goodman, G.S., & Aman, C.J. (1987 April). Children's use of anatomically correct dolls to report an event. In M. Steward (Chair), *Evaluation of suspected child abuse: Developmental, clinical and legal perspectives on the use of anatomically correct dolls.* Symposium conducted at the meeting of the Society for Research in Child Development, Baltimore, MD.

Goodman, G.S., Aman, C.J., & Hirschman, J. (1987). Child sexual and physical abuse: Children's testimony. In S.J. Ceci, M.P. Toglia, & D.F. Ross (eds.), *Children's eyewitness memory* (pp. 1–23). New York: Springer-Verlag.

Goodman, G.S., Golding, J.M., & Haith, M.M. (1984). Jurors' reactions to child witnesses. *Journal of Social Issues, 40*(2), 139–156.

Goodman, G.S., Golding, J.M., Helgeson, V.S., Haith, M.M., & Michelli, J. (1987). When a child takes the stand: Jurors' perceptions of children's eyewitness testimony. *Law and Human Behavior, 11*, 27–40.

Goodman, G.S., Hirschman, J., & Rudy, L. (1987 April). Children's testimony: Research and policy implications. In S. Ceci (Chair), *Children as witnesses: Research and policy implications.* Symposium conducted at the meeting of the Society for Research in Child Development, Baltimore, MD.

Goodman, G.S., Jones, D.P.H., Pyle, E., Prado, L., Port, L.P., England, P., Mason, R., & Rudy, L. (1988). Emotional effects of criminal court testimony on child sexual assault victims: A preliminary report. In G. Davies & J. Drinkwater (eds.). *Issues in criminological and legal psychology.* Leicester, England: British Psychological Society.

Goodman, G.S., & Michelli, J. (1981). Would you believe a child witness? *Psychology Today, 15*, 82–95.

Goodman, G.S., & Reed, R.S. (1986). Age differences in eyewitness testimony. *Law and Human Behavior, 10*, 317–332.

Johnson, M.K. (1986 August). On the credibility of child eyewitnesses: The jury is still out. In S. Ceci (Chair), *Children as witnesses: Juror's perceptions of credibility and guilt.* Symposium conducted at the meeting of the American Psychological Association, Washington, DC.

Kahn, A., Gilbert, I.A., Latta, R.M., Deutsch, C., Hagen, R., Hill, M., McGaughey, T., Ryan, A.N., & Wilson, D.W. (1977). Attribution of fault to a rape victim as a function of respectability of the victim: A failure to replicate or extend. *Representative Research in Social Psychology, 8*, 98–107.

Kaplan, M.F., & Miller, L.E. (1978). Effects of jurors' identification with the victim depend on likelihood of victimization. *Law and Human Behavior, 2*, 353–361.

Krulewitz, J.E., & Nash, E.J. (1979). Effects of rape victim resistance, assault outcome, and sex of observer on attributions about rape. *Journal of Personality, 47*, 557–574.

L'Armand, K., & Pepitone, A. (1982). Judgments of rape: A study of victim-rapist relationship and victim sexual history. *Personality and Social Psychology Bulletin, 8*, 134–139.

Leippe, M.R., & Romanczyk, A. (1987). Children on the witness stand: A communication/persuasion analysis of jurors' reactions to child witnesses. In S.J. Ceci, M.P. Toglia, & D.F. Ross (eds.). *Children's eyewitness memory* (pp. 155–177). New York: Springer-Verlag.

Leippe, M.R., Wells, G.L., & Ostrom, T.M. (1978). Crime seriousness as a determinant of accuracy in eyewitness identification. *Journal of Applied Psychology*, *63*, 345–351.

Lenehan, G.E., & O'Neill, P. (1981). Reactance as determinants of a judgment in a mock jury experiment. *Journal of Applied Social Psychology*, *11*, 231–239.

Lindsay, R.C.L., Wells, G.L., & Rumpel, C. (1981). Can people detect eyewitness identification accuracy within and across situations? *Journal of Applied Psychology*, *66*, 79–89.

Luginbuhl, J., & Mullin, C. (1981). Rape and responsibility: How and how much is the victim blamed? *Sex Roles*, *7*, 547–559.

Marin, V., Holmes, D.L., Guth, M., & Kovac, P. (1979). The potential of children as eyewitnesses. *Law and Human Behavior*, *3*, 295–305.

Melton, G.B., & Thompson, R.A. (1987). Getting out of a rut: Detours to less traveled paths in child-witness research. In S.J. Ceci, M.P. Toglia, & D.F. Ross (eds.). *Children's eyewitness memory* (pp. 209–229). New York: Springer-Verlag.

Nigro, G.N., Buckley, M.A., Hill, D., Nelson, J. (in this volume). When juries "hear" children testify: The effects of eyewitness age and speech style on jurors' perceptions of testimony.

Ross, D.F., Miller, B.S., & Moran, P.B. (1987). The child in the eyes of the jury: Assessing mock jurors' perceptions of child witnesses. In S.J. Ceci, M.P. Toglia, & D.F. Ross (eds.). *Children's eyewitness memory* (pp. 142–154). New York: Springer-Verlag.

Rudy, L. (1986). *The effects of participation on children's eyewitness testimony.* Unpublish Honors Thesis submitted to the University of Denver, Denver, CO.

Russell, D.E.H. (1983). The incidence and prevalence of intrafamilial and extrafamilial sexual abuse of female children. *Child Abuse and Neglect*, *7*, 133–146.

Wells, G.L. (1985). The eyewitness. In S.M. Kassin & L.S. Wrightsman (eds.). *The psychology of evidence and trial procedure* (pp. 43–66). Beverly Hills, CA: Sage.

Wells, G.L., Ferguson, T.J., & Lindsay, R.C.L. (1981). The tractability of eyewitness confidence and its implications for triers of fact. *Journal of Applied Psychology*, *66*, 688–696.

Wells, G.L., & Leippe, M.R. (1981). How do triers of fact infer the accuracy of eyewitness identifications? Using memory for peripheral detail can be misleading. *Journal of Applied Psychology*, *66*, 682–687.

Wells, G.L., Lindsay, R.C.L., & Ferguson, T.J. (1979). Accuracy. confidence and juror perceptions in eyewitness identification. *Journal of Applied Psychology*, *64*, 440–448.

Wells, G.L., Lindsay, R.C.L., & Tousignant, J.P. (1980). Effects of expert psychological advice on human performance in judging the validity of eyewitness testimony. *Law and Human Behavior*, *4*, 275–286.

Wells, G.L., Turtle, J.W., & Luus, C.A.E., (in this volume). The perceived credibility of child eyewitnesses: What happens when they use their own words?

Whipple, G.M. (1912). Psychology of testimony and report. *Psychological Bulletin*, *9*, 264–269.

Whitcomb, D., Shapiro, E.P., & Stellwagen, C.D. (1985). *When the victim is a child: Issues for judges and prosecutors.* Washington, DC: National Institute of Justice.

Wigmore, J.H. (1909). Professor Munsterberg and the psychology of evidence. *Illinois Law Review, 3,* 339–445.

Wrightsman, L.S. (1987). *Psychology and the legal system.* Belmont, CA: Wadsworth.

2
The Perceived Credibility of Child Eyewitnesses: What Happens When They Use Their Own Words?

GARY L. WELLS, JOHN W. TURTLE, and C.A. ELIZABETH LUUS

How do triers-of-fact judge the credibility of children versus that of adults as eyewitnesses? We argue that there are two processes to consider in answering this question and that previous research has examined only one of these processes, namely, biases and stereotypes possessed by triers-of-fact. The first process, and the one that separates our's from previous research, involves the inferences about accuracy or believability that triers-of-fact discern from the qualities of the testimony itself. If a child appears to have little confidence and pauses at inappropriate points in response to questions, for example, that child might be judged to be less credible than an adult who is more confident or pauses less frequently. On the other hand, a child who appears more confident than an adult might be judged to be more credible than the adult. In other words, we propose that the factors that seem to drive the credibility of adult eyewitness testimony (such as confidence; see Wells, Ferguson & Lindsay, 1981) also drive the credibility of child eyewitness testimony. If children and adults differ systematically on these quality-of-testimony variables, their testimony should be differentially credible as well.

Surprisingly, little is known about the quality of eyewitness testimony given by children versus that given by adults. Although numerous experiments have measured children's versus adults' accuracy of memory in eyewitness settings (e.g., Ceci, Ross & Toglia, 1987; King & Yuille, 1987; Marin, Holmes, Guth & Kovac, 1979; Saywitz, 1987; Zaragoza, 1987), these studies have not examined how children perform in a courtroomlike test situation involving oral responses to direct and cross-examination. Are children less confident than adults on the stand? Do their responses to direct- and cross-examination questions somehow lack the power of persuasion? Do they use different words from adults? We cannot answer such questions merely by converting testimony into accuracy scores.

The other process by which the eyewitness credibility of children and adults might be perceived differently is through the biases, stereotypes, or implicit theories of the triers-of-fact. Thus, even when children give testimony as confidently and competently as adults, they might be perceived as less credible because the triers-of-fact believe children's memories are inferior. Previous research has addressed this latter process, which we simply call the stereotype hypothesis.

Although the stereotype studies are somewhat informative, our concern was with the "bottom line." That is, we were interested in how credible children are judged to be compared with adults when both populations give eyewitness testimony in their own words. We were not concerned with separating the two processes (stereotype process vs. quality-of-testimony process) in our experiment; we were interested in allowing both processes to assume their natural levels of variation and covariation. The bottom line for us was the perceived credibility of children versus that of adults when both processes were naturally mixed as they are in actual courtroom testimony.

Previous Research

Previous research, although sometimes billed as assessing the perceived credibility of children's testimony, has in fact assessed only one component of the perceived credibility issue, namely, the stereotype component. These studies have used paradigms in which the testimony was scripted and, therefore, constant across ages. Two variations have been used: Some studies used written transcripts in which the subject-jurors were told that the eyewitness was a particular age; other studies have had a child or an adult deliver the scripted testimony on videotape. Recent research by Goodman, Golding, & Hegelson (1987) exemplifies both of the basic paradigms used to test the stereotype process. In a series of three experiments, subject-jurors read a description of testimony about a car–pedestrian accident (Experiment 1) or a murder (Experiment 2), or observed a videotaped mock trial of the car–pedestrian accident case (Experiment 3). The presumed age of the eyewitness was manipulated in Experiments 1 and 2 by the written assertion that the eyewitness was six-, ten-, or thirty-years old. The age variable was manipulated in Experiment 3 by the use of a six-, ten-, or thirty-year-old actor-witness in the videotape. The results were consistent across the three experiments: the young child was judged to be significantly less credible than the adult, and the ten-year old child's credibility was judged to be between those of the young child and the adult.

Similar results were reported in two experiments conducted by Leippe and Romanzcyk (1987). In both experiments, transcripts of a case described the eyewitness as having been six, ten, or thirty years old. In both experiments, the young eyewitness was rated as less credible than the adult eyewitness, especially if the eyewitness demonstrated inconsistency in his testimony.

The findings of the studies by Goodman et al. (1987) and Leippe and

Romanczyk (1987) contrast somewhat with the results obtained by Ross, Miller, and Moran (1987). Ross et al. manipulated the age of the key eyewitness for the prosecution in a videotaped, simulated court case by using an eight-year-old, twenty-one-year-old, or seventy-four-year-old actor. Except for the specific choice of ages and the fact that Goodman et al.'s subject-jurors deliberated, the Ross et al. study is conceptually equivalent to Experiment 3 in the Goodman et al. study. Interestingly, however, Ross et al. found no age differences in credibility and found that the eight-year-old witness was rated as more accurate, forceful, consistent, truthful, confident, and intelligent than the twenty-one-year-old, whereas the ratings of the eight-year-old and seventy-four-year-old eyewitnesses did not differ.

These previous studies are important, but they fall somewhat short of providing a clear indication of how the average child's testimony will be evaluated by triers-of-fact. Studies using *written* transcripts are reasonable tests of subject-jurors' stereotypes of the child eyewitness in that they require the subject-jurors to construct an examplar (e.g., of an eight-year-old eyewitness) and evaluate the examplar. However, we think it is safe to argue that few people have ever actually observed an eight-year-old child deliver eyewitness testimony. Thus, there might be a large gap between subject-jurors' imagined exemplar of eight-year-olds' testimony and actual eight-year-olds' testimony. Using videotaped testimony of an actual eight-year old is an improvement over using a written transcript, but only if we can assume that the selected eight-year-old is somehow typical of his or her eight-year-old peers. Typicality is difficult to assess, in part, because the relevant dimension or dimensions have not been articulated in the eyewitness testimony literature. A child who obtains an average SES score or an average intelligence test score would perhaps satisfy the typicality criterion. However, we favor the use of a sample of children and adults rather than the use of any one child or any one adult, because of the possibility that the testimonies of a given child and adult might differ for numerous reasons other than their ages. The study by Ross et al. (1987) could be a case in point. It is possible that the accuracy of the eight-year-old was perceived as greater than that of the adult in the Ross et al. study because either the child or adult actor-witness was unrepresentative of his age (i.e., the child actor might have been especially believable for his age or the adult especially unbelievable). Indeed, research indicates that there is considerable variation in the believability of adults' eyewitness testimony (Wells, Lindsay, & Ferguson, 1979), and we see no reason to expect less variation within samples of children's testimony. We suspect that children do not give testimony in the same way as adults (e.g., choice of words, qualifying clauses) and that the use of scripted testimony, which masks these differences, makes it difficult to know the extent to which children's testimony is perceived as less credible than the testimony of adults.

As far as we know, the study we report in this chapter is the first to examine differences between samples of child eyewitness testimony and samples of adult eyewitness tesimony under courtroomlike conditions. [Goodman, Bottoms, & Herscovici (this volume) describe courtroomlike questioning of child eyewitnesses in their first experiment, but no adult sample was included in that experiment.] Although numerous experiments have examined differences in the memory of child eyewitnesses and adult eyewitnesses, those experiments have not actually examined how children testify orally, but instead have simply scored the witnesses' accuracy on tasks of recognition or recall. We were interested in assessing their oral testimony under conditions of direct and cross-examination in a manner that simulates a courtroom experience.

Experiment 1

The paradigm we used was similar to that used by Wells and his colleagues in examining the oral testimony of adult eyewitnesses (e.g., Lindsay, Wells, & Rumpel, 1981; Wells, Lindsay, & Ferguson, 1979). All witnesses were exposed to a staged criminal event (a videotaped abduction of a child from a playground) and one day later were subjected to direct and cross-examination by separate persons. The examinations were videotaped and later presented to subject-jurors whose task was to evaluate the accuracy, believability, and confidence of the eyewitnesses. Separate accuracy scores were calculated by the experimenters who, of course, knew the actual facts of the witnessed event, and these "performance scores" were compared with subject-jurors' estimates of eyewitness accuracy.

Phase 1

The sample of subjects who served as eyewitnesses consisted of fourteen children in grade 3 (mean age = 7.9 years), fourteen children in grade 7 (mean age = 11.8 years), and fourteen adult university students. The children were sampled from four separate classrooms and represented a diversity of socioeconomic backgrounds. We avoided selecting children who were unrepresentative of their age group in that we did not sample the children only from advanced-achievement or only from lower-achievement school programs.

Each of the forty-two eyewitnesses viewed the staged abduction on a 60-inch (152.4-cm) video screen. Until the time of the questioning (one day after viewing) subjects did not know they would be examined regarding their memories of the witnessed event. To keep the subject-witnesses from thinking they would tested on these memories, they were first shown a videotaped tennis match and asked to estimate such things as the effort and ability displayed by each player. Witnesses were given no indication that the questions to be asked of them the following day would be memory questions rather than the attribution-like questions asked on the first day. Thus, whatever subject-witnesses remembered about the subsequent abduction tape was not a result of intentional memory encoding, but instead was incidental to what they thought our interests were. The abduction involved an eleven-year-old boy playing on a playground with a thirteen-year-old friend. A man, sitting on a bench watching the children play, approached the eleven-year-old, talked to him briefly, coaxed him into a car, and sped away. After viewing the abducting tape, the child witnesses were given a "safety message" advising them not to get involved with or accept rides from strangers. Subjects were scheduled for their return visit and told "tomorrow, you will be doing something similar to what you did today." We assume that the subjects were perhaps thinking about the tape occasionally over the next 24 hours with some idea of forming impressions of the people in the tape. But the sessions were scheduled in such a way as to preclude or make unlikely the subject-witnesses anticipating we were interested in their memories and their abilities to communicate those memories. This mimics what we consider to be a common eyewitness situation; eyewitnesses do not have a "memory set" at the time they witness an event and might not learn until later that their testimony is important to authorities.

When they returned for their session, one day after having viewed the event, the witnesses were greeted by the same experimenter who had conducted the first session the day before. The first experimenter explained that the witness was going to be asked some more questions regarding the film shown yesterday about the man and the boys at the playground. The witness was told that the first experimenter would ask some initial questions and a second experimenter, who had yet to interact with the witness and had not been present the day before, would then ask some more questions. Each witness was told that accuracy and completeness in answering the questions were important, but no specific consequences to either the witness or the accused were mentioned to the witness. The witness was also asked for his or her permission to be videotaped while responding to the questions; all the witnesses agreed.

The direct examination consisted of ten questions regarding the number of children at the playground, a general description of the boys and the man in the film, and color of the car in which the man and one of the boys left the scene. After asking these first ten questions, the first experimenter asked the other experimenter if he or she had any further questions at that time. The second experimenter then asked seven more questions representative of the kinds of things that a witness might be asked under cross-examination, for example: "You claimed before that the playground was fairly crowded, is that correct?" "In which hand was the man carrying his wallet?" (a wallet was never visible in the scene) "Would you agree that the man in the film was fairly short?" (the man was actually 6 ft., 2 in. tall) "Isn't it true, though, that the man was facing away from you for most of the time?" (the man was actually in full view of the camera for more than half the time). Both the direct and the cross-examination questions were cast in a way that allowed the questioners to follow their examination format regardless of how the witness responded. At the conclusion of the cross-examination, the witness was thanked and fully debriefed. In the case of the child eyewitnesses, the experimenters discussed some measures the child might take to remember details of events they suspect might be dangerous to themselves or others (e.g., try to write down the license number of suspicious cars, in the dirt or snow if necessary).

Phase 2

The purpose of Phase 1 was to generate clear records of the forty-two eyewitnesses' testimony by videotaping their direct and cross-examinations. The purpose of Phase 2 was to evaluate those videotapes using subject-jurors who judged the credibility of the eyewitnesses' testimony. Independently, we were also able to score the testimony tapes for their actual accuracy.

Each of 294 subject-jurors (university students) evaluated one of the forty-two testimony tapes. Thus, each eyewitness was evaluated by an average of seven subject-jurors. The instructions to subject-jurors emphasized that their evaluations were important but did not describe specific consequences of their evaluations. We used five measures of perceived credibility; two were measures of the perceived accuracy of the eyewitness and three were measures of their believability. In addition, we had subject-jurors estimate the confidence of the eyewitness. Subject-jurors were aware of the fact that the witnesses recollections were based on a one-day retention interval.

The two perceived accuracy measures asked subject-jurors to estimate the number of questions the eyewitness answered correctly during the examination; this was asked after viewing the direct examination (subject-jurors were told that there was a total of ten direct-examination questions) and again after viewing the cross-examination (subject-jurors were told that there was a total of seven cross-examination questions). Similarly, subject-jurors were asked to assess the believability (on a seven-point scale on which 1 = not at all believable and 7 = totally believable) of the witness's testimony after direct examination, again after cross-examination, and finally "overall." A parallel format was used for subject-jurors' estimates of the eyewitnesses' confidence; confidence (on a seven-point scale, with 1 = not at all confident and 7 = completely confident) was estimated after direct examination, after cross-examination, and overall. The tape was stopped for subject-jurors after the direct examination, and the three direct-examination measures (perceived accuracy, believability, and confidence of direct testimony) were solicited before they were shown the cross-examination testimony.

Accuracy of Testimony: Phase 1 Results

The examination included seventeen questions; ten direct-examination questions and seven cross-examination questions. Answers to these questions were scored by determining definite boundaries on the range of possible replies to each question. For instance, only "purple" or "burgundy" were acceptable descriptions of the color of the getaway car. Interjudge reliability was virtually perfect because the scoring criteria were very explicit.

We assigned each of the forty-two eyewitnesses two accuracy scores, one for the ten direct-examination questions and one for the seven cross-examination questions. The mean accuracy of witnesses, as functions of age and type of examination, is graphed in Figure 2.1. (Note that these scores have been converted to percentages to control for the different numbers of questions for direct and cross-examination.) Univariate ANOVAs (with age as the factor) indicated that accuracy did not differ significantly with age for the direct-examination responses $[F(2,39) = 2.23, p = .12]$. There was, however, a significant age difference in the accuracy of the cross-examination responses $[F(2,39) = 8.91, p = .007]$. A subsequent Neuman–Keuls analysis revealed that the eight-year-old children were significantly less accurate on cross-examination than were the twelve-year-

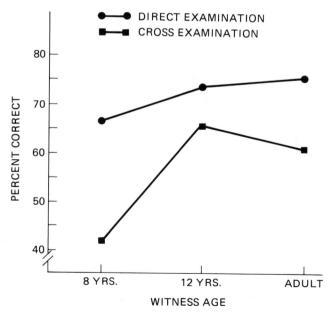

FIGURE 2.1 Actual accuracy scores under direct and cross-examination as a function of the age of the witness.

old or adult eyewitnesses at the .01 level. The twelve-year-old and adult eyewitnesses did not differ in the accuracy of their cross-examination responses.

A second analysis of accuracy scores was conducted using bivariate regression with age groupings as the predictor variable. Bivariate regression can be more sensitive than the ANOVAs in this case, because it tests specifically for the linear component of age. This analysis indicated a significant relationship between age and accuracy for both direct- and cross-examination accuracy scores. Age accounted for 9 percent of the variance in direct-examination accuracy ($r = .299, n = 42, p < .05$), 16 percent of the variance in cross-examination accuracy ($r = .399, n = 42, p < .01$), and 20 percent of the variance in the witnesses' total-accuracy scores ($r = .452, n = 42, p < .01$).

We conclude that the eight-year-old witnesses were not as accurate as the twelve-year-old witnesses and adults. This difference in accuracy as a function of age seems to be somewhat stronger for cross-examination questions than for direct-examination questions, but the linear trend relating age to accuracy was significant for both types of questions.

The large decline in accuracy of eight-year-olds under cross-examination is consistent with Ceci et al.'s (1987) findings regarding young children's susceptibility to misleading information. Ceci et al. found that very young children (three-year-olds) were drastically worse than twelve-year-olds, and their three-year-old control group counterparts, in their ability to resist incorporating misleading information into their responses. Ceci et al. demonstrated, however, that at least some of this increased susceptibility is due to the young children's desire to conform to what they perceive to be the expectations of an adult "authority" figure; when the same misleading information was provided by seven-year-olds, the young children were significantly more resistant to it, although they were still less accurate than the misled twelve-year-olds or the three-year-olds who were not asked misleading questions. It makes sense to view the social pressures present during cross-examination as analogous in many ways to the misleading-question situation, and the fact that the eight-year-olds were much less accurate under cross-examination might be interpreted as being a function of the same source-credibility effect demonstrated by Ceci et al.

Perceived Credibility and Confidence: Phase 2 Results

Credibility and confidence ratings by the subject-jurors were averaged over the approximately seven subject-jurors who evaluated each witness. This provided a stable estimate of the perceived credibility and confidence for each of the forty-two eyewitnesses. We then conducted analyses of variance on each measure, using age as a between-subjects variable. In addition, we calculated eight bivariate regressions (one for each measure), with age as the predictor variable. Neither technique produced a significant

TABLE 2.1 Subject-jurors' mean credibility and confidence ratings of witnesses as a function of witness age.

	Witness Age		
	8 Years	12 Years	Adult
Credibility			
Perceived accuracy/direct	6.73	6.87	6.87
Perceived accuracy/cross	6.10	6.16	6.35
Belief/direct	4.96	4.99	5.08
Belief/cross	4.52	4.44	4.59
Belief/overall	4.64	4.73	4.65
Confidence			
Confidence/direct	4.33	4.43	4.81
Confidence/cross	3.96	3.99	4.06
Confidence/overall	4.30	4.22	4.33

TABLE 2.2 Correlations among measures.

		PAD	PAC	BD	BC	BO	CD	CC	CO
Credibility									
Perceived accuracy/direct	(PAD)	X	.45	.81	.36	.67	.66	.38	.58
Perceived accuracy/cross	(PAC)		X	.54	.72	.63	.29	.71	.64
Belief/direct	(BD)			X	.59	.79	.75	.59	.73
Belief/cross	(BC)				X	.67	.34	.79	.67
Belief/overall	(BO)					X	.58	.77	.79
Confidence									
Confidence/direct	(CD)						X	.52	.77
Confidence/cross	(CC)							X	.87
Confidence/overall	(CO)								X

effect for the age of the eyewitness. Although these differences were not significant, we present the means in Table 2.1 as interocular evidence to support these inferential statistics; clearly, the age of the eyewitness was unrelated to any of the five credibility or the three confidence measures.

We were sensitive to the possibility that our measures were not reliable, in spite of their high face validity, which could account for our null results. Inspection of the correlations in Table 2.2 seems to put that concern to rest. There is a great deal of coherence in our measures, all of which are closely related and statistically significant. These correlations illustrate, for example, that the subject-jurors tended strongly to believe eyewitnesses who were perceived as confident, and that confident eyewitnesses were given higher accuracy estimates than were low-confidence witnesses. Also, the perceived accuracy and believability of direct-examination testimony were related more to the perceived confidence of the direct testimony ($rs = .66$ and $.75$) than to the perceived confidence of the cross-examination testimony ($rs = .38$ and $.59$). A complementary pattern emerges with regard to the measures of the perceived accuracy and believability of the cross-examination testimony, which were related more to the perceived confidence of the cross-examination testimony ($rs = .71$ and $.79$) than to the perceived confidence of the direct testimony ($rs = .29$ and $.34$). The magnitudes and general coherence of these patterns of correlation indicate that our measures were sensitively and meaningfully tapping subject-jurors' impressions of the credibility and confidence of the eye-witnesses' testimony.

Actual vs. Perceived Accuracy

Although the actual accuracy of the witnesses' testimony varied with age, subject-jurors' estimates of accuracy did not. This phonomenon is a graphically represented in Figure 2.2, which is shown only for its descriptive value. The scores for actual and perceived accuracy are on comparable

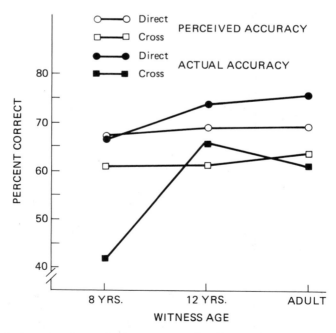

Figure 2.2 Actual and perceived accuracy under direct and cross-examination as a function of witness age.

scales in that they reflect the percentage of questions subject-jurors thought the witnesses answered correctly and the percentage that witnesses actually did answer correctly. These data indicate that subject-jurors' estimates of accuracy were fairly close to the actual accuracy of witnesses in all cases except for the eight-year-olds' cross-examinations. Although we are not yet prepared to conclude that triers-of-fact overestimate the accuracy of eight-year-olds' cross-examination testimony, these data suggest that this might be one of the areas in which triers-of-fact are especially likely to misperceive the relevance of age. The notion that people may not be sensitive to young children's susceptibility to misleading or suggestive questions is supported in part by survey results reported by Yarmey and Jones (1983). In response to a question asking how and eight-year-old would be likely to respond to questions in court, the majority of student-jurors indicated that they thought the child would be likely to reply accurately. In contrast, all but one of the eyewitness "experts" surveyed indicated that they thought the child would reply in the way the adult led them to answer.

Conclusions

We propose that eight-year-old, twelve-year-old, and adult eyewitnesses are nearly equivalent in the perceived accuracy and believability of their testimony. Although a negative stereotype of the young eyewitness probably exists (as found by Goodman et al., 1987; Leippe & Romanczyk, 1987), we propose that this stereotype is mitigated when triers-of-fact observe actual testimony delivered by young eyewitnesses. In other words, our findings are not inconsistent with the idea that a negative stereotype exists in how people imagine a young child's testimony; however, the actual testimony by the average eight-year-old is at odds with this stereotype. Indeed, the eight-year-old and twelve-year-old eyewitnesses in our study gave much better testimony than we had anticipated, and we think this was the general impression among subject-jurors as well. The idea that a significant gap could exist between people's abstract view of the credibility of child eyewitnesses and how they judge the credibility of actual, concrete cases of child testimony should not be particularly surprising; after all, probably no one in our study or in previous studies had ever actually observed children give eyewitness testimony.

Regarding previous studies, we argue that the use of a single child's versus single adult's videotaped testimony runs the risk of that child or adult being unrepresentative of the credibility of their respective ages. Figure 2.3 shows the variance within ages on the measures of perceived accuracy and perceived believability. Had we chosen only one eight-year-old, one twelve-year-old and one adult, we might have reached any number of conclusions, including the conclusion that children are *more* credible than adults. In addition, studies that give a child and an adult identical, scripted testimony to act out might be providing the child with unnatural language;

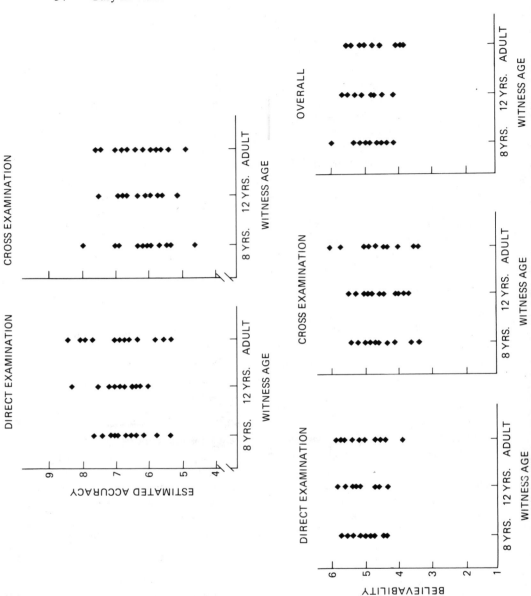

FIGURE 2.3 Distributions of subject-jurors' estimates of accuracy and believability as functions of witness age.

at the very least, scripted testimony is not a product of the child's actual memories of a witnessed event.

Our measures were sensitive to the differences in the way subject-jurors perceived the eyewitnesses in that there was appreciable variance in confidence, perceived accuracy, and believability across the forty-two eyewitnesses. Nevertheless, no significant proportion of this variance was accounted for by the age of the eyewitnesses (as evidenced by the ANOVAs and the bivariate regression analyses). On the other hand, the overall confidence of the eyewitnesses accounted for a low of 35 percent and a high of 62 percent of the variance in the five credibility scores. These data strongly suggest that we need not concern ourselves with age in predicting the credibility of an eyewitness on the witness stand, but the confidence of the witness could be a powerful predictor of testimony credibility. This conclusion might change if the age variable were tested outside the ranges we used (e.g., younger than eight years). Specifically, we suspect that there is some age, perhaps as low as four to five years old, at which triers-of-fact are reluctant to find eyewitness testimony credible regardless of the confidence of the eyewitness.

Summary

Data were collected from 294 subject-jurors on several measures of the perceived credibility of forty-two videotaped direct and cross-examinations of eyewitnesses to a filmed abduction. The ages of the eyewitnesses (mean ages of 7.9, 11.8, and university age, $n = 14$ for each group) were unrelated to the perceived accuracy, believability, or confidence of the eyewitnesses under either direct or cross-examination. The overall confidence of the eyewitnesses, however, accounted for between 35 and 62 percent of the variance in the perceived accuracy and believability of the eyewitnesses.

Because we sampled from normal populations of eight-year-old and twelve-year-old witnesses (rather than especially advanced or slow populations), used reasonable sample sizes for all three ages (rather than one example of an eyewitness from each age), and had them testify in their *own* words using their *own* memories (rather than using scripted testimony), we feel confident that our results approximate what might be found in actual cases involving testimony by eyewitnesses of these ages. Specifically, we would not expect a normal sample of eight-year-olds or twelve-year-olds to give testimony that is perceived as less credible by triers-of-fact than that given by adults.

Acknowledgment. This research was supported in part by a grant to the first author from the Social Sciences and Humanities Research Council of Canada. The authors thank teachers Murphy, Feniak, Turner, Konduc, and Barret for their support in helping obtain our samples of children.

Thanks are also due to Aaron Wells, who agreed to be abducted, Tim Jackson, who played the abducted child's acquaintance, and Brian Taylor, who agreed to be the abductor.

References

Ceci, S.J., Ross, D.F., & Toglia, M.P. (1987). Age differences in suggestibility: Narrowing the uncertainties. In S.J. Ceci, M.P. Toglia, & D.F. Ross (eds.) *Children's eyewitness memory*. New York: Springer-Verlag.

Goodman, G.S., Bottoms, B.L., Herscovici, B.B., & Shaver, P. (in this volume). Determinants of the child victim's perceived credibility.

Goodman, G.S., Golding, J.M., Hegelson, V.S., Haith, M.M., & Michell, J. (1987). When a child takes the stand: Jurors' perceptions of children's eyewitness testimony. *Law and Human Behavior, 11,* 27–40.

King, M.A., & Yuille, J.C. (1987). Suggestibility and the child witness, In S.J. Ceci, M.P. Toglia, & D.F. Ross (eds.) *Children's eyewitness memory*. New York: Springer-Verlag.

Leippe, M.R., & Romanczyk, A. (1987). Children on the witness stand: A communication/persuasion analysis of jurors' reactions to child witnesses. In S.J. Ceci, M.P. Toglia, & D.F. Ross (eds.). *Children's eyewitness memory*. New York: Springer-Verlag.

Lindsay, R.C.L., Wells, G.L., & Rumpel, C. (1981). Can people detect eyewitness identification accuracy within and across situations? *Journal of Applied Psychology, 66,* 79–89.

Marin, B.V., Holmes, D.L., Guth, M., & Kovac, P. (1979). The potential of children as eyewitnesses: A comparison of children and adults on eyewitness tasks. *Law and Human Behavior, 3,* 295–306.

Ross, D.F., Miller, B.S., & Moran, P.B. (1987). The child in the eyes of the jury: Assessing mock jurors' perceptions of the child witness. In S.J. Ceci, M.P. Toglia, & D.F. Ross (eds.) *Children's eyewitness memory*. New York: Springer-Verlag.

Saywitz, K.J. (1987). Children's testimony: Age-related patterns of memory errors. In S.J. Ceci, M.P. Toglia, & D.F. Ross (eds.). *Children's eyewitness memory*. New York: Springer-Verlag.

Zaragoza, M.S. (1987). Memory, suggestibility, and eyewitness testimony in children and adults. In S.J. Ceci, M.P. Toglia, & D.F. Ross (eds.) *Children's eyewitness memory*. New York: Springer-Verlag.

Wells, G.L., Ferguson, T.J., & Lindsay, R.C.L. (1981). The tractability of eyewitness confidence and its implications for triers of fact. *Journal of Applied Psychology, 66,* 688–696.

Wells, G.L., Lindsay, R.C.L., & Ferguson, T.J. (1979). Accuracy, confidence, and juror perceptions in eyewitness identification. *Journal of Applied Psychology, 64,* 440–448.

Yarmey, A.D., & Jones, H.P.T. (1983). Is the psychology of eyewitness identification a matter of common sense? In S.M.A. Lloyd-Bostock & B.R. Clifford (eds.). *Evaluating eyewitness evidence*. Chichester: John Wiley & Sons.

3
Age Stereotypes, Communication Modality, and Mock Jurors' Perceptions of the Child Witness

DAVID F. ROSS, DAVID DUNNING, MICHAEL P. TOGLIA, and STEPHEN J. CECI

In the American legal system today, few issues are as timely as the debate over the credibility of the child witness. As the number of child and spousal abuse cases in America continues to rise, courts are increasingly forced to turn to the testimony of children (Beach, 1983; Finkelhor, 1984). The courts do so with some trepidation, for both lawyers and judges recognize some potentially serious issues centering on the child witness: Are children able to render accurate testimony about the crimes they witness? Are they dangerously open to suggestibility on the part of attorneys and the police? Can they adequately distinguish between reality and fantasy?

For the research psychologist, these questions provide exciting opportunities to conduct work that is both theoretically provocative and of practical importance. It is not surprising that an increasing number of researchers have concentrated on the child witness. On one front psychologists have started to explore the ability of children to provide accurate eyewitness testimony (see Ceci, Ross, & Toglia, 1987, for a recent review).

This chapter focuses on another front of psychological research, namely, how jurors perceive and evaluate the testimony of the child witness. We will first review recent studies that explore this issue. Specifically, we will examine whether jurors give the testimony of the child more or less weight than comparable testimony offered by an adult. Then our focus will shift to an important factor that has been relatively neglected by research to date. That factor is *communication modality*, or rather the "medium," whether written or visual, by which the eyewitness testimony of the child is presented to the court and the juror. We will discuss why modality may be important, describe an experiment that investigated its impact on jurors' perceptions of the child witness, and finally conclude by examining the implications for future research.

Juror Perceptions of the Child Witness: A Review

Do jurors discount eyewitness testimony when it is given by a child as opposed to an adult?

We should note at the outset that the legal community has long held the opinion that children's memories are too prone to error and vulnerable to misleading suggestion to provide accurate testimony (Whipple, 1911). In many jurisdictions, a child must pass a competency examination before testifying, though this requirement has been relaxed as the number of cases involving child abuse has grown (Goodman, 1984; Melton, 1984). But do triers-of-fact, those likely to be called as actual jurors in a case, share the legal community's viewpoint of the child witness?

One answer to this question comes from surveys of laypeople. In a survey we conducted, fifty college students were asked whether they believed a child witness would be more or less likely to render accurate testimony than an adult. Specifically, we asked our college-age respondents to consider hypothetical six-, eight-, twenty-one-, and seventy-four-year-old witnesses, and asked them to rate all witnesses on how accurate their testimony was likely to be, how open they were to suggestion, and how likely they were to be honest. Finally, each respondent reported how much weight they would give to the testimony of each eyewitness. Respondents answered these questions on seven-point scales.

As can be seen in Table 3.1, our subjects held a rather negative stereotype of the child witness. They believed the child witness, whether six or eight years old, was less likely to be accurate and more likely to be open to suggestion than witnesses of adult age (either young or old). Furthermore, they reported that they would give less weight to testimony offered by a child than to that offered by an adult. However, the elderly witness was viewed more negatively than the young adult witness on these same dimensions. These results are consistent with past surveys that have addressed this issue (Leippe & Romanczyk, 1987; Yarmey & Jones, 1983).

Additional queries, not displayed in Table 3.1, reinforced the unfavorable image that our respondents held of the child witness. In our survey, respondents were asked two questions based on a recent survey by Leippe

TABLE 3.1 Mock-jurors' beliefs about age differences in eyewitness ability.[a]

Witness Characteristic	Age of Hypothetical Witness			
	6	8	21	74
Witness accuracy	3.28 (c)	4.22 (b)	5.92 (a)	4.74 (b)
Suggestibility	2.14 (d)	3.06 (c)	5.30 (a)	4.20 (b)
Honesty	4.94 (b)	4.94 (b)	5.14 (ab)	5.72 (a)
Weight given to testimony	3.06 (d)	4.10 (c)	5.96 (a)	4.98 (b)
Total score	13.42 (d)	16.32 (c)	22.32 (a)	19.64 (b)

[a] Means with a different letter are statistically significantly different, at least at the $p < .05$ level, by a Bonferroni multiple comparision test. Higher scores indicate more positive reactions: greater witness accuracy, less suggestibility, more honesty, greater weight given to testimony. $N = 50$; range of potential responses, 1 to 7.

& Romanczyk (1987). First, at what age do people become capable of providing accurate and credible eyewitness testimony? And second, is there an age at which people become too old to be trusted as witnesses? Subjects estimated that children become competent to testify at 16.1 years (S.D. = 7.2). Thirty-four percent of the sample (16/50) indicated that there was an age of incompetency, which was estimated at 75.3 years (S.D. = 8.3).

We should note that our survey revealed that the stereotype of the child witness is not uniformly more negative than perceptions of the adult. When our respondents considered the issue of honesty, they consistently reported that the child was *equally* likely to be sincere in his or her testimony as a *young* adult, while the elderly witness was viewed as the most likely to be honest of all four age groups. Leippe and Romanczyk (1987) report a similar finding. This finding is our first hint, to be discussed at length later, that the age of the witness has a complex, though orderly, effect on jurors' perceptions of credibility.

Experimental Studies

Given these survey results, it was expected that people's generally negative beliefs about child memory would influence their judgments about the testimony of a specific witness in a straightforward fashion: Jurors should perceive child witnesses as less credible than their adult counterparts, and thus should be less likely to convict a defendant based on their testimony. Initial research on this topic has only been partially consistent with this expectation. Goodman, Golding, Helgeson, Haith, and Michelli (1987) presented college students (and citizens at large in a later study) with a trial in which the key prosecution witness was a six-, ten-, or thirty-year-old individual. Juror-subjects consistently rated the child witness as less credible than the adult, even though, surprisingly, witness age failed to influence ratings of guilt or innocence. Leippe and Romanczyk (1987) reported similar findings in a mock robbery trial.

Other data have suggested that witness age does indeed influence guilt judgments, albeit by an indirect route. Goodman et al. (1987) asked subject-jurors to assess the credibility of all witnesses offering testimony in the trial they presented. The correlation between the credibility of the key witness and guilt did not change whether the witness was described as a child or an adult. How much jurors relied on the testimony of other witnesses, however, did change. When the key witness was a child, the correlations between the credibility of other witnesses and final guilt judgments were much higher than when the key witness was an adult. Goodman et al. (1987) termed this the "importance displacement hypothesis," and suggested that jurors give more weight to testimony of other witnesses when the key witness is a child and not an adult.

Ross, Miller, and Moran (1987) found that the influence of witness age on perceptions of credibility is not uniformly negative. In that study, juror-subjects evaluated the testimony given in a cocaine possession case. The prosecution's key witness was a neighbor who had seen the cocaine in the defendant's bedroom, and who was described as eight, twenty-one, or seventy-four years old. The factor of witness age had a dramatic influence on credibility ratings—but in a completely unexpected variable fashion. When subjects rated the credibility of this neighbor, they rated the twenty-one-year-old as least credible, the seventy-four-year-old as moderately credible, and the eight-year-old as the most credible. These are not isolated findings; similar findings have been reported by a number of researchers (Goodman, Bottoms, Herscovici, & Shaver, this volume; Leippe & Romanczyk, in press; Ross, Dunning, Toglia, & Ceci, in press; Nigro, Buckley, Hill, & Nelson, this volume; and Duggan, Aubrey, Doherty, Isquith, Levine, & Scheiner this volume).

A Theoretical Analysis of Juror Perceptions of the Child Witness

What are we to make of these contradictory findings? Do juror stereotypes of the child witness really matter after all? Do they have any orderly effect on perceptions of witness credibility? One explanation for these complex findings centers on how stereotypes (here, of the child eyewitness) influence social judgment. A second explanation centers on whether the credibility of a witness rests primarily on the accuracy of their memory or the sincerity of their intentions. These explanations are not new, they have been suggested by a number of researchers (Goodman et al., this volume; Leippe & Romanczyk, in press; Ross et al., 1987; Ross et al., in press).

An Explanation Centering on the Role of Stereotypes

Hundreds of studies have shown that stereotypes have a dramatic influence on social judgment. Put simply, if people expect to see a characteristic in an individual (such as dependence in a child, crankiness in a senior citizen, aggressiveness in a New Yorker), they usually see it. In the parlance of social psychology, this is called an "assimilation effect"—judgments assimilate toward the relevant stereotype.

But assimilation does not occur all the time, only when the behavior of the relevant individual conforms to the stereotype or is at least open to interpretation. Consider the case of the student who glowingly praises the lecture of a professor after every class. If we have reason to think the "ingratiator" stereotype is relevant, we will quickly label the student's actions as manipulative or insincere.

Now consider the courtroom. People expect the child witness to be hesitant, vague, easily distracted, or quite eager to please the attorney questioning him or her. To the extent that the behavior of the child witness conforms to these expectations, or is ambiguous enough to be interpreted as conforming to them, jurors will naturally discount the veracity of the child's testimony. This may have occurred in the Goodman et al. (1987) study. Mock jurors viewing the videotaped testimony of a child witness may have been watching a more hesitant and confused witness. Or, when presented with a written transcript of a trial, they may have assumed that the child witness acted in a vague and unforceful manner.

Jurors perceptions of credibility, however, might be quite different when they observe a child who violates every expectation they hold of the child witness. Consider a child who testifies forcefully and in very precise detail. Such a child would be truly impressive, and perhaps even more credible than an adult counterpart exhibiting the same behavior. Many social psychological studies have shown that when stereotypes are violated, a rebound or "contrast" effect occurs: the individual is rated as less similar to the relevant stereotype than a member of a different group displaying the same behavior (Condry & Ross, 1985; Jussim, Coleman, & Lerch, 1987; Manis, Paskewitz, & Cotler 1986). In the psycholegal literature, this phenomenon has been referred to as a "perceptual adaption" effect (Ross et al., 1987), whereby jurors use different standards to evaluate the testimony of a child and an adult:

If an adult witness describes an event that is fairly complex, jurors may report that the witness is only average in terms of both intelligence and accuracy because jurors expect such abilities from an adult. However, if a child gives the identical description, then jurors are likely to rate the child as being extremely intelligent and as having an excellent memory because they do not expect children to remember complex events. (Ross et al., 1987, p. 149).

In sum, stereotypes matter—they do guide impression formation. But the specific behavior of the child also matters. To the extent that the behavior conforms to the stereotype of the child witness, the witness' testimony is discounted. To the extent that the behavior of the witness violates jurors' expectations, the child is viewed as extremely credible and convincing.

An Explanation Centering on the Components of Credibility

Classic work in social psychology (Hovland, Janis, & Kelley, 1953) has demonstrated that a person's credibility rests on two separate components: (a) that person's expertise and (b) his or her sincerity. The notion that an *eyewitness'* credibility is based on these components has already been proposed by several researchers (Goodman et al., this volume; Leippe & Romanczyk, 1987; Leippe & Romanczyk, in press; Ross et al., in press). The idea is that the relative impact of child and adult testimony depends on which of these components, expertise or honesty, is most salient in a trial. Recall that in our survey data, children were seen as less likely to render accurate testimony and more open to suggestibility. They were, however, seen as equally likely to provide sincere testimony, while Leippe & Romanczyk (1987) found children to be viewed as *more* honest than adults. Some types of trials and some sets of circumstances place a premium on a person's ability to remember. Consider, as an example, a convenience store robbery in which a child witness is called on to remember the exact sequence of events and to identify the assailant from a lineup. In this type of situation, children are less likely to be seen as credible. Consider, instead, a crime for which the honesty of the witness is the critical issue. Trials of sexual abuse, as pointed out by Goodman et al. (this volume), might fall into this category. Jurors might believe that an adult has an ulterior motive for accusing someone of abuse. The child, however, will be seen as incapable of producing the elaborate lies necessary to carry out any deception. This can be seen in several studies reported in this volume (Goodman et al., Duggan et al.). For example, Goodman et al. had subjects read a summary of a sexual abuse case in which the victim was described as a six-, fourteen-, or twenty-two-year-old female. When subjects rated the credibility of the victim, they rated the six-year-old as the most credible and the twenty-two-year-old as the least credible. In addition, subjects were more likely to convict the defendant when the victim was described as a child or adolescent than when the victim was described as an adult.

Summary

Several tentative conclusions can be drawn concerning how age stereotypes influence jurors' perceptions of children. First, the testimony of a child will be evaluated more positively than the testimony of an adult under two conditions: (1) when the child's testimony violates, in a positive manner, the juror's expectation about children's eyewitness abilities or (2) when witness credibility depends more on honesty than cognitive ability. Second, the testimony of a child will be viewed more negatively than the testimony of an adult when neither of these conditions are present, and when (1) the child acts like a typical youngster or (2) credibility rests mainly on the ability to remember events.

Communication Modality and Perceptions of the Child Witness

The analysis suggested in the preceding section, and the research it draws on consistently show that the age of the witness has a dramatic, although complex, impact on jurors' perceptions of that witness. A careful review of the extant studies on perceptions of the child witness, however, reveal a curious anomoly: The age of the witness influences perceptions (whether positively or negatively) of the witness' credibility, but has only a sporadic impact on more important judgments of guilt and innocence. Witness credibility should directly affect judgments of guilt, and witness age does influence credibility—so why does age often fail to sway decisions concerning guilt or innocence?

Our attempt to answer this question centered on one factor that has been relatively ignored in the literature to date: communication modality. Modality refers to the "medium" by which jurors have been exposed to eyewitness testimony. In some studies, jurors are presented testimony in a written format (e.g., Goodman et al., 1987; Leippe & Romanczky, 1987). In others, the jurors are shown a videotaped display of the eyewitness testimony (e.g., Ross et al., 1987). Could the modality of the testimony affect how jurors perceive the credibility of the eyewitness? It should be noted that visual displays are more persuasive than written displays (Chaiken & Eaglely, 1980). But could modality also mediate the effect of witness age on perceptions of credibility and guilt? Drawing from recent social psychological literature and Leippe and Romanczyk's (1987) "Communication/Persuasion" model of eyewitness testimony, the answer is yes. Recent studies of communication modality suggest that witness age should influence perceptions of credibility, and also decisions concerning guilt, when the testimony is *displayed visually* rather than in a written format.

Such reasoning is based on Leippe and Romanczyk's (1987) "Communication/Persuasion" model of eyewitness testimony. These researchers argue that "eyewitness testimony can be seen as a one-way communication that travels from the witness (source) to the jury (audience). The witness, in a sense, is an influence agent, attempting to persuade or convince the juror of his or her account of the what and who of the criminal event" (p. 156). Furthermore, whether or not that witness is persuasive to a great extent depends on his or her credibility. But credibility becomes a more salient issue when the communication is presented visually.

Why is this so? Leippe and Romanczyk (1987) point out that videotaped messages produce more *heuristic* processing—in which the audience makes its judgment to accept or reject a message based primarily on characteristics of the communicator (Chaiken & Eagley, 1980). Written messages, on the other hand, are evaluated by means of *systematic* processing, based solely on the coherence and force of the actual arguments presented, regardless of who presented them. Why does videotape prompt greater reliance on the characteristics of the communicator, as opposed to the message itself? According to Chaiken and Eagley (1983), "in many persuasion settings, it is not the persuasive message itself that is made more vivid (and thus more persuasive) in videotaped and audiotaped (vs. written) modalities, but, rather, *information about the communicator*" (p. 37, italics added), for example, whether the person is an expert or is physically attractive. Or—most relevant to our present concerns—whether the persuasive agent is a child or an adult. (See Leippe & Romanczyk (1987) for a more detailed discussion of the importance of heuristic versus systematic processing of child witness testimony.)

In sum, an analysis of past research on communication modality would lead us to expect that the age of the witness is more likely to affect perceptions of credibility and also judgments of guilt and innocence when the testimony is presented in a visual (videotaped) rather than written form. Such visual testimony simply makes the age of the witness more salient, which then should have a much greater impact on the judgments that jurors must reach.

The Impact of Communication Modality: A Direct Test

These hypotheses concerning the role of communication modality lead quite naturally to a simple experiment, one in which the same trial was presented in a videotaped versus a written format. We pursued this experiment, presenting subjects with a trial, based on an actual transcript, concerning a cocaine possession charge, in which the age of a key witness was varied. (The case is the same as that used by Ross, Miller, & Moran, 1987, and therefore it is only briefly described here.) We compared the data from the Ross et al. (1987) study, which used a videotape modality, with a replication study in which the same trial information was presented to mock jurors using a written trial transcript. The two studies are discussed as if they were a *single* experiment in which witness age and modality (videotape/written transcript) are the independent variables. This comparison allows us to assess any influence that modality may possess and to gauge the generalizability of the Ross et al. (1987) findings. In that experiment the perceptual adaption/contrast effect that was observed may have been caused by specific characteristics of the individuals who played the witness roles in the videotape. For instance, perhaps the child witness appeared "angelic" whereas the young adult witness had shifty eyes. By employing a written transcript, we can be assured that any witness age effects result from age stereotypes about eyewitness ability and not from extraneous factors such as unique physical appearance or notable body language of he actors employed.

The case used in the study involved a woman who was charged with possessing approximately $12,000 worth of cocaine in her apartment. There was no question in the case that the cocaine was present in her apartment. Rather, the issues were who brought it into the apartment and whether the defendant was aware of its presence. At the time of her arrest, the defendant was dating a previously convicted drug dealer who testified under a grant of immunity that the cocaine belonged to him, and that he brought the cocaine in full view of the prosecution's witness.

The prosecution's case was based on an eyewitness who testified, contrary to the drug dealer's testimony, that the drug dealer had not entered the apartment with the cocaine. Thus, the prosecution argued that the cocaine must have been in the defendant's apartment the entire time, and that she must have known that it was being stored there and perhaps had stored it there herself. Of interest in the present study was the age of the prosecution's key witness, which was described as eight, twenty-one, or seventy-four years.

In this study, witness age was crossed with the factor of communication modality (video vs. written). Subjects in the video condition saw a 50-minute videotape of a court trial in which an actual judge and two practicing criminal trial lawyers played the respective roles of judge, prosecution, and defense attorneys. The role of the prosecution witness was played by an eight, twenty-one-, or seventy-four-year-old person. The remaining subjects were presented with a written transcript of the trial. The transcript was fifteen single-spaced pages in length and took approximately 30 to 40 minutes to read. Consistent with the videotape condition, the age of the prosecution's key eyewitness was presented as eight, twenty-one, or seventy-four years. (In addition, the sex of the witness was manipulated but had no effect on the results reported here; therefore, the results discussed are collapsed across this variable.)

After watching the videotape or reading the transcript, subjects were asked to rate the guilt or innocence of the defendant on a seven-point scale, with 1 = not at all guilty and 7 = extremely guilty. In addition, subjects were given the opportunity to indicate that they were "undecided" about the defendant's guilt or innocence using an additional response category. This category was employed to differentiate between subjects who felt that the defendant was innocent because the evidence in the case failed to prove guilt beyond a reasonable doubt and subjects who were undecided about a verdict. Only 6.0 percent of the subjects (13 out of 217) reported that they were undecided. These subjects are excluded from any analyses involving guilt ratings, but are included in the analyses of witness characteristic ratings.

In addition, subjects were asked to rate the prosecution's key eyewitness on a variety of dimensions related to credibility: accuracy of witness memory, witness confidence, forcefulness of response, amount of manipulation by defense and prosecution attorneys, consistency of testimony, truthfulness of response, credibility, objectivity, intelligence, and trustworthiness. Finally, subjects rated the amount of influence the eyewitness' testimony had in their decision of guilt or innocence. Subjects were also asked to rate the defendant and the drug dealer on a subset of the same dimensions: truthfulness, credibility, accuracy of memory, confidence, and influence of testimony.

This study was designed to examine the effects of witness age and communication modality on witness credibility as well as on judgments of guilt and innocence. Juror-subjects' guilt ratings were submitted to a 3 (age of witness: 8, 21, 74 years) × 2 (communication modality: videotape versus written) analysis of variance (ANOVA), while the witness characteristic measures were submitted to a 3 (age of witness) × 2 (modality) multivariate analysis of variance (MANOVA).

An examination of the responses of subject-jurors in both the written

TABLE 3.2 Mean ratings of the prosecution's key witness by condition.[a]

Variable	Child	Young Adult	Elderly
Accuracy of memory	3.84 (a)	3.32 (b)	3.74 (ab)
Witness confidence	5.04 (a)	4.13 (b)	4.58 (ab)
Forcefulness of response	3.86 (a)	2.98 (b)	3.29 (b)
Manipulation by defense	3.10	3.21	3.16
Manipulation by prosecution	4.43	4.23	4.62
Consistency of testimony	4.21 (a)	3.46 (b)	3.94 (ab)
Telling truth	5.15 (a)	4.15 (b)	5.14 (a)
Credibility	4.06	3.64	4.05
Bias/objectivity	5.96	5.53	6.00
Intelligent	5.01 (a)	3.05 (c)	4.29 (b)
Trustworthy	5.13 (a)	4.00 (b)	5.09 (a)
Influential	4.01	3.98	3.92
Total score	53.86 (a)	45.73 (b)	51.86 (a)

[a] Means with a different letter are statistically significantly different by a Bonferroni multiple comparison test, at least at the $p < .05$ level, except for witness accuracy, which is significant only at the $p < .10$ level. Higher scores indicate more positive responses: greater perceived confidence, intelligence, and so on. Range of potential responses, 1 to 7; sample sizes by condition: child ($n = 66$), young adult ($n = 76$), and elderly ($n = 75$).

and videotaped trial conditions reveals that witness age had a profound effect on perceptions of credibility. More specifically, a contrast/perceptual adaptation effect was observed. A reliable overall main effect for witness age in the MANOVA revealed that the child witness was generally rated as the most credible, the young adult was rated as the least credible, and the elderly witness was rated as moderately credible.

Table 3.2 displays the mock jurors' responses to the specific questions we asked. As can be seen in the table, the child witness was perceived as more confident, forceful, consistent, intelligent, trustworthy, and accurate than the twenty-one-year-old. The ratings of the elderly witness were similar, but slightly less positive, than the ratings for the child witness.

A look at mock jurors' responses also suggests the specific mechanism responsible for the contrast effect we obtained. Recall, from our previous analysis, that two separate mechanisms can prompt jurors to judge the child witness as more credible than a *young adult*: (1) the child's behavior can violate the jurors' stereotypes, and (2) jurors may define credibility in terms of honesty rather than cognitive ability. These data suggest that the former mechanism was primarily responsible for producing this contrast effect (when looking at the child–young adult comparison). People believe that child witnesses should be hesitant and confused, but our juvenile witness was seen as markedly confident, forceful, consistent, and intelligent. The second mechanism received only modest support. Although the child witness was seen as more trustworthy and truthful than the young adult, juror-subjects did not rate the child as more objective. Perhaps these results are best viewed in terms of an interaction between the two mechanisms. Subjects may have attributed greater credibility to the child's tesimony because it violated their expectations about child witnesses, and to a lesser extent, there was no concern that the child was in any way involved in the drug transaction or trying to cover up for his friend and neighbor. Both of these factors may have enhanced the credibility of the child's testimony.

A similar explanation appears appropriate for the young adult/elderly comparison. As seen in Table 3.1, our survey findings show that both the eight- and seventy-four-year-old were viewed as less credible than a twenty-one-year-old in terms of accuracy of memory, suggestibility, and other factors. The elderly witness was, however, viewed as the most honest of all four age groups. Perhaps the positive ratings given to the elderly witness were also a result of a positive violation of subjects' age stereotype in regard to cognitive ability (i.e., intelligence) and to viewing the elderly witness as a very honest, trustworthy person, who would not be involved in a drug transaction. Finally, the similarity between subjects' reactions to the child and elderly witness could be attributed to a similarity in the age stereotype—both age groups are generally viewed as less credible witnesses (with the exception of honesty) than a young adult.

But although witness age had a dramatic effect on witness credibility, it failed to influence ratings of guilt. Whether the key prosecution witness was a child, a young adult, or an elderly individual, subject-jurors were equally likely to convict the defendant in this cocaine possession case. Given our results on witness credibility, this finding is surprising, yet completely consistent with past research on this topic (Goodman et al., 1987).

Communication Modality

As hypothesized previously witness age may have an impact on guilt decisions when testimony is presented visually, but not when the testimony is presented in a written transcript. Did the format of the testimony have an impact on perceptions of credibility and guilt?

As can be seen in Table 3.3, modality did have an overall main effect on eyewitness credibility. Regardless of the age of the witness, the witness was seen as more credible when the testimony was provided in a videotape than in a written transcript. However, modality did not influence ratings of guilt. Subjects in the video condition were no more likely to convict the defendant than subjects in the written condition.

Our investigation of communication modality, however, was designed to answer whether the potentially negative (or positive) views the jurors held of the child were exaggerated when testimony was offered visually, and

TABLE 3.3 Mean ratings of the prosecution's key witness by modality.[a]

Variable	Video	Written
Accuracy of memory	3.78	3.43*
Witness confidence	4.92	4.41**
Forcefulness of response	3.47	3.13*
Manipulation by defense	2.88	3.66**
Manipulation by prosecution	4.49	4.01*
Consistency of testimony	4.13	3.60**
Telling truth	5.04	4.54**
Credibility	4.02	3.66*
Bias/objectivity	6.00	5.74
Intelligent	3.93	4.21
Trustworthy	4.96	4.52**
Influential	3.74	4.15
Total score	51.40	49.13*

*$p < .10$.
**$p < .05$.
[a] Means with an asterisk are statistically significantly different as a function of a univariate F test. Higher scores indicate more positive responses: greater perceived confidence, intelligence, and so on. Range of potential responses, 1 to 7.

whether these perceptions would then spill over into judgments of guilt. On this score, the results were clear: Communication modality did not exaggerate the different perceptions that jurors held of child and adult witnesses. Moreover, it did not influence the relationship between witness age and guilt. In both modality conditions, witness age had absolutely no effect on jurors' ultimate decisions on the fate of the defendant.

What do these findings on communication modality suggest? On the one hand, they suggest that modality matters: all witnesses were seen as more convincing and credible when their testimony was videotaped than when it was written. This suggests that videotape simply makes any judgment of the witness more extreme. If a witness' written testimony is mildly credible, his or her testimony presented visually is more convincing. If the witness is hard to believe, a videotaped testimony only heightens a juror's disbelief.

Communication modality, however, does not mediate the influence of witness age on credibility. When testimony is videotaped, juror perceptions of child and adult witnesses do not diverge any more than when the testimony is written. Moreover, when the testimony is videotaped, witness age does not influence judgments concerning the guilt of the defendant. Indeed, the influence of witness age on juror perceptions is remarkably consistent across modalities.

Further Explorations of the Weight Given to Child Testimony

In one final analysis, we explored the "importance displacement" phenomenon, in which subjects discount the testimony of a child by relying more on the testimony of other witnesses in making their decision regarding the guilt or innocence of the defendant. To test this notion, we computed the correlations between the credibility of each witness (including the defendant and her boyfriend) and ratings of guilt. Goodman and her colleagues (1987) have suggested such correlations index the eyewitness' influence in juror decision making. These correlations, which are presented in Table 3.4, were computed separately for each age of witness condition and modality. Although in previous analyses communication modality did not modify the influence of witness age on ratings of guilt, in this analysis a strikingly different pattern was observed in the two modality conditions.

As seen in Table 3.4, we find no support for the importance displacement hypothesis as stated by Goodman et al. (1987). Whether the key witness is a child, young adult, or senior citizen, our subject-jurors give roughly equal weight to the testimony of other witnesses.

Looking at the correlations in the video condition, we see a pattern that indicates that subject-jurors were giving less weight to the testimony of the

TABLE 3.4 Correlation between witness credibility and guilt, broken down by witness age and modality.[a]

Witness	Witness Age		
	8 Years	21 Years	74 Years
Video Trial			
Prosecution's key witness	.02	.43**	.48**
Defendant	−.38*	−.36*	−.68**
Drug dealer (defense witness)	−.53**	−.45**	−.75**
Written Trial			
Prosecution's key witness	.67**	.16	.49**
Defendant	−.57**	−.40*	−.64**
Drug dealer (defense witness)	−.47**	−.41*	−.62**

*$p < .05$
**$p < .001$

[a] These correlations exclude thirteen subjects (five from the video condition and eight from the written) or 6.0 percent of the total sample, who responded "undecided" when asked to rate the guilt or innocence of the defendant. Sample sizes range from thirty to forty-one in each cell. Higher scores indicate greater perceived guilt of the defendant and witness credibility (measured as a single dimension). Range of potential responses, 1 to 7.

child. Although the child witness was viewed more positively than the young adult or the elderly witness, when it came to making a final decision of guilt, it appears that the child's testimony was not weighed heavily, whereas those of the young adult and the elderly witness do appear to have been given ample weight, as indicated in their higher correlations.

But this straightforward picture goes awry when we turn our attention to the written testimony condition. The testimonies of the child and (to a slightly less extent) the elderly witness appear to be weighed heavily in making the final decision of guilt, whereas the young adult's testimony is given no weight at all. This pattern follows directly from the results seen in Table 3.1, where the child and the elderly witness were viewed more positively than the young adult.

How do we explain these striking differences in guilt–credibility correlations across modalities? These findings are clearly surprising and quite puzzling, and we can find no parsimonious explanation for them. One potential explanation, which we offer hesitantly, centers on which aspect of the child testimony each modality made salient. In the written condition, perhaps subjects paid more attention to the consistency, detail, and overall quality of the child's testimony, and noted how much it violated their expectations of the eyewitness abilities of a child. This attention, in turn, resulted in their giving the child's testimony a great deal of weight. Subjects in the video condition apparently noticed that the child's testimony was exceptional given their expectations about children (since their reactions were similar to those found in the written condition), but the visual modality may have provided a constant reminder that it was a child who was testifying. These thoughts may have prompted a simple decision rule that said "don't trust a child's testimony." And thus the constant visual image of the child may have "overpowered" any positive impression made by the quality of the child's testimony. This reasoning is consistent with research on the systematic versus heuristic routes to persuasion. When presented with written messages, people attend to the quality and internal consistency of the arguments (systematic processing). When confronted with a persuasive message using a visual modality (videotape), people attend to source characteristics, such as witness age, in judging whether to accept or reject the message (Chaiken & Eagley, 1980; 1983). Therefore, the striking differences in the observed patterns of correlations may be produced by differences in the attentional focus of the jurors.

Extreme caution should be taken before accepting this explanation. First, we have no way to measure what aspects of the testimony subject-jurors were attending. In our explanation, we are guided only by past research which shows that people pay attention to the message when it is presented in a written format and to the message-giver when it is presented visually. Second, there are interpretive problems with guilt–credibility analyses in general. It is often assumed in this line of research that correlations between guilt and credibility indicate something about the weight given to the testimony of each witness in a trial (Goodman et al, 1987). This may be inappropriate for several reasons. First, in most studies on this topic the impact of witness age on guilt ratings, and the correlation between guilt and credibility do not show a one-to-one correspondence. For example Goodman et al. (1987) found that witness age had no impact on guilt ratings, yet guilt–credibility correlations suggested that the testimony of the child was not given as much weight as the testimony of the adult. If a child is a witness for the prosecution, and his or her testimony is discounted by a jury, then jurors should be less likely to convict the defendant than when the witness is an whose testimony is given a great deal of weight. In other studies the opposite occurs, when witness age has significant effects on guilt ratings, but guilt–credibility correlations do not differ by witness age (Leippe & Romanczyk, 1987). If correlational analyses truly reflect a decision making process, why is it that guilt ratings and guilt–credibility correlations do not tell the same story?

Another difficulty with guilt–credibility analyses is that witness credibility is often treated as a unidimensional construct. Wigmore (1935) and Ross et al. (1987) have argued that witness credibility is multidimensional and should be measured accordingly. As seen in Table 3.2, there are no age differences in the unidimensional credibility measure, but a strong age effect is seen in the summation score, which collapses over multiple witness characteristics and represents a more accurate reflection of general credibility. Relying on mono-method measures in guilt–credibility correlations may suffer both in terms of reliability and construct validity, which may be contributing to the conflicting results seen in the literature (Cook & Campell, 1979).

In the experiments reported here, we attempted to overcome some of these methodological problems by asking subjects directly to rate how much the testimony of each witness in the trial influenced their decision regarding the guilt or innocence of the defendant. As can be seen in Table 3.1, there were no age differences in the subjects' ratings of the influence of the prosecution's key eyewitness, and correlations between influence ratings and guilt (following the same format as shown in Table 3.4 with guilt–credibility correlations) failed to show any consistent pattern. Although influence ratings appear to be a straightforward solution to this issue, they too may be inappropriate. Nisbett and Wilson (1977) found that people are often inaccurate in their reports of what factors they used in making a decision about a given issue (see also Nisbett & Bellows, 1977; Nisbett & Ross, 1980).

In any event, certainly one direction for future research in this area is to develop more adequate measures of how a child's testimony is being weighed in the jury decision-making process. For example, given the problems we have discussed here concerning correlational tests of the importance displacement hypothesis, we suggest that importance displacement should be studied *experimentally*. By that, we mean that future experimenters should manipulate the credibility of various witnesses in a trial (e.g., by changing the occupation of one witness from a Sunday school teacher to a prostitute). If the credibility of these other witnesses begins to sway guilt judgments more when the key witness is a child rather than an adult, then we would have strong support for the existence of importance displacement. Until that type of experiment is conducted, we are left with statistical tests that include a number of interpretive problems.

Conclusions

These data indicate that witness age has a dramatic impact on jurors perceptions of credibility, even though witness age has virtually no impact on guilt ratings. In this specific study, subjects reacted more positively to the child witness than to either the young adult or the elderly witness. Communication modality (video versus written) did not modify this finding. There were, however, two modality effects. First, subjects' ratings of the prosecution's witness were more extreme in the video condition, regardless of witness age. And second, strikingly different patterns of correlations between guilt and credibility for the child's testimony were found in the two modalities. However, it remains *extremely* difficult to make inferences about the weight given to the child's testimony, given the complexity of the findings and the methodological difficulties with guilt–credibility analyses in general.

The findings of the present experiment suggest several issues one should consider before conducting an experiment on jurors' perceptions of eyewitness testimony. Specifically, the results of any one study on jurors' perceptions of the child witness depend, in large part, on *the specific behavior of the child or adult witness*. Therefore, psychologists should pay particular attention to what they are manipulating in their studies—the behavior of the witness or simply the age-label applied. As our analysis suggests, if a child witness in a psychological study acts like a typical child, then jurors will discount his or her credibility. If the child witness acts more "adult-like," juror-subjects may be favorably impressed. Thus, researchers should not automatically attempt to hold the statements of the adult and child witness as constant as possible (Wells et al., this volume). When they do, they are, in essence, creating an adultlike child (or a childlike adult) and therefore ensuring a contrast effect in which the child is seen as unduly credible (or the adult is seen as not at all credible). However, as Wells et al. (this volume) illustrate, there is enormous individual variability within a given age range in terms of witness confidence, accuracy, and other factors. Undoubtedly there are situations in which "adultlike" children are asked to testify, and when they do, perceptual adapation may enhance their credibility. The broader point to be made here is that researchers should be very attentive to the interaction between the age of the witness and individual differences in witness performance when asking mock jurors to evaluate the credibility of children.

The research reported here, however, raises two difficult and intriguing questions. First, how accurate are jurors at evaluating the testimony of a child? Second, are jurors' stereotypes about child witnesses warranted or accurate? Some attempts have been made to answer these questions. Goodman, Bottoms, Herscovici, & Shaver (this volume) videotaped children who were three to six years of age as they answered direct- and cross-examination questions concerning a visit they made nine to twelve months earlier to a medical center to receive an innoculation shot. The videotapes were shown to mock jurors who were asked to make judgments about the accuracy of each witness. In general, there was no correlation between mock jurors' perceptions of children's accuracy and the children's actual accuracy scores. In a similar study, Wells, Turtle, & Luus (this volume) videotaped eight-year-olds, twelve-year-olds, and college students answering direct- and cross-examination questions about a crime they had observed. The videotapes were shown to mock jurors who were asked to estimate the accuracy of each witness. Wells et al. (this volume) found that children's performance scores increased with age, and although the mock jurors' estimates of witness performance were fairly accurate on the direct-examination questions, they grossly overestimated the performance of the eight-year-olds on the cross-examination questions. Finally, Leippe and Romanczyk (1987) found that adults were accurate in their estimates of children's face recognition performance, but they underestimated young children's ability to recall events.

These findings are consistent with research showing that jurors tend to have difficulty estimating the accuracy of adult witnesses as well (Brigham & Bothwell, 1983; Lindsay, Wells, & Rumpel, 1981; Wells, Lindsay, & Tousignant, 1980, Wells & Leippe, 1981; Leippe & Romanczyk, 1987). One possible explanation for these findings is that there are no quick and easy markers or "traits" that distinquish accurate from inaccurate witnesses. Memory researchers over the last several decades have shown that memory performance is context specific and not cross-situationally consistent (e.g., Ceci, 1987; Ceci & Bronfenbrenner, 1985; Gardner, 1983; Neisser, 1982). Because no memorial traits can be observed across all contexts to differentiate accurate from inaccurate witnesses, jurors use markers such as witness confidence, facial expressions, and memory for irrelevant details to make judgments about witness accuracy. Unfortunately many of these markers, such as witness confidence, have been shown to be unrelated to accuracy (Deffenbacher & Loftus, 1982).

A similar situation appears to exist in relation to age differences in eyewitness performance. Leippe & Romanczyk (1987) point out that widespread disagreement exists among memory researchers over whether there are age differences in certain types of face-recognition or other memory-related abilities. In many situations, as Wells et al. (this volume) suggest, variability in eyewitness performance may be greater within age groups than between them. Therefore, using age as a "marker" to judge witness accuracy and credibility may lead jurors to make erroneous assumptions.

In sum, these studies suggest that a seemingly straightforward issue can, with some reflection and empirical study, become quite complex. Jurors do not have uniformly simple age stereotypes or reactions to the child witness. Although in general, subject-jurors have a negative stereotype concerning child witnesses (with the exception of beliefs about honesty), this can produce both negative and positive reactions to a particular child witness because of assimilation and contrast effects that are based on the performance of the witness and other case characteristics. This line of investigation would benefit greatly from the isolation of factors that produce these divergent results. A successful study of this type would provide enormous insight not only into juror reactions to the child witness, but into the more general issue of how stereotypes influence, impression formation and social judgment.

References

Beach, B.H. (January 31, 1983). Out of the mouth of babes. *Time*, p. 58.

Brigham, J.C., & Bothwell, R.K. (1983). The ability of prospective jurors to estimate the accuracy of eyewitness identifications. *Law and Human Behavior*, 7, 19–30.

Ceci, S.J. (1987). On Intelligence . . . . more or less: A bio-ecological theory of individual differences in cognition. Unpublished manuscript.

Ceci, S.J., & Bronfenbrenner, U. (1985). Don't forget to take the cupcakes out of the oven: Prospective memory, strategic time-monitoring, and context. *Child Development*, 56, 152–164.

Ceci, S.J., Ross, D.F., & Toglia, M.P. (1987). Suggestibility of children's memory: Psycholegal implications. *Journal of Experimental Psychology: General*, 116, 38–49.

Chaiken, S., Eagley, A.H. (1980). Heuristic versus systematic information processing and the use of source versus message cues in persuasion. *Journal of Personality and Social Psychology*, 37, 1387–1397.

Chaiken, S., & Eagley, A.H. (1983). Communication modality as a determinant of persuasion: The role of communicator salience. *Journal of Personality and Social Psychology*, 39, 752–766.

Condry, J.C., & Ross, D.F. (1985). Sex and aggression: The influence of gender label on the perception of aggression in children. *Child Development*, 56, 225–233.

Cook, T.D., & Campbell, D.T. (1979). *Quasi-experimentation: Design and analysis issues for field settings*. Chicago: Rand McNally.

Deffenbacher, K., & Loftus, E.F. (1982). Do jurors share a common understanding concerning eyewitness behavior? *Law and Human Behavior*, 6, 15–30.

Duggan, L.M., Aubrey, M., Doherty, E., Isquith, P., Levine, M., & Scheiner, J. (in this volume). The credibility of children as witnesses in a simulated child sex abuse trial.

Finkelhor, D. (1984). *Child sexual abuse*. New York: The Free Press.

Gardner, H. (1983). *Frames of mind: The theory of multiple intelligences*. New York: Cambridge University Press.

Goodman, G.S. (1984). Children's testimony in historical perspective. *Journal of Social Issues, 40*, 9–31.

Goodman, G.S., Bottoms, B.L., Hersocvici, B.B., & Shaver, P. (in this volume). Determinants of the child victim's perceived credibility.

Goodman, G.S., Golding, J.M., Helgeson, V., Haith, M., & Michelli, J. (1987). When a child takes the stand: Jurors' perceptions of children's eyewitness testimony. *Law and Human Behavior, 11*, 27–40.

Hovland, C.I., Janis, I.L. & Kelley, H.H. (1953). *Communication and persuasion*. New Haven, CT: Yale University Press.

Jessum. L., Coleman, L., Lerch, L. (1987). The nature of stereotypes: A comparison and integration of three theories. *Journal of Personality and Social Psychology, 52*, 536–546.

Leippe, M.R., & Romanczyk, A. (1987). Children on the witness stand: A communication/persuasion analysis of jurors' reactions to child witnesses. In S.J. Ceci, M.P. Toglia, & D.F. Ross (eds.). *Children's eyewitness memory*. New York: Springer-Verlag.

Leippe, M.R. & Romanczyk, A. (In press). Reactions to child (versus adult) eyewitnesses: The influence of jurors' preconceptions and witness behavior. *Law and Human Behavior*.

Lindsay, R.C.L., Wells, G.L., & Rumpel, C. (1981). Can people detect eyewitness identification accuracy within and between situations? *Journal of Applied Psychology, 66*, 79–89.

Manis, M., Paskewitz, J., Cotler, S. (1986). Stereotypes and social judgment. *Journal of Personality and Social Psychology, 50*, 461–473.

Melton, G.B. (1984). Child witnesses and the First Amendment: A psycholegal dilemma. *Journal of Social Issues, 40*, 109–125.

Neisser, U. (1982). *Remembering in natural context*. San Francisco: W.H. Freeman.

Nigro, G.N., Buckley, M.A., Hill, D.E., & Nelson, J. (in this volume). When juries "hear" children's testimony: The effects of eyewitness age and speech style on jurors perceptions of testimony.

Nisbett, R.E., & Bellows, N. (1977). Verbal reports about causal influences on social judgments: Private access versus public theories. *Journal of Personality and Social Psychology, 35*, 613–624.

Nisbett, R.E., Ross, L. (1980). *Human inferences: Strategies and shortcomings of social judgment*. Englewood Cliffs, NJ: Prentice-Hall.

Nisbett, R.E., & Wilson, T.D. (1977). The halo effect: Evidence for unconscious alteration of judgments. *Journal of Personality and Social Psychology, 35*, 250–256.

Ross, D.F., Miller, B.S., & Moran, P. (1987). The child in the eyes of the jury: Assessing mock jurors' perceptions of the child witness. In S.J. Ceci, M.P. Toglia, & D.F. Ross (eds.). *Children's eyewitness memory*. New York: Springer-Verlag.

Ross, D.F., Dunning, D., Toglia, M., & Ceci, S.J. (in press). The child in the eyes of the jury: Assessing mock jurors' perceptions of the child witness. *Law and Human Behavior*.

Wells, G.L., & Leippe, M.R. (1981). How do triers of fact infer the accuracy of eyewitness identification? Using memory for detail can be misleading. *Journal of Applied Psychology*, *66*, 682–687.

Wells, G.L., Lindsay, R.C.L., & Tousignant, J.P. (1980). Effects of expert psychological advice on human performance in judging the validity of eyewitness testimony. *Law and Human Behavior*, *4*, 275–285.

Wells, G.L., Turtle, J.W., Luus, C.A. (in this volume). The perceived credibility of child eyewitnesses: What happens when they use their own words?

Whipple, G.M. (1911). The psychology of testimony. *Psychological Bulletin*, *8*, 307–309.

Wigmore, J.H. (1935). *A student's textbook of the law of evidence*. Brooklyn: The Foundation Press.

Yarmey, A.D., & Jones, H.P.T. (1983). Is the psychology of eyewitness identifications a matter of common sense? In S.M.A. Lloyd-Bostock & B.R. Cliffords (eds.). *Evaluating witness evidence: Recent psychological research and new perspectives*. Chichester: Wiley.

4
When Juries "Hear" Children Testify: The Effects of Eyewitness Age and Speech Style on Jurors' Perceptions of Testimony

GEORGIA N. NIGRO, MAUREEN A. BUCKLEY,
DINA E. HILL, and JENNIFER NELSON

Although eyewitnesses appear in few trials (Kalven & Zeisel, 1966), juries decide only a fraction of these (Cole, 1975), and child witnesses are rarer still (Ross, Miller, & Moran, 1987), jurors' reactions to children's testimony deserve study for several reasons. One reason is the role played by the anticipated reaction of a jury at different stages of the criminal justice process (Stasser, Kerr, & Bray, 1982). As Stasser et al. (1982) point out, jurors' probable reactions figure in decisions to arrest, indict, and enter into plea bargaining. What are jurors' probable reactions to children's testimony? Although it has been widely assumed that jurors would not believe a child (Yarmey & Jones, 1983), recent evidence suggests that this assumption is too simplistic. Another reason to study jurors' reactions to children's testimony is the growing number of cases in which a child is the key witness (Goodman, Golding, Helgeson, Haith, & Michelli, 1987). As prosecutors face more cases in which key testimony is provided by a child, and as legislatures change laws to accommodate the young witness, the need for systematic information about jurors' perceptions grows.

Is the child witness more credible under some circumstances than others? In an attempt to answer this question, we survey the recent literature concerning jurors' perceptions of children's eyewitness testimony. We then report the results of a study designed to examine a variable that may mediate the effects of age on jurors' reactions to a child eyewitness—that is, the power of an eyewitness's speech style. The eyewitness in our study delivered his testimony in either a powerful or powerless speech style (Conley, O'Barr, & Lind, 1978; Erickson, Lind, Johnson, & O'Barr, 1978; Lind & O'Barr, 1979; O'Barr 1982). The powerless style is characterized by hedges (e.g., "kind of," "I guess"), hesitation forms (e.g., "uh," "well"), intensifiers (e.g., "surely," "definitely"), and a questioning intonation in normally declarative contexts. These features are less common in the powerful style. The inclusion of the speech style variable followed from the assumption that how something is said is often as important as what is said. How something is said in a courtroom is especially important because trials are literally "heard" (Lind & O'Barr, 1979); speech is the dominant medium of both civil and criminal trials. Even material evidence such as documents and photographs is usually introduced through the spoken testimony of a witness.

The powerful and powerless speech styles were first identified by O'Barr (1982) and his colleagues after ethnographic analysis of more than 150 hours of court speech taped in a North Carolina Superior Court. These researchers then examined the effects of these stylistic variations on trial processes in a series of studies. For example, Erickson et al. (1978) found that the powerful style resulted in increased credibility of an adult witness as well as heightened attractiveness of the witness and increased damage awards. O'Barr (1982) reported that many of these effects persisted even after jurors were instructed to disregard speaking styles.

Why is the speech style of a child witness of interest? As Goodman et al. (1984) point out, children probably appear more powerless than adults, especially in the stressful atmosphere of a courtroom. Their voices are not as audible as adults', and they probably use more powerless expressions, such as "uh" and "um." Although there are no data to support the claim that children's testimony is less powerful than adults', trial practice manuals (e.g., Bailey & Rothblatt, 1971) often describe tactics that take advantage of children's linguistic vulnerabilities. Jurors may react to the power of a child's delivery in several ways. They may evaluate a child's delivery in the same way they evaluate an adult's, penalizing a powerless style and rewarding a powerful one. A more interesting possibility is that jurors may evaluate a child's delivery differently from that of an adult. They may be especially harsh on a child's powerlessness, much as jurors in a recent study by Leippe and Romanczyk (1987) did not excuse a child witness's inconsistencies. Conversely, they may be especially impressed by a child's powerful delivery, much as jurors in a recent study by Ross et al. (1987) rated a child witness more positively than an adult who delivered the same testimony. Alternatively, jurors might discount the power of a child's delivery, viewing powerlessness in a child as undiagnostic of the child's memory abilities (Leippe & Romanczyk, 1987). Finally, jurors might view with suspicion a child's powerful delivery. A child who speaks in a powerful style may appear more rehearsed than a child who speaks in a powerless style.

In our review of the literature, we begin with research on the effects of age alone on jurors' reactions to children's testimony. Then we turn to research, including our own, in which age has been studied in conjunction with other variables that may play an important role in mediating the effects of age on jurors' perceptions of a eyewitness.

The "Main Effect" Model: Jurors' Reactions to the Age of an Eyewitness

In several recent studies, researchers have varied the age of an eyewitness to a crime and examined the effect of this manipulation on jurors' ratings of defendant guilt and witness credibility. In three experiments, Goodman et al. (1987; see also Goodman, Golding, & Haith, 1984) manipulated the age of an eyewitness who provided crucial testimony in a trial. In their first experiment, mock jurors read a description of a trial concerning a fatal car–pedestrian accident; the only eyewitness to the accident was described as six, ten, or thirty years old. Subjects rated the defendant's degree of guilt and the credibility of the defendant, the eyewitness, and three other witnesses. The credibility of the eyewitness increased with age: the six-year-old eyewitness was rated as least credible and the thirty-year-old eyewitness most credible. The defendant's degree of guilt, however, was not affected by the age of the eyewitness.

In their second experiment, Goodman et al. demonstrated that the results generalized to another type of trial, in this case, a murder trial. Again, the credibility of the eyewitness increased as a function of age, but the defendant's degree of guilt did not.

The third experiment employed a videotaped trial based on the scenario from the first experiment and potential jurors from the surrounding community. This time, jurors rated the defendant's degree of guilt and the witnesses' credibility before and after groups of twelve jurors deliberated over the case. Once again, the findings confirmed earlier results: the six-year-old eyewitness was less credible than the thirty-year-old eyewitness, but eyewitness age had no effect on the defendant's degree of guilt. Further analyses revealed that the credibility of both the thirty-year-old and the ten-year-old eyewitnesses predicted subjects' guilt ratings better than did the credibility of the other witnesses. However, the credibility of the six-year-old eyewitness was no more predictive than that of the other four witnesses. When Goodman et al. examined jurors' comments during deliberations, they found that the proportion of negative statements about the eyewitness (e.g., "I think her memory is confused") decreased as eyewitness age increased. Taken together, these experiments support the suspicion that adults attribute less credibility to a child than to an adult. But contrary to Goodman et al.'s initial predictions, adults did not attribute greater guilt to a defendant when an adult eyewitness testified.

Ross et al. (1987) also varied the age of an eyewitness in a videotaped trial based on an actual court transcript of a case involving narcotics possession. The eyewitness was an eight-year-old boy, a twenty-one-year-old man, or a seventy-four-year-old man. After mock jurors viewed the videotape, they rated each of three witnesses (including the eyewitness) on a variety of dimensions including credibility, objectivity, consistency, truthfulness, and attractiveness. They also rated the defendant's degree of guilt. In contrast to the findings of Goodman et al. (1987), Ross et al. found no effect of age on eyewitness credibility. Subjects judged the eight-year-old child's testimony to be as credible as that of the twenty-one-year-old and the seventy-four-year-old. Eyewitness age also had no effect on the defendant's degree of guilt, replicating Goodman et al.'s (1987) finding. However, age of the eyewitness did have an impact on jurors. A multivariate analysis across the dimensions of objectivity, consistency, truthfulness, and other factors revealed that jurors viewed the child witness much more positively than the twenty-one-year-old witness. Ratings of the elderly witness more closely resembled those for the child witness than those for the twenty-one-year-old witness. Ross et al. suggested that jurors' expectations for children (and the elderly) may differ from their expectations for young adults. Thus, a twenty-one-year-old man who recounts a fairly complex event may be rated as average in intelligence and accuracy, whereas an eight-year-old boy who gives the same account may be rated as highly intelligent and accurate. Despite the jurors' positive view of the child witness, the child's credibility ratings were not significantly correlated with ratings of the defendant's guilt. In contrast, for both the seventy-four-year-old and the twenty-one-year-old witness, credibility and guilt were reliably correlated.

The results of these two studies suggest there are no easy answers to the question of jurors' reactions to the age of an eyewitness. On the one hand, there was agreement in finding that the age of an eyewitness had no effect on the defendant's degree of guilt. But, as Ross et al. (1987) cautioned, this finding may not be as generalizable as it appears at first glance. Perhaps eyewitness age has no effect on jurors' verdicts when the trial evidence favors the prosecution or the defense (as it may have in the two studies). Possibly, eyewitness age affects guilt ratings when a case is ambiguous.

On the other hand, the results of the two studies diverged on the question of whether age of an eyewitness has an effect on witness credibility. Ross et al. (1987) noted that the source of the discrepancy may be subjects' reactions to particular characteristics of the persons who played the witnesses in the videotapes of the two studies. They suggested that the child witness in their study may have been more "angelic" than the one in Goodman et al.'s (1987) study, and thus made a more favorable impression on mock jurors. Another possibility is that the child witness in the Ross et al. study may have used a more powerful speech style than the child in the other study.

These areas of agreement and disagreement underscore the need for research that extends beyond the "main-effect" model, in which only the age of the eyewitness varies (Ross et al., 1987). It is imperative that experimental designs include variables such as the nature of the evidence in a case, eyewitness characteristics, juror characteristics, trial type, and other factors that may mediate jurors' reactions to the age of an eyewitness. The investigations to which we now turn our attention are, we believe, a first step in this direction.

Beyond the "Main Effect" Model

In two recent studies, researchers have examined the impact of other variables in the investigation of mock jurors' reactions to eyewitness age. In the first of two experiments, Leippe and Romanczyk (1987) varied eyewitness age and strength of evidence in a robbery–murder case. Mock jurors read a summary of the case in which the only eyewitness was described as a six-year-old boy, a ten-year-old boy, or a thirty-year-old man. In addition, incriminating evidence was manipulated to create a strong, ambiguous, or weak case against the defendant. A control group read a strong version of the case that did not include eyewitness testimony. Subjects gave a dichotomous judgment of the defendant's guilt and provided ratings of the credibility of the eyewitness and two other witnesses.

The results showed that age reliably affected ratings of eyewitness credibility. The six-year-old eyewitness was rated as least credible and the thirty-year-old as most credible. Age did not have a similar effect on guilty verdicts, but, more interestingly, it interacted with case strength. Eyewitness age made no difference when the case against the defendant was weak. However, age had some influence when the case was ambiguous, and it was a key factor when the case was strong. In particular, when the case was strong and the eyewitness was an adult, the verdict was always guilty. When the case was strong but the eyewitness was six or ten years old, guilty verdicts occurred no more frequently than when there was no eyewitness.

Thus, contrary to Ross et al.'s (1987) suggestion that eyewitness age would have the greatest effect when a case was ambiguous, it appears that jurors take eyewitness age into consideration when the evidence is particularly strong. Leippe and Romanczyk (1987) offer two possible interpretations of this finding. One is that jurors may first notice eyewitness age and then selectively process other incriminating evidence according to the age of the eyewitness. An adult eyewitness may induce a selective focus on other incriminating evidence, whereas a child eyewitness may not. Alternatively, jurors may first recognize strong evidence from other sources and then process eyewitness evidence according to the age of the witness. Strong incriminating evidence may enhance jurors' acceptance of an adult's testimony but leave untouched their suspicion of a child's testimony.

In their second experiment, Leippe and Romanczyk (1987) included eyewitness consistency and severity of the defendant's possible sentence in their study of jurors' reactions to the age of an eyewitness. Mock jurors read a summary of a case involving a mugging and murder. The only eyewitness to the crime was a six-year-old boy, a ten-year-old boy, or a thirty-year-old man. Subjects read a version of the case in which consistency between the eyewitness's original statement to the police and testimony in court was either high or low. In addition, subjects learned that, if convicted, the defendant faced either a light sentence (five to seven years, with possible parole after two years) or a heavy sentence (life, with no parole). After reading the case summary, subjects judged the defendant's guilt and rated the credibility of the eyewitness. Leippe and Romanczyk found that neither eyewitness age, eyewitness consistency, nor the severity of the defendant's possible sentence affected guilty verdicts. Guilty verdicts were fairly high in all conditions. Eyewitness consistency did affect credibility ratings: the consistent eyewitness was judged more credible than the inconsistent eyewitness. More important, eyewitness consistency and age had an interactive effect on credibility. Consistency of the testimony did not influence the credibility of the ten-year-old or the thirty-year-old; only the six-year-old paid a price for inconsistency. Specifically, the inconsistent six-year-old witness was perceived as less credible than the consistent six-year-old and less credible than the inconsistent ten-year-old and thirty-year-old. According to Leippe and Romanczyk, it appears that adults are unforgiving of a child's inconsistencies. Rather than discounting a child's inconsistencies as undiagnostic of the child's memory abilities, mock jurors seem to demand high internal consistency in the testimony of a child witness.

A recently completed study in our laboratory was also designed to examine issues that extend beyond the main-effect model. In our experiment, 192 college students read a twelve-page description of a case involving a fatal car–pedestrian accident (based on the trial used by Goodman et al. [1987] in their first experiment). The subjects first read opening statements by the judge, the prosecuting attorney, and the defense attorney, and then read testimony from five witnesses. Three witnesses offered circumstantial evidence, and one offered eyewitness testimony. The eyewitness testified that he saw the defendant run a red light. The fifth witness, the defendant, claimed that the pedestrian ran out in front of his car as he proceeded through a green light. Closing arguments by the two attorneys and the judge's instructions completed the description.

Four versions of the trial description were required, one corresponding to each of the conditions of a 2×2 between-subjects design. Forty-eight subjects served in each treatment condition. One between-subjects variable was the age of the eyewitness. The eyewitness was either an eight-year-old boy or a twenty-five-year-old man. The other between-subjects variable was the power of the eyewitness's speech style. The eyewitness testified in either the powerful or the powerless speech style, described earlier. For example, in answer to a question about what happened in the late afternoon of August 11 regarding the accident on 3rd and Vine Streets, the powerful eyewitness in our study said, "I was coming home from a friend's house, and I was getting ready to cross the street, and I saw a car go through a red light and hit a man." In contrast, the powerless eyewitness answered, "Well, I was coming home from a friend's house, and uh, I was just about to cross the street, and . . . then I saw a car go through a red light and, you know, hit a man." In a pilot test of the four versions of the trial description, subjects rated the eyewitness who spoke in the powerful style as more credible, trustworthy, and intelligent than the eyewitness who delivered testimony in the powerless style. The only nonsignificant effect of speech style in the pilot testing was for consistency. The powerful eyewitness was rated as no more consistent than the powerless one.

After subjects read the trial description, they rated the defendant's

TABLE 4.1 Mean credibility ratings of the eyewitness before and after deliberation.[a]

Eyewitness Age, Years	Speech Style	
	Powerful	Powerless
	Before Deliberation	
8	5.04	4.25
25	4.40	4.08
	After Deliberation	
8	4.38	3.50
25	3.75	3.25

[a] $N = 48$ subjects in each treatment condition before deliberation and 8 juries in each treatment condition after deliberation.

degree of guilt and the credibility of the eyewitness and other witnesses on seven-point scales, ranging from 1 for not credible or not guilty to 7 for very credible or very guilty. Following the individual ratings, the jurors deliberated in groups of six for 45 minutes, or until they reached a unanimous verdict of guilt or innocence. Eight juries of six served in each of the treatment conditions. Deliberations were tape recorded. Finally, after deliberation, jurors completed a set of individual ratings identical to the set they had filled out before deliberation.

Beginning with jurors' individual ratings of eyewitness credibility and defendant guilt, we found that eyewitness age and speech style affected both. Table 4.1 shows the mean credibility ratings of the eyewitness before and after jury deliberation. An analysis of variance calculated on the before-deliberation credibility ratings revealed significant main effects of eyewitness age and style of speech. Specifically, subjects viewed the child witness as more credible than the adult witness and the powerful witness as more credible than the powerless one. There was no interaction between the two variables. An analysis of variance on the after-deliberation credibility ratings was performed using the mean rating for each jury as the dependent variable. This analysis showed that even after deliberation, subjects perceived the powerful speaker as more credible than the powerless one.

Table 4.2 displays the mean guilt ratings of the defendant both before and after jury deliberation. An analysis of variance on the guilt ratings revealed an interesting pattern of results. A main effect of speech style was found for the before-deliberation guilt ratings. Subjects gave higher ratings when the eyewitness spoke in the powerful style. However, this finding was qualified by a significant interaction between age and speech style. The defendant received the highest guilt ratings when the eyewitness was a child who spoke in the powerful style and the lowest ratings when the

TABLE 4.2 Mean guilt ratings of the defendant before and after deliberation.[a]

Eyewitness Age, Years	Speech Style	
	Powerful	Powerless
	Before Deliberation	
8	4.10	3.02
25	3.38	3.27
	After Deliberation	
8	3.75	1.75
25	1.88	1.88

[a] $N = 48$ subjects in each treatment condition before deliberation and 8 juries in each treatment condition after deliberation.

eyewitness was a child who testified in the powerless style. Speech style had little effect on guilt when the adult eyewitness testified. Similar findings emerged when the after-deliberation guilt ratings were analyzed using the mean rating for each jury as the dependent variable. Again, when the eyewitness spoke powerfully, the defendant received higher guilt ratings. In this instance, the defendant also received higher guilt ratings when the eyewitness was a child. Most important, however, the significant interaction between eyewitness age and speech style persisted. The defendant again received the highest guilt ratings when a child testified in the powerful style and the lowest when a child spoke in the powerless style. Speech style had no effect on guilt when an adult eyewitness testified.

Unlike all previous studies, the present one uncovered circumstances under which mock jurors judge a child witness to be more credible than an adult witness and a defendant more guilty based on a child's tesimony than on an adult's. Speech style appears to be a potent factor mediating the effects of eyewitness age on adults' perceptions of eyewitness credibility and defendant guilt. Adults do not seem to discount a child's speaking style; on the contrary, they generously "reward" the child who delivers testimony in a powerful style and "punish" the child who speaks in the powerless style probably more typical of children. In other words, adults appear to be very vigilant in their scrutiny of a child witness. Leippe and Romanczyk (1987) reported a similar vigilance in their subjects' unwillingness to excuse inconsistencies in a young child witness.

The mediating effect of speech style had an especially strong impact on the guilt ratings. Its effect was not as strong for the credibility ratings, however, in which no interaction between eyewitness age and speech style emerged. In an attempt to find out why the pattern of results differed for the credibility and guilt ratings, we computed correlations between ratings of witness credibility and defendant guilt for each condition. (Only the before-deliberation ratings were used in these analyses.) The results indicated significant positive correlations between eyewitness credibility and defendant guilt in every condition. When partial correlations between eyewitness credibility and defendant guilt were computed, controlling for the credibility of the other witnesses, only in the case of the child who testified in the powerless style did the correlation fall to zero. In the other three conditions, eyewitness credibility and defendant guilt remained significantly correlated after partialing out the effects of the credibility of other witnesses. These results suggest that although jurors found the child who testified in the powerless style fairly credible, when it came to assigning guilt to the defendant, they may have sought corroborating evidence in the testimony of the other witnesses. The child who testified in the powerful style did not seem to prompt jurors to consider corroborating evidence. The same was true of the adult eyewitness, regardless of speech style.

Turning next to the tape-recorded jury sessions, we found that the deliberations lasted from 1.10 to 45.0 minutes, with a mean length of 12.15 minutes. An analysis of variance on the deliberation times indicated no differences among the four treatment conditions. To examine the content of the deliberations, we categorized jurors' statements according to a scheme proposed by Wells and Lindsay (1983). Wells and Lindsay suggested that jurors rely on three types of information to infer the accuracy of another's memory: (1) witnessing conditions, such as lighting and length of exposure; (2) consistency of information both within the remembering person and across persons who shared the experience; and (3) response-bias information, such as the rememberer's confidence or willingness to admit memory failures. We implemented this scheme in the following manner. Under witnessing conditions, we coded two types of statements: statements influenced by self-based judgments (e.g., Would I have remembered that?) and all other statements about witnessing conditions. Under consistency of information, we also coded two types of statements: statements about within-witness consistency and statements about across-witness consistency. Under response-bias information, we coded statements about the eyewitness's confidence. A second coder scored 30 percent of the statements. The reliability coefficient across coders was .95. Because each jury deliberated for a different length of time, each jury's total number of statements in each category was divided by the length of that jury's deliberations. Table 4.3 shows the mean number of statements per minute by information type. Analyses of variance were performed on these means. (Analyses of covariance performed on the total number of statements, using deliberation time as a covariate, yielded the same results.)

A few significant findings emerged from these analyses. For witnessing conditions, eyewitness age and speech style interacted in their effect on statements influenced by self-based judgments. Subjects made more such statements when the eyewitness was an adult who spoke in the powerful

TABLE 4.3 Mean number of juror statements per minute by information type.[a]

Information Type	Powerful Speech Style		Powerless Speech Style	
	8-year-old	25-year-old	8-year-old	25-year-old
Witnessing Conditions				
Self-based judgments	0.07	0.22	0.13	0.05
Other statements	2.66	2.83	1.98	2.16
Consistency of Information				
Within-witness	0.04	0.01	0.17	0.15
Across-witness	0.13	0.15	0.09	0.16
Response-Bias Information				
Eyewitness confidence	0.06	0.06	0.27	0.42

[a] $N = 8$ juries in each treatment condition.

style than in any other condition, suggesting that subjects may have identified with this eyewitness more than with the others. Although subjects made many other statements about witnessing conditions, as can be seen in Table 4.3, neither eyewitness age nor speech style affected statements about witnessing conditions that excluded self-based judgments. For information consistency, the only finding was a marginally significant effect of speech style on within-witness consistency. Subjects commented more on the consistency of the powerless witness than on that of the powerful one. It is interesting that, contrary to what one might have expected based on the correlation results, neither eyewitness age nor speech style affected across-witness consistency. For response-bias information, we found that eyewitness speech style affected statements about the eyewitness's confidence. Juries discussed witness confidence more when the witness spoke in the powerless style than when he spoke powerfully. Overall, these findings demonstrate further the important contribution of presentational style to jurors' reactions to eyewitness testimony. Seemingly small variations in speech style produced significantly different patterns of deliberations as well as trial outcomes.

In examining the verdicts reached by the juries, we found that only three of the thirty-two juries voted to convict. All three pro-conviction juries had read testimony by the child who testified in the powerful style, and all three deliberated at or above the mean deliberation time. Three juries hung. One of these juries also read testimony by the child who spoke powerfully, and two read testimony by the powerless adult. The three hung juries all deliberated well above the mean deliberation time. The remaining twenty-six juries voted to acquit. A chi-square test on the verdicts did not reach significance.

Conclusions

The study reported here demonstrated what others (e.g., Goodman et al., 1987) have suspected: under some circumstances, children are more credible witnesses than adults. We showed that a characteristic of the eyewitness—speech style—mediated the effects of age on jurors' reactions to a witness. When the eyewitness was a child, mock jurors' ratings of a defendant's guilt depended on the child's presentational style. Style did not have a similar effect when the eyewitness was an adult. What is especially surprising about these results is that they demonstrate that speech style has an impact not only on evaluations of the witness, but on the perception of trial information as well. The latter is not a common finding in this literature (Lind & O'Barr, 1979).

It remains for future research to determine which features of the powerful and powerless speech styles affect judgments of credibility and guilt in the case of the child witness. Although O'Barr (1982) claims that the features of the powerless style tend to covary, others claim that certain features contribute more to the effects of each style than others (Bradac & Mulac, 1984) and that the effects of some features differ depending on the sex of the speaker (Wright & Hosman, 1983). Bradac and Mulac (1984), for example, found that subjects judged intensifiers such as "really" and "surely" as relatively powerful and effective, whereas they judged hesitations as clearly powerless. The confounding of powerful (intensifiers) and powerless (hesitations) features in the present study may have inadvertently diminished the difference between the powerful and powerless presentations. Alternatively, in a single message with hesitations and other powerless features, intensifiers may connote relatively low power after all. Researchers could examine these alternatives by systematically varying the features and comparing the effects of these variations.

It also remains for future research to probe the consequences for the child witness of other speech styles in the courtroom. The narrative versus fragmented testimony styles seem especially promising candidates for study (Lind & O'Barr, 1979; O'Barr, 1982). Ethnographic research by O'Barr (1982) has revealed substantial variation in the length of witnesses' responses to questions posed by lawyers. Some witnesses give habitually longer, narrative answers; others give briefer, more fragmented answers. According to O'Barr, at times it appears as if the witness's style is shaped by the examining lawyer, who sometimes wants the witness to speak fully and other times desires brief, nonelaborated answers. Experimental investigation of the narrative and fragmented styles has shown that when reactions to the two styles differ, the narrative style receives more favorable responses (O'Barr, 1982). O'Barr speculates that the narrative style conveys to jurors the impression that the attorney has willingly surrendered some control over evidence presentation to the witness. In other words, the attorney who permits a witness to respond at length holds a favorable opinion of a witness, and jurors might be inclined to accept the attorney's evaluation.

How are these stylistic variations relevant to the child witness? Based on developmental research on referential communication, we can speculate that children use a more fragmented style when they are younger and a more narrative style as they get older. Greenfield and Dent (1980), for example, found that when children had to describe complex actions to someone who could not see the actions, ten-year-olds verbalized more than six-year-olds. In particular, they verbalized more of the communicatively important elements of the actions. If children naturally use a more fragmented testimony style, this stylistic variation, like the powerful versus powerless one, might mediate the effects of age on jurors' reactions to a child witness. Researchers could examine this possibility by employing a design similar to that of the present study.

Of course, certain design features of the present study could be improved in future investigations. For one, jurors in this study were college students, a sample that is not representative of the population from which jurors are drawn (Weiten & Diamond, 1979). College students may differ from potential jurors on a variety of variables important in the deliberation process (Feild & Barnett, 1978), and they may also have less experience with children than potential jurors. In addition, jurors in this study read the trial description; they did not have an opportunity to see and hear the principal characters in the case. Although spoken delivery might prove more salient than written presentation of the speech styles, we note the strength of our findings with the written format. In related work, Erickson et al. (1978) have also found effects of powerful and powerless speech in both written and tape-recorded formats, and Goodman et al. (1987) have obtained consistent effects of eyewitness age across subject samples and presentational formats.

Speech styles are just one class of eyewitness characteristics that may mediate the effects of age on jurors' reactions to a witness. Race, sex, socioeconomic status, and demeanor are a few of the others that might affect jurors' perceptions of children's testimony. Not only do eyewitness characteristics influence jurors, but a variety of other factors probably come into play when jurors consider children's testimony. Goodman et al. (1987) mention the type of trial, juror characteristics, the witness's role, and trial features, such as the use of expert testimony, as factors that might mediate the effects of age on jurors' reactions. Ross et al. (1987) add to this list the ambiguity of the evidence in the case. Leippe and Romanczyk's (1987) research suggests that eyewitness consistency is another important mediating influence. Clearly, there will be no one verdict on jurors' responses to the age of an eyewitness. As research includes more and more of these factors, a richer understanding of jurors' reactions to the child witness will take shape.

References

Bailey, F.L., & Rothblatt, H.B. (1971). *Successful techniques for criminal trials.* Rochester, NY: The Lawyers Co-operative Publishing Company.

Bradac, J.J., & Mulac, A. (1984). A molecular view of powerful and powerless speech styles: Attributional consequences of specific language features and communicator intentions. *Communication Monographs, 51,* 307–319.

Cole, G.F. (1975). *The American system of criminal justice.* North Scituate, MA: Duxbury.

Conley, J.M., O'Barr, W.M., & Lind, E.A. (1978). The power of languages: Presentational style in the courtroom. *Duke Law Journal, 1978,* 1375–1399.

Erickson, B., Lind, E.A., Johnson, B.C., & O'Barr, W.M. (1978). Speech style and impression formation in a court setting: The effects of "powerful" and "powerless" speech. *Journal of Experimental Social Psychology, 14,* 266–179.

Feild, H.S., & Barnett, N.J. (1978). Simulated jury trials: Students vs. "real" people as jurors. *Journal of Social Psychology, 104,* 287–293.

Goodman, G.S., Golding, J.M., & Haith, M.M. (1984). Jurors' reactions to a child witness. *Journal of Social Issues, 40,* 139–156.

Goodman, G.S., Golding, J.M., Helgeson, V.S., Haith, M.M., & Michelli, J. (1987). When a child takes the stand: Jurors' perceptions of children's eyewitness testimony. *Law and Human Behavior, 11,* 27–40.

Greenfield, P.M., & Dent, C.H. (1980). A developmental study of the communication of meaning: The role of uncertainty and information. In K.E. Nelson (ed.). *Children's language* (Vol. 2, pp. 563–598). New York: Gardner Press.

Kalven, H., Jr., & Zeisel, H. (1966). *The American jury.* Boston: Little, Brown & Company.

Leippe, M.R., & Romanczyk, A. (1987). Children on the witness stand: A communication/persuasion analysis of jurors' reactions to child witnesses. In S.J. Ceci, M.P. Toglia, & D.F. Ross (eds.). *Children's eyewitness memory* (pp. 155–177). New York: Springer-Verlag.

Lind, E.A., & O'Barr, W.M. (1979). The social significance of speech in the courtroom. In H. Giles & R.N. St. Clair (eds.). *Language and social psychology* (pp. 66–87). Baltimore: University Park Press.

O'Barr, W.M. (1982). *Linguistic evidence.* New York: Academic Press.

Ross, D.F., Miller, B.S., & Moran, P.B. (1987). The child in the eyes of the jury: Assessing mock-jurors' perceptions of the child witness. In S.J. Ceci, M.P. Toglia, & D.F. Ross (eds.). *Children's eyewitness memory* (pp. 142–154). New York: Springer-Verlag.

Stasser, G., Kerr, N.L., & Bray, R.M. (1982). The social psychology of jury deliberations: Structure, process, and product. In N.L. Kerr & R.M. Bray (eds.). *The psychology of the courtroom* (pp. 221–256). New York: Academic Press.

Weiten, W., & Diamond, S.S. (1979). A critical review of the jury simulation paradigm. *Law and Human Behavior, 3,* 71–93.

Wells, G.L., & Lindsay, R.C.L. (1983). How do people infer the accuracy of eyewitness memory? Studies of performance and a metamemory analysis. In S.M.A. Lloyd-Bostock & B.R. Clifford (eds.). *Evaluating witness evidence* (pp. 41–55). New York: John Wiley & Sons.

Wright, J.W., II, & Hosman, L.A. (1983). Language style and sex bias in the courtroom: The effects of male and female use of hedges and intensifiers on impression information. *The Southern Speech Communication Journal, 48*, 137–152.

Yarmey, A.D., & Jones, H.P.T. (1983). Is the psychology of eyewitness identification a matter of common sense? In S.M.A. Lloyd-Bostock & B.R. Clifford (eds.). *Evaluating witness evidence* (pp. 13–40). New York: John Wiley & Sons.

5
The Credibility of Children as Witnesses in a Simulated Child Sex Abuse Trial[1]

L. MATTHEW DUGGAN III, MOSS AUBREY, ERIC DOHERTY, PETER ISQUITH, MURRAY LEVINE, and JANINE SCHEINER[2]

Child sexual abuse is presently the focus of a great deal of public attention. Although there is no commonly accepted definition (Brant & Tisza, 1977; Kelly, 1984), sexual abuse of children is illegal in all fifty states (Fraser, 1981) and indeed throughout the world (Doek, 1981). All states have mandatory reporting statutes (Meriwether, 1986); however, only thirteen have attempted to define child sexual abuse (Fraser, 1981). In New York State the definition of child sexual abuse hinges on the age of the child as well as the term "sexual contact" (New York State Penal Law, 130.000–130.60). The term "sexual contact" is defined as any touching of the sexual or other intimate parts of a person not married to the actor for the purposes of gratifying the sexual desire of either party. It includes the touching of the actor by the victim as well as the victim by the actor, whether directly or through clothing (New York State Penal Law 130.00).

The attitude that sexual contact between adults and children is abominable conduct for rational adults is relatively modern (deMause, 1974; Mrazek, 1981). In England around the sixteenth century, legislation prohibited adults from engaging male children in forced sodomy and female children under ten years of age in rape (Radzinowicz, 1948). In the late nineteenth century children were regarded as undisciplined "animals" who needed protection from themselves and others (Schultz, 1982). This theme

[1] This research was supported by the Baldy Center for Law and Social Policy, SUNY Buffalo. The Baldy Center provided a dissertation year fellowship for Duggan and some research support. The project was also supported by BSRG funds made available through the Faculty of Social Sciences, SUNY Buffalo, and from funds allocated by the Research Center for Children and Youth, SUNY Buffalo.
[2] This report is based on a doctoral dissertation designed by L. Matthew Duggan, a second dissertation by Moss Aubrey, and a Master's thesis by Janine Scheiner. The research group conducted the study, jointly designed the content analysis coding system, and participated in the coding, analysis, and write-up of the project. The project was under the general direction of Murray Levine. With the exception of Duggan, coauthors are listed alphabetically to reflect the joint contribution of all members to the study.

was especially strong in America, where as early as 1894, in New York, children could legally by removed from their parents if the parents were found to be sexually abusing them. England followed this lead and in 1908 declared incest a crime (Mrazek, 1981). In more recent times, within the mental health viewpoint, the sexual abuse of children by adults was characterized as pathological rather than criminal (Schultz, 1982). Although sex between children and adults has not always been condemned, and even today some groups advocate that adults and "consenting children" be allowed to engage in sexual relations (Densen-Gerber & Hutchinson, 1978), at present sex between adults and children is deemed a serious and deleterious act subject to criminal penalty.

Ten years ago reports of child sexual abuse were quite rare. Today, sexual abuse of children is the fastest growing form of reported child abuse (MacFarlane & Bulkley, 1982). It is hard to compile an accurate estimate of the number of sexual abuse cases each year. As many of 50 percent of sexual abuse cases known to some authorities are never officially reported (Burgdorf, 1980; Burgess, Groth, Holmstrom, & Sgroi, 1978; Finkelhor, 1983). In 1981, a special report by the National Center on Child Abuse and Neglect estimated that at a minimum, the incidence of child sexual abuse is in excess of 100,000 cases each year. In 1978, 6096 cases of child sexual abuse were reported. The age range of the children varied from under one to just under eighteen years; 38 percent of the cases fell in the thirteen-to-sixteen-year-old range. Childhood sexual abuse occurs in all social, ethnic, economic, and racial groups (Finkelhor, 1979).

Generalizing to the entire nation from reported cases in Brooklyn, Conneticut, Minneapolis, and Washington, D.C., Sarafino (1979) estimated that 74,725 children are sexually abused each year. However, since experts agree that the actual number of cases is usually three to four times higher than the reported incidents, he estimated that 261,500 cases of child sexual abuse go unreported each year. His grand estimate of the annual incidence of child sexual abuse is 336,225. DeFrancis (1969) estimated that the rate of sexually abused female to sexually abused male children was roughly 10 to 12:1, although Fritz, Stoll, & Wagner (1981) concluded that the ratio of sexually abused females to males is closer to 2:1, rather than 10 to 12:1. De Jong, Hervada, and Emmett (1983) reviewed the records of 566 children ranging in age from six months to sixteen years who presented to a sexual assault crisis center. Nearly 82 percent of the sample was female. The National Center study found that 87 percent of reported cases involved female victims (see also Russell, 1983). The National Center on Child Abuse and Neglect also claims that the incidence of child sexual abuse is increasing each year (Knight, 1980). We do not know if the rate is increasing or if the increase in reporting is a result of better supervision and greater public awareness. Whatever the reason, the apparent increase adds pressure on the legal system and on mental health workers to deal with the problem.

The identity of the perpetrator might help explain why child sex abuse is so rarely reported. The system of justice is adult oriented. Children themselves do not bring cases to court. If a child has been wronged, we assume the parents will act in his or her best interest and bring the situation to the attention of the authorities. Many of the alleged perpetrators, however, are parents, other relatives, guardians, or family friends (DeFrancis, 1969; De Jong et al., 1983; Finkelhor, 1983; Goldberg and Goldberg, 1976; Jorne, 1979; Khan & Sexton, 1982; MacFarlane, 1978), and the likelihood that a parent will prosecute a spouse or a close relative is low.

Surprisingly, physical injury in child sexual abuse is rare (Quinsey, 1977; Sgroi, 1978). The most commonly reported type of child sexual abuse is nonviolent genital manipulation, which would rarely cause any physical damage (Finkelhor, 1979).

Numerous studies have assessed both the short- and long-term emotional and behavioral effects of childhood sexual abuse (Browne & Finkelhor, 1986; Kelly and Tarran, 1983; Mrazek and Mrazek, 1981). These studies tend to show that short-term adverse effects of childhood sexual abuse are common, though not inevitable; the frequency of long-term effects is not absent, but substantially lower.

At present, each state has at least two statutes governing child sexual abuse: a criminal statute, whose purpose is to punish and deter the perpetrator, and a child protection statute (Fraser, 1981). Reported cases can be processed either through the family court system or through the criminal courts. The guilt or innocence of the accused is determined in criminal court. A defendant found guilty receives the penalty determined by statute, as imposed by the judge. The child's well-being and the consequences for the family of a guilty verdict are of secondary concern in the criminal system. The family court tries to take into account what would be best for the child and the family and uses methods it hopes will be rehabilitative. Presently, most cases of child sexual abuse are funneled through the family courts.

Criticism of the limits of the family court in preventing repeated episodes of abuse, accompanied by increased reporting of child sexual abuse, has resulted in more of these cases going to criminal court. With increasing numbers of cases, we have seen changes in law designed to ease prosecution and to protect the child victim's rights. New York State, for example, has amended its criminal code to allow children to give uncorroborated testimony, which was previously inadmissable, on their own behalf in child sexual abuse cases (N.Y.S. Penal Law, 130.16). This change will probably bring many more cases to criminal court. Because most child sexual abuse occurs with only the victim and the perpetrator present, in the absence of physical evidence of sex abuse, a great number of cases depend wholly on a child victim's testimony. However, this law's effects will be nullified if district attorneys fail to bring cases to trial on the assumption that jurors will not believe the unsupported word of children (Rogers, 1982). Moreover, the intention of the legislation to punish and deter could well backfire if jurors do not credit children's testimony. Defendants would then choose to go to trial and seek vindication, with the assumption that juries will not convict on the supported word of a child.

Because acts of sexual abuse occur in private and leave little physical evidence the typical case involves a child victim witness on one side and an adult, on the other, insisting that no sexual abuse has occurred. Will jurors believe children who claim they have been sexually abused? Will younger children be believed as readily as older children?

In 1911 psychologist J. Varendonck summed up the feeling of the time by asking "When are we going to give up, in all civilized nations, listening to children in courts of law?" (Goodman, 1984). Then and probably today, many people believed that children are innocent and truthful yet also manipulable and devious (Goodman, 1984). Skepticism regarding children's abilities to give valid testimony is manifest in the evidentiary rule that children are incompetent to testify until they prove otherwise (American Jurisprudence, 1960; Goodman, 1984; Wigmore, 1976). On the other hand, recent attempts to accommodate the presumed psychological limitations of children by allowing leading questions may be of questionable benefit, because leading questions increase inaccuracy in recall in both children and adults (Loftus and Davies, 1984). Decisions made about the validity of children's testimony have been based on untested assumptions about children's capacities and about whether adult jurors will believe children.

At present, there has been an increase in psyhological research on legally relevant issues and the courts have been receptive to such work (Loh, 1981). Issues about children's capacities to recall events, to recognize faces, and to resist suggestion and their inclination to tell the truth have all been subject to experimental study. These are the very questions that jurors are likely to consider when weighing the evidence provided by a child witness. Questions about children's memory have been subjected to experimental analysis. The adequacy of a child's recall may be a function of familiarity with stimulus conditions (Chi, 1978; Lindberg, 1980). Children may attend to a wider range of stimuli and may be better than adults at recalling seemingly irrelevant detail (Neisser, 1979). Children do not confuse their imaginations with real experiences any more than adults do (Johnson, Bransford & Solomon, 1973; Johnson & Foley, 1984). Much of the research has not been conducted under conditions of strong emotional arousal, and therefore generalization from the laboratory to real life circumstances may be hazardous. Children's ability to recognize faces, an important issue in identification, has also been subject to extensive study. In general, it appears that children's memory for faces is quite good in real-life situations (Chance & Goldstein, 1984; Marin, Holmes, Guth, & Kovac, 1979). However, because most perpetrators of sexual abuse are well known to their child victims, the accuracy of the child's identification of the perpetrator is not usually at issue in a criminal prosecution. Loftus & Davies (1984) provide an extensive review of susceptibility to suggestion. It is apparent that adults are subject to suggestion under some conditions, and memory can be altered and transformed. However, there are no clear developmental trends in susceptibility to suggestion. Burton (1976) and Strichartz (1987) conclude that under most circumstances young children are truthful and that children as young as four years approximate an adult understanding of the difference between the truth and lies. The experimental literature offers some measure of confidence in children's testimony. It is an open question whether the stress of testifying is emotionally harmful or helpful to children (Bauer, 1983; Berliner & Barbieri, 1984; Jones, Gruber, & Freeman, 1983; Pynoos & Eth, 1984.)

The important issue is not so much what the psychological literature has to say about children's testimonial capacities, but rather how adult jurors will weigh children's testimony, and whether prosecutors think jurors will accept children's testimony (Goodman, Golding, & Haith, 1984). Goodman et al. (1984) have found that younger children are significantly less credible as eyewitnesses in a simulated vehicular homicide case than are adults. Goodman, Golding, Hegelson, Haith, & Michelli (1987) report several replications of the finding that jurors judge children to be less credible eye witnesses than adults. However, the age of the eyewitness did not affect the degree of guilt assigned to the defendant. The Goodman et al. studies used children in the role of eyewitnesses, not as victims. We do not know how credible children will prove to be as complaining witnesses, nor do we know how the issue of sex abuse will affect jurors' perceptions of children's credibility. There is reason to believe that the nature of a sexual crime will stir different emotions in potential jurors (Kelly, 1984; Kelly & Tarran, 1983, 1984). Aubrey (1986) has summarized a great deal of evidence showing that, under many circumstances, responsibility for rape is attributed to the female rape victim. Those attitudes have not been studied as they affect juror perceptions of children as victims of sex abuse. There is an extensive literature on extraevidentiary factors that affect jury decision making (e.g., authoritarian attitudes, attitudes towar the dealth penalty, attractiveness of the defendant). However, Visher (1987) points out that evidence is critical in determining judgments of guilt or innocence and that in most studies evidence far outweighs extraevidentiary factors. Extraevidentiary factors are likely to have an effect when evidence is ambiguous.

The study reported here was designed to assess the credibility of children of different ages as witnesses in a child sex abuse trial. The elements of the trial were based on common reports that sexual abuse often occurs in private contact with an adult male known to the child, and without physical harm to the child. The study varied the incestuous or nonincestuous nature of the crime by varying the relationship between the victim and the perpetrator. It was further designed to assess the significance of corroboration for the credibility of a child's testimony, and in view of the possibility that the corroborator may be another child, to test the effectiveness of a child as corroborator compared with that of an adult.

Because most reported cases of childhood sexual abuse involve female victims, it was deemed important to include an equal number of males and females on each jury. Jurors were randomly selected from voters in our community. We presented all trials in videotape format to enhance the reality of the experience for jurors, and we videotaped the deliberations to provide a data base for understanding how the jurors considered the children's testimony. We designed a coding scheme to assess many of the issues of credibility discussed earlier. In particular we asked (1) would jurors convict an adult of sexual abuse based on the testimony of a child?; (2) How would their judgments be affected by the child's age?; and (3) How would their judgments be affected by partial corroboration of the child's story?

Procedure

Overview

In all there were eighteen trial tapes reflecting the $3 \times 3 \times 2$ design (child victim/witness ages: five, nine or thirteen years) × (no corroboration, corroboration by a nine-year-old child, corroboration by an adult); × (stepfather defendant, neighbor defendant). The variables are described in the following paragraphs. Each tape was viewed by two juries selected randomly from the voting rolls. The following instructions were read to them:

Please be seated and make yourself comfortable. This research deals with juror reactions to court cases. All of the information collected here will be confidential and anonymous. You are the six members of a jury assigned to the case you are about to view. This will entail paying close attention to the trial in order to form some opinion as to the guilt or innocence of the defendant.

After you have viewed the trial you will be asked to fill out a short questionnaire assessing your views of the case. Following this you will deliberate as an actual jury would and these deliberations will be recorded. The deliberations will not last less than 15 minutes nor more than 45 minutes. Finally, you will fill out a very brief questionnaire. It is important to note that each of you is sitting in a chair with a number on the backboard. Please put this number on each of your questionnaires in the space provided. This is very important since it is the only way we have of matching the first questionnaire with the second one. Are there any questions?

Although no formal *voir dire* was conducted, jurors were given the explicit option of withdrawing from participation at this or any other point during the experiment. Jurors were assured that payment for participation would be provided whether they completed the study or not. No one exercised his or her option to withdraw from the study.

After reading the instructions, the experimenter showed one of the eighteen child sexual abuse trial videotapes to the jurors. Following the viewing of the tape, half the juries filled out a questionnaire, deliberated, and then repeated the questionnaire. The other half of the juries filled out the questionnaire only after deliberating. Finally, jurors were debriefed, paid, and thanked for their help.

The jury literature has been criticized for methodological flaws (e.g., absence of deliberations; use of paper and pencil stimuli, nonrepresentative jurors, etc.), which raise questions about external validity. An attempt was made to correct these limitations. This study used videotapes of a child sexual abuse trial developed in cooperation with lawyers familiar with sex abuse cases. We selected jury-eligible citizens from the community and included a period of deliberation, which was videotaped.

We employed child actresses obtained through advertising to serve as witnesses. Each child actress had parental consent to participate in the study. The basic trial scenario involved a child's allegation that she had been touched illicitly while sitting on the lap of an adult male who was telling her a ghost story in the woods behind her home. To protect the child participants against any possible adverse effects deriving from participation in a trial whose subject matter involves sexual abuse, care was taken to create a script in which the children's lines, taken alone, were quite innocuous. The children were also filmed apart from the other cast members, further limiting their exposure to the nature of their roles. The child's filmed lines were then edited into the final tape and were seen by the jurors as testimony given in response to questions asked by the judge or the attorneys.

In each of the videos, the jurors viewed the same actors and heard the same script lines for the parts of judge, prosecutor, and defense attorney. Three different actresses, aged five, nine and thirteen years were employed to play the victim role. An adult actress played the adult corroborating witness role, and a different female child played the corroborating witness role. The defendant role was played by the same actor. He was identified either as the child's stepfather or as a neighbor. We kept exactly the same story line and allegations in each version. Each version was produced by editing the tape using exactly the same footage as much as possible.

Selection of Jurors

A random sample of voters in the districts surrounding the SUNY Buffalo campus was taken from the voter registration rolls. Each person selected received a letter on university letterhead requesting their participation in a jury study. The letter offered a juror fee of $12 for approximately two hours of work. The letter did not specify the nature of the trial, but indicated it might be one of four types, including childhood sex abuse. A few days later, each prospective juror received a telephone call. Approximately one in four jurors agreed to serve when called. We constructed the juries so that three members were male and three were female. The questionnaire distributed to jurors at the end of the deliberation requested juror age, sex, occupation, education, and past experience with children.

The jurors ranged in age from twenty to eighty years (mean age was forty-two). Ninety-eight pecent were Caucasian, reflecting the racial composition of the districts around the university. Forty-seven percent had at least a high school education, and 51 percent had at least a college education. Eighteen percent reported at least one previous experience as a juror.

Design

Independent Variables

In addition to the three independent variables already mentioned—(1) age of the victim-witness, (2) the presence and source of corroborative testimony, (3) relationship of defendant to the victim-witness—a fourth was included: (4) gender of juror.

1. Age of Victim-Witness

Although in some jurisdictions, children as young as three years may testify, the lower age of five was chosen because this is the age at which children are usually deemed competent to testify (Melton, 1981; Flin, Davies, & Stevenson 1987). A nine-year-old should be viewed as more competent intellectually than a five-year-old, and a thirteen-year-old should be viewed as having still greater intellectual competence. In addition to these considerations, research has shown that people have different reactions to adult–child sex as a function of the age of the child (Kelly & Tarran, 1983).

2. Corroborative Testimony

Recently, New York State changed its laws to allow children to give uncorroborated testimony in child sexual abuse cases (Penal Law 130.16). Other states have similarly changed their laws. At present, we do not know how corroborative testimony, or its absence, will affect juror's perceptions. Similarly, the source of the corroborating testimony (i.e., from another child or from an adult) may also be important to jurors (See Goodman et al., 1987; Ross et al., 1987). One set of tapes had no corroborating witness. Another set had corroboration in the form of testimony from a nine-year-old female identified as a friend of the victim/witness. The third set of tapes showed corroboration by an adult female identified as the victim/witness' neighbor.

3. Relationship of the Victim/Witness and the Defendant

Because the overwhelming percentage of childhood sex abuse cases involve an adult male (DeFrancis, 1969), the defendant in this trial was a male. The alleged perpetrator was identified as either the child's step-father or as a neighbor. Thus the act was either incestuous or nonincestuous. Kelly (1984) reported that respondents in a survey felt that incestuous adult–child sex was more immoral and more psychologically harmful than nonincestuous adult–child sex and wanted longer prison sentences for defendants found guilty of incestuous adult–child sex (Kelly & Tarran, 1984). Finkelhor and Redfield (1982; cited by Kelly, 1984), however, did not believe that the incest–nonincest factor is a significant consideration in cases of this kind.

4. Gender of Juror

Many studies have assessed the effect of juror gender on perceptions of crime in general and, more specifically, on perceptions of sex crimes (Deitz & Byrnes, 1981; Kelly, 1984; Villemur & Hyde, 1983). The effect of juror gender on juror decision making has varied greatly in different studies. In this study, we examined the effect of juror gender on votes of guilty or not guilty, and on attitudes toward various facets of the testimony and the crime. Because a sex crime involving a female child might be highly salient for female jurors, we examined the participation of male and female jurors in the deliberative process.

Dependent Variables

Most of the dependent variables were assessed through the use of a questionnaire completed after viewing the videotaped trial. We also examined group verdicts and individual votes.

1. Witness Credibility

Subjects assessed the child witness' credibility on a seven-point scale from 1 = not at all believable to 7 = totally believable.

The issue of credibility has special relevance in a case of this kind because the central witness is a child. Present research suggests that children, in general, are seen as less credible witnesses than adults (Goodman, Golding, & Haith, 1984; Goodman, Golding, Helgeson, Haith, & Michelli, 1987; see, however, Ross, Miller, & Moran, 1987). Much of the previous research studied the credibility of a child who reported events he or she had witnessed. Would the child victim in a sex abuse case have reduced credibility when testifying about her victimization?

2. Memory

One question assessed jurors' perceptions of the child's memory. The jurors rated the reliability of the child's memory for this event on a scale from 1 = not at all reliable to 7 = totally reliable. Research (see, e.g., Johnson & Foley, 1984) on the accuracy of children's memories has produced mixed conclusions, as has research on adult perceptions of children's memories (Yarmey & Jones, 1983).

3. Understanding

Three questions assessed jurors' beliefs about the child witness' understanding of what had occurred. The jurors rated the probability that the witness misinterpreted the defendant's actions on a scale from 1 = no chance of this to 7 = this is a certainty. The jurors also assessed the degree to which the child understood the gravity of this situation on a scale from 1 = totally unaware to 7 = totally aware. Finally, the jurors rated how responsible the child was for the sexual abuse having occurred, on a scale from 1 = not at all responsible to 7 = totally responsible.

These issues are important for a number of reasons. Defendants in sex abuse cases often attempt to show that the child victim has misinterpreted the situation. Thus, one question assessed the jurors' susceptibility to this defense. Similarly, it is often stated that children do not understand the gravity of the charge and thus may be less concerned about telling the full truth on the stand. Would jurors be affected by the belief that children do not understand the seriousness of the charge? Finally, although there is no legal issue of consent in a child sex abuse case, would juror attributions of responsibility to the child affect their decision making (see Kelly, 1984; Aubrey, 1986)?

4. Harm

Jurors assessed how harmful the sexual abuse was to the child on a scale of 1 = not at all harmful to 7 = as harmful as can be imagined. They were also asked how harmful it is to the child to testify in a case of this kind, on a scale from 1 = not at all harmful to 7 = as harmful as can be imagined. Some have suggested that the mere act of a child's testifying in a case of this kind can have negative psychological consequences. Would jurors believe testifying is harmful to the child and would that belief affect their decisions and perceptions?

5. Decisions

Each juror voted guilty or not guilty.

6. Punishment

Jurors were asked to assign a fair prison term from 0 to 100 years. These ratings may reflect both jurors' anger at the crime as well as their perceptions of the validity of the evidence.

Results

Because only one measure was affected by whether the jurors voted and made their ratings before or after deliberating, data from both conditions were combined in all subsequent analyses.

Group Verdicts

Did the age of the victim and the presence of corroborating testimony influence how likely jurors were to convict the defendant? The most relevant data are the juries' verdicts. Of the thirty-six juries, thirteen reached a unanimous verdict, twelve finding the defendant guilty and one finding the defendant not guilty. All unanimous verdicts favored guilt, with the exception of one verdict in the no-corroboration, thirteen-year-old alleged victim, nonincestuous condition, which favored acquittal.

Results of a hierarchical log linear analysis of unanimous verdicts only suggested that, of the three independent variables in study (age of witness, corroboration, and incestuous–nonincestuous nature of the offense), the best-fitting model included only the corroboration variable [likelihood ratio, X^2 (12, $N = 36$) = 6.57; $p = .885$]. Corroboration resulted in more guilty verdicts than no corroboration. Although two-thirds of all the guilty verdicts were returned when a nine-year-old child corroborated the complaining witness, the analysis did not yield a statistically significant interaction. The small number of cases may have limited the power of the analysis.

Only 36 percent of our juries reached a unanimous verdict. The result may reflect the reluctance of some jurors to convict based on a child's testimony. However, because of practical restrictions, each jury was allotted a minimum of 15 and a maximum of 45 minutes to deliberate. If the period of deliberation had been extended, more juries might have reached unanimous verdicts. The large percentage of hung juries may also be a reflection of the deliberately ambiguous evidence presented during the trial. We turn now to an analysis of the individual votes to try to clarify how the conditions of the study affected individual jurors.

Individual Votes

One hundred fifty-three, or 73.9 percent, of the 207 jurors who completed questionnaires voted to convict the defendant. (Nine jurors failed to indicate their vote on the questionnaire.)

What is the effect of corroboration on individual jurors' guilty votes? Hierarchical log linear analysis of individual juror votes suggests that the best-fitting model includes only the corroboration and alleged victim age variables separately with no higher-order interactions (likelihood ratio,

TABLE 5.1 Individual votes by corroboration condition.

Vote		No Corroboration	Child Corroboration	Adult Corroboration	N
			Corroboration condition		
Guilty	N	40	62	51	153
	%	57%	89.9%	75%	
Not guilty	N	30	7	17	54
	%	43%	10.1%	25%	
N =		70	69	68	207

x^2 (2, $N = 207$) = 19.35, $p < .0001$.

X^2 (26, $N = 207$); $p = .80$). Odds ratios indicate that the chances of an individual juror voting guilty were approximately 8:1 in the child corroboration condition, 3:1 with the adult corroborator, and 1.5:1 with no corrobation.

Because there were no interactions, chi-square tests of significance were used to examine differences among the corroboration and victim age conditions. There was a significant effect for corroboration [X^2 (2, $N = 207$) = 19.35, $p < .0001$] (Table 5.1). The child corroboration condition produced significantly more guilty votes (89.9%) than either the adult corroboration (75%) condition [X^2 (1, $N = 137$) = 4.25, $p < .05$] or the no corroboration (57%) condition (X^2 (1, $N = 139$) = 17.40, $p < .0001$]. Furthermore, the adult corroboration condition produced significantly more guilty votes than the no corroboration condition [X^2 (1, $N = 138$) = 4.13, $p < .05$].

What is the relationship between guilty votes and the age of the alleged victim? The chances of jurors voting guilty were highest for the nine-year-old victim (odds ratio, 6:1), next highest for the five-year-old victim (4:1), and lowest for the thirteen-year-old victim (3:1) (Table 5.2). When we probed the age groups, the nine-year-old alleged victim elicited more guilty votes (81%) than the thirteen-year-old (65%) alleged victim [X^2 (1, $N = 139$) = 3.88, $p < .05$). The five-year-old alleged victim drew a number (75%) falling directly between the nine-year-old and thirteen-year-old guilty votes, and was not statistically significantly different from either.

There was no difference in the number of guilty votes with respect to the nature of the act. Those who viewed the incestuous trial returned 48.4 percent of all the guilty votes, while those who viewed the nonincestuous trial returned 51.6 percent of all the guilty votes.

Although in surveys females have been found to react more negatively to child sexual abuse than males (Kelly & Tarran, 1984), in this study males

TABLE 5.2 Individual votes by age of alleged victim.

Vote		Age of Witness			
		5-year-old	9-year-old	13-year-old	N
Guilty	N	51	57	45	153
	%	75%	81%	65%	
Not guilty	N	17	13	24	54
	%	25%	19%	35%	
N =		68	70	69	207

x^2 (2, $N = 207$) = 4.80, $p = .09$.

produced 46.4 percent of the guilty votes and the females returned 53.6 percent. This difference is not statistically significant.

Jurors completed a questionnaire assessing their perceptions of the evidence and their attitudes toward some aspects of the crime. It is interesting to assess whether jurors who voted guilty differed from those who voted not guilty on the dependent measures.

Jurors who found the defendant guilty believed the child witness to a greater extent [$t(77) = 11.55$, $p < .001$], thought the child's memory was better [$t(61) = 6.80$, $p < .001$], thought the child misunderstood the defendant's actions less [$t(202) = -6.39$, $p < .001$], believed the child understood the seriousness of the accusation to a greater extent [$t(203) = 4.28$, $p < .001$], thought the child was less responsible for the abuse, assuming it had occurred [$t(79) = -3.04$, $p < .005$], felt more confident that the defendant was guilty [$t(60) = 16.06$, $p < .001$], believed the child more on reassessment of this variable following deliberation [$t(101) = 7.51$, $p < .001$], believed the inclusion of corroborating testimony was a more important factor in their decisions [$t(135) = 2.27$, $p < .05$], and believed that the absence of corroborating testimony was a less important factor in their decisions [$t(59.98) = -9.00$, $p < .001$] than those people who voted to acquit the defendant.

Factor Analysis of Dependent Variables

As noted, jurors completed eleven 7-point Likert scale questionnaire items designed to assess their perceptions of the evidence and attitudes toward various aspects of the offense. A factor analysis using the principal component method for extraction with varimax rotation was performed on the eleven questionnaire items plus the individual vote of guilty or not guilty. This procedure resulted in four factors.

The first factor included five of the items and accounted for 30.3 percent of the variance. The items included were confidence in the guilt of the defendant, guilty or not guilty vote, believability of the alleged victim, perception of the memory capabilities of the alleged victim, and degree to which the child misinterpreted the defendant's actions. This cluster of variables is referred to as the credibility factor.

The second factor contained two items and accounted for 14.0 percent of the variance. It included jurors' perceptions of a fair sentence for someone convicted of this crime as well as their perception of the sentence the defendant would most likely receive if found guilty in this case. This factor is referred to as the sentencing factor.

The third factor included three items and accounted for 10.7 percent of the variance. The factor variables included the perceived harm to the child of the abuse assuming it had occurred, the perceived harm to the child of testifying, and the perceived awareness the alleged victim had regarding the gravity of the accusation. This factor is referred to as the emotional-cognitive factor.

The fourth factor accounted for 9.2 percent of the variance and included the effect the jurors felt the age of the child had on their perceptions, and the perceived responsibility of the child for the abuse, assuming it had occurred. This factor is referred to as the age-responsibility factor.

The resulting four factors were then used as the dependent variables in a $2 \times 3 \times 3$ MANOVA. The independent variables were (1) age of the complaining witness (five, nine, thirteen), (2) corroboration (no corroboration, child corroborator, adult corroborator), and (3) juror gender. (The reader interested in a still more fine-grained analysis of these data is referred to Duggan, III, 1987.) The multivariate F on the witness age by corroboration interaction was significant [Hotellings test: $F(16, 1074) = 1.95$, $p = .013$]. The univariate F test for the witness age by corroboration interaction was significant for the credibility factor [$F(4, 273) = 4.37$, $p = .002$]. The thirteen-year-old alleged victim testifying in the uncorroborated condition had the lowest credibility factor score. However, with corroboration, the credibility factor score for the thirteen-year-old alleged victim was not significantly different from the credibility factor scores of the nine-year-old and the five-year-old alleged victims (see Figure 5.1).

We examined the jurors' ratings of the importance of corroborating testimony, or lack of it, for their decisions. Post hoc probing of the relationship shows that corroboration was rated as significantly more important when the nine-year-old alleged victim testified ($M = 4.94$) than when the five-year-old ($M = 3.85$) or thirteen-year-old alleged victims ($M = 3.88$) testified [$F(2, 142) = 6.26$, $p < .005$]. The rating on the importance of lack of corroborating evidence showed that the lack was significantly more important to those jurors who viewed the thirteen-year-old alleged victim ($M = 5.83$) than for those who viewed the five- ($M = 3.96$) or nine-year-old alleged victim ($M = 3.92$) [$F(2.71)] = 5.90$, $p < .005$].

The univariate F test for the witness age by corroboration interaction on

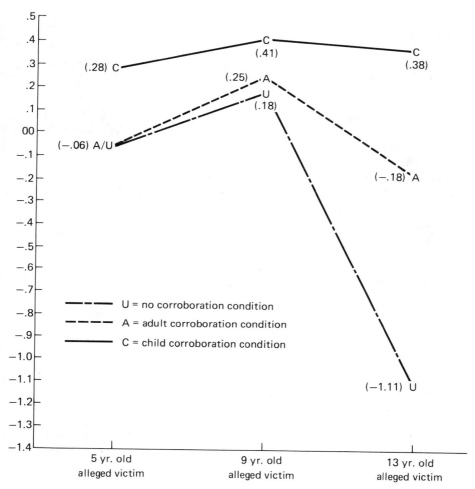

FIGURE 5.1 Witness age by corroboration interaction for credibility factor.

the age–responsibility factor showed a trend toward significance [$F(4,273)$ = 2.01, $p = .093$]. The jurors tended to attirbute more responsibility to the thirteen-year-old alleged victim than to the nine- and five-year-old alleged victims, especially with no corroboration. The finding for the age–responsibility factor mirrored those for the credibility factor.

Taken together these findings shed some light on the interaction between corroboration and age of the alleged victim. In particular, these results suggest that when a thirteen-year-old child accuses a man of sexual abuse, jurors may feel the thirteen-year-old bears some responsbility in the situation; this limits the child's credibility, especially if there is no corroboration.

Gender of the Juror

In general, the effect of juror gender has produced inconsistent results (Deitz & Byrnes, 1981; Villemur & Hyde, 1983). In the area of child sexual abuse, Kelly and Tarran (1984) noted that women were more offended by this act than men, and Foss-Goodman and Wright (1987) found female mock jurors believed child testimony on sexual abuse to a greater extent than the male jurors did. Assuming that women are more offended by an act of sexual abuse committed against a female child, how does that attitude affect their votes as jurors?

The multivariate F test for juror gender across the four factors was highly significant [Hotellings: $F(4,270) = p < .0001$]. The univariate F tests showed significant differences between the men and women jurors on the credibility factor [$F(1,273) = 4.02$, $p = .046$; (z score $M = -.11$, $M = .13$, respectively)] and on the emotional-cognitive factor [$F(1,273) = 18.78$, $p < .001$, (z score $M = -.21$, $M = .28$, respectively)].

The gender differences were mirrored in several of the items comprising the factor scores. In particular, females found the alleged victim to be more cognizant of the seriousness of the accusation [$t(210) = -2.10$, $p < .05$], more harmed by the act [$t(209) = -2.85$, $p < .005$], and more harmed by testifying [$t(211) = -2.39$, $p < .05$] than did males. Females found the alleged victim to be more believable initially [$t(213) = -3.13$, $p < .005$] and on reassessment of this variable following deliberation [$t(106) = 2.87$, $p < .005$]. It is very interesting to note that despite these differences in the degree to which males and females believed the child witnesss, and the degree to which they believed the child was harmed, there was no statistically significant difference in the votes rendered by men and women. Seventy-eight percent of the female and 70 percent of the male jurors voted guilty [X^2 (1, $N = 207$) = 1.52, $p = .22$].

Gender Differences in the Deliberation Process

We also examined how the two genders participated in the deliberation process. A male and female rater, blind to the hypothesis of the study, were trained to use the SYMLOG system for rating group interaction (Bales & Cohen, 1979). The raters independently coded eighteen of the videotapes. We analyzed gender differences for the three dimensions of the SYMLOG system: D–U (dominance–submissiveness), B–F (emotionally expressive–instrumental/task orientation) and N–P (display of positive or negative affect).

We found no significant gender difference for number of lines spoken or for the first speaker in each group. However, a significant main effect emerged on the D–U factor for gender ($p < .05$) and for rater ($p < .01$). There was also a significant interaction between gender of the rater and gender of the juror ($p < .01$). Both male and female raters rated the male jurors as more dominant than the female jurors, but the effect was more pronounced for the male rater.

By breaking the B–F variable into its components of emotional expressiveness and task orientation, we found a significant gender effect for task orientation, but not emotional expressiveness. Both the male and female rater saw the male jurors as more task oriented than the female jurors ($p = .056$). Although the trends were the same for both male and female raters, the results were complicated by differences between the male and female raters in this study.

In general, the results support previous work showing that males tend to be more dominant and more task oriented in jury deliberations than women (Hastie et al., 1983; Strodtbeck & Mann, 1956), but we did not replicate previously reported gender differences in emotional expressiveness. Further, despite apparent gender differences in the mode of participation during deliberations, analysis of the guilty and not guilty *votes* did not indicate that men and women responded differently to the evidence included in the videotaped trials. They did respond differently on the credibility factor and on the emotional–cognitive factor, as well as on a number of the separate items making up the factors. However, the guilty or not guilty vote may reflect an additional weighing of the evidence. It is interesting that the guilty-not guilty vote loaded only on the credibility factor along with items assessing the believability and accuracy of testimony. In other words, jurors' attitudes toward the crime may be less important in determining a vote of guilty or not guilty than their views of the evidence, for both male or female jurors.

Neither the nature of the act (incestuous or not), nor the amount of experience the jurors had with children affected their votes or their rating.

Content Analysis of Jury Deliberations

To help us understand how the jurors reacted to the conditions of the experiment, we developed an elaborate scheme for the analysis of the deliberation tapes. We were less interested in the process aspects of the deliberation than we were in the content of the deliberations. As a result, the techniques and instruments developed by others provided only general guidance. We videotaped and transcribed the deliberations. Because the deliberations were videotaped, we had little problem in identifying which juror was speaking. Deliberations lasted from 15 to 45 minutes and resulted in written transcripts that varied from 8 to 26 pages in length.

We decided to use the "turn" as the unit of analysis, allowing coders to decide when the juror was discussing more than one content theme. (This procedure presented no unusual problems for us. A preliminary analysis revealed 96 percent agreement among fifteen rater pairs for the use of single versus multiple codes.) The coding system also required that we identify the witness (i.e., child victim, corroborator, or defendant) the juror was discussing. Our rater pairs agreed on that determination 99 percent of the time.

The actual content codes were based on our desire to trace the effects of the independent variables in the deliberations. For example, we developed a content category labeled "Disbelief Based on Cognitive Distortion" to reflect the hypothesis that jurors who viewed the trial with the five-year-old victim/witness would question her ability to accurately and consistently report details of the event. In addition, we developed other content categories by reviewing a small sample of the transcriptions, and creating additional categories until we no longer needed new categories to classify the statements in subsquent transcriptions. We also reviewed the literature for variables others have found of interest that might be pertinent. The category "witness demeanor" is one example.

The complex coding system resulted in seventy-nine codes. The content codes were used with different frequency; some were easier to code reliably than others. In a test of reliability, using a different transcription than the one on which we had developed the codebook, agreement among six coders for the assignment of juror statements averaged 60 to 71 percent when using the full seventy-nine categories. Our experience suggests that the hermeneutic process of coding is far more complex than simple disagreement suggests. For purposes of quantitative analysis, we have developed an elaborate scheme to wash out the effects of individual coder bias. Each transcription will be coded by pairs of trained coders assigned from among a set of six coders. Disagreements will be resolved by a third person who will resolve the discrepancy by assigning the code from among the two selected by the pair of coders who were in disagreement. Because we do not yet have quantitative results, our discussion here is restricted to our impressions of the factors that occupied jurors' attention during deliberation.

With respect to the age of the complaining witness, jurors discussed the susceptibility of young children to external influences such as television, sexual abuse prevention programs in the schools, suggestion from attorneys or parent, and the propensity of children to fantasize. The countering argument asserted that the child's testimony was detailed, and that the details lent credibility to the story. Moreover, jurors emphasized that young children were sexually naive and probably could not make up such a story. Jurors examined the degree of motivation to lie that each witness had. The story told by the thirteen-year-old witness was examined closely for the appropriateness of the child's actions in relation to the defendant. Some jurors were impressed with the possibility that the thirteen-year-old was sexually attracted or sexually involved with the defendant and therefore had motivation to lie to avoid punishment. Although the judge's charge made it clear that the only issue was whether the defendant had engaged in an illegal touching of the child's genitals, some jurors were concerned with the possibility that the thirteen-year-old had some responsibility for the episode. Such speculation by jurors is consistent with the findings from rating scale data that jurors attributed responsibility to the thirteen-year-old, and found the thirteen-year-old less credible, especially in the noncorroborated condition.

One surprising result was that the adult corroborator appeared to have had less of an effect on jurors' votes than did the child corroborator. Two factors appeared to be important in the perception of the adult corroborator. First, some jurors developed a poor opinion of that witness because the scenario had the witness on the scene, with the witness hearing the child say the defendant was hurting her, but she did not intervene. That poor opinion may have undermined her credibility with the jurors. Second, many jurors speculated on the possible relationship of the witness to the defendant or to the victim's mother. The trial scenario presented no data on familial relationships, and the jurors frequently speculated on those issues, including the role the neighbor might have played.

Jurors were sensitive to the corroboration issue. Many of their statements included questions as to why additional forms of corroboration and additional testimony about the family, the character of the children, or the character of the defendant was not presented. We are currently analyzing the data to determine whether statements indicating that specific corroboration was missing came more often in the uncorroborated condition.

There was hardly any discussion of the fact that the defendant was either a neighbor or a step-father. Discussion related to this issue dealt with the appropriateness of the interaction between defendant and child, as described in the defendant's and the child's testimony. What was appropriate for a step-father might not have been appropriate for a neighbor. However, there was only an occasional comment on the incestuous aspect of the offense, and when jurors displayed moral indignation, it was in relation to any adult sexually abusing a child.

Jurors were sensitive to the demeanor of the witnesses, but for each person who inferred guilt from the defendant's demeanor or lying from the child's demeanor, another juror would make a case for inferring the opposite from the same behavior. Jurors certainly paid attention to demeanor, and it is possible that witness demeanor had a heavier weight in determining juror votes than we think at present. It is certainly true that a number of jurors remarked on the smiling, coy manner and lack of distress with which the five-year-old presented her testimony. It is possible that it was the five-year-old's manner rather than her age that undermined her credibility to some degree. Another child showing more affect might have drawn even more guilty votes than did our five-year-old. Our quantitative analysis of the codes may shed some light on this point. It is also possible that what jurors perceived as the defendant's lack of vigor in denying the charge, and the defendant's poor eye contact resulted in their disbelief of him. Our conclusion on this point awaits further analysis.

We were impressed that jurors, especially those who seemed to be in favor of a "not guilty" vote, emphasized the issue of proof beyond a reasonable doubt. (We are currently examining the appearance of "reasonable doubt" statements in the transcriptions.) Some jurors expressed the opinion that the defendant was probably guilty, but then went on to state that the evidence was insufficient to warrant a guilty verdict. Most of the jurors' statements were appropriate discussions of evidence, and possible inferences from evidence. Jurors were frequently very skillful in pointing out the limits of logical inference from some piece of evidence, or in pointing out the irrelevancy of some statements. We did develop content codes for inappropriate juror statements (i.e., statements made by jurors during deliberation about issues that were proscribed by the judge's instructions), but those statements were relatively infrequent, and it is our impression that they were often followed by another juror's reminder of what the rules of deliberation were. Some jurors appeared to enjoy the role of intellectual gadfly. They served the useful function of forcing the jurors to review all of the evidence. It was not always apparent from observing the juror's actions and words during the deliberation how he or she was going to vote.

We developed content codes that dealt with the jurors' perceptions of the realism of the videotaped trial. A small percentage of the jurors' comments focused on various aspects of that issue, although issues of experimental realism were mentioned at least once in 94 percent of the transcriptions. We are in the process of analyzing these statements as well. Jurors sometimes prefaced their remarks by saying, "In a real trial . . . ." Some referred to the shortness of the trial, and to the fact that we were videotaping their deliberations. Although we have every reason to believe that most of the jurors participated seriously, attended carefully to the trial video, and deliberated wholeheartedly, the fact that comments such as these appeared indicates that even this method cannot fully overcome the artificiality of a simulation. On the other hand, when comments were made about experimental realism, jurors would remind one another that they were to make decisions as if this were a real case. Even though the conditions were artificial, we cannot say that artificiality either affected or failed to affect the deliberation process or the outcome. It is our impression that, in general, jurors took their roles seriously, and we do not believe the perceived artificiality strongly affected the way evidence was received and discussed.

We were concerned that the results showing less credibility and greater attribution of sexual responsbility the thirteen-year-old witness and greater credibility for the nine-year-old witness may have been artifacts of the particular script we used and the particular child actors employed. To assess the generalizability of these results, we provided groups of college and

TABLE 5.3 The believability of the child witness, to student and community jurors combined, as measured by a questionnaire.

	Most Believed		Least Believed	
Age of Child	N	%	N	%
Five	29	34.1	33	36.3
Nine	26	30.6	12	13.2
Thirteen	30	35.3	46	50.5

See text for details of the statistical analysis.

community subjects with a questionnaire that asked at what age (five, nine, or thirteen years) they would "most believe" and "least believe" a child witness in a case of alleged sexual abuse. Neither the college nor community subject groups showed any significant difference in who was most believed among the three groups. However, the nine-year-old was least often (13%) selected as the least believed, while thirteen-year-old was selected 50 percent of the time. The five-year-old was selected as least believed 37 percent of the time. The departure from randomness was statistically significant by a chi-square test for both the college subject (df, 2; $N = 76$, $p < .005$) and community subject groups (df, 2; $N = 15$, $p < .005$). (Table 5.3).

The subjects were also asked to rate (the degree to which they would convict on a 7 point scale where 7 = definitely convict) if they thought the five-year-old, the nine-year-old, or the thirteen-year-old bore any responsibility for the sexual abuse. Although most of the raters said they would tend to vote guilty regardless of the child's age, the agreement was significantly less strong when the thirteen-year-old was involved ($\bar{X} = 2.53$) than when the five year-old ($\bar{X} = 3.69$) or nine-year-old ($\bar{X} = 3.57$) were involved ($F (2, 41) = 11.43$, $p = .001$).

The questionnaire data support the results obtained using the videotape simulation format. Apparently, the age of the child is a salient concern for jurors assessing the credibility of a child victim's testimony in a case of child sexual abuse. We also believe that the context-free method we used to check the results from those obtained with the videotapes is a useful control for the limitations of generalization resulting from the use of one actor and one script.

Summary and Conclusions

Will juries convict a defendant based on the word of a young child? The five-year-old witness drew four guilty verdicts. The nine-year-old drew six, while the thirteen-year-old drew but two guilty verdicts and one guilty verdict. The majority of juries hung. We can say that a jury is very unlikely to convict without some corroboration, especially if the victim is an adolescent or very young, although that judgment has to be tempered by the limitations of the simulation method.

Seventy-five percent of jurors viewing the five-year-old alleged victim voted to convict, and 81 percent of those viewing the nine-year-old alleged victim voted to convict. Only 65 percent of those viewing the thirteen-year-old alleged victim voted to convict. It appears that it is not the very youngest child who is the least credible witness, but rather the teenager.

The finding that the nine-year-old alleged victim is the most effective witness makes sense. The five-year-old's testimony may be discounted to some extent because of her susceptibility to influence. The nine-year-old, on the other hand is perceived as old enough to understand the nature of the encounter, yet young enough that sexual responsibility is not attributed to her. The fact that we find a younger child (nine-year-old) is more effective as a complaining witness than an older child indicates that the literature on eyewitness effectiveness as a function of age has not taken into account the child's role as witness or as complaining victim or the nature of the offense involved.

The finding that the thirteen-year-old is the least believed is disheartening. The issue of responsibility is not a factor in this crime. The statute places responsibility for refraining from sex with a child wholly on the adult. These data suggest that regardless of the law, jurors are sensitized to the notion that a thirteen-year-old might be partly responsible for what occurred and may use this judgment in arriving at a verdict. Age does not have a linear relationship to the credibility of a child witness. The increased age of the victim is not necessarily a positive factor affecting victim credibility. As girls approach their teenage years, jurors may look on them with greater suspicion in sexual abuse cases. The tendency to blame the victim has been shown to exist primarily in rape cases involving adult women (Aubrey, 1986). Our data suggest the tendency to blame the victim of a sexual assault may affect the credibility of females as young as thirteen. These data also suggest that posing the question of the relationship of age of witness to credibility to adults oversimplifies the issues. Because of the nature of the trial's subject matter, here is an instance in which an older witness is less credible than a younger witness, a finding contrary to that reported by Goodman et al. (1987).

The group verdicts and the individual votes reveal that corroboration was important. Most of the unanimous, guilty verdicts came in a corroborated condition, in particular the condition in which a nine-year-old child provided the corroboration. The one acquittal with the thirteen-year-old came in an uncorroborated condition. Seventy-four percent of guilty votes were cast in the two corroborated conditions, while 56 percent of the not guilty votes were cast in the no corroboration condition. The effect of corroboration was most pronounced when the thirteen-year-old was the alleged victim. The nine-year-old corroborating witness was more effective in producing guilty votes than a corroborating adult. Again, the result that a child is a better witness than an adult contradicts the data Goodman et al. (1987) have reported. The subject matter of the trial is clearly important, as is the specific script. However, our specific result needs to be replicated.

These data suggest that corroboration continues to be important in sexual abuse trials, despite the change in law allowing cases of child sexual abuse to proceed without corroborating evidence. These data also suggest, however, that a child as corroborating witness can prove effective in producing guilty verdicts.

Given that corroboration had a demonstrable effect on vote, how cognizant of this effect were the jurors? We found no difference in the degree of importance jurors assigned to the presence or absence of corroboration under the three conditions of corroboration in this study. These findings suggest that the effect of corroboration is quite subtle. Jurors appear to credit the decision to the alleged victim's testimony rather than to the corroboration. The effect of corroboration may be to add weight to the alleged victim's testimony, without the juror's being aware of it. Other explanations are possible. There is an effect of corroboration, but the mechanisms by which it works are unclear. This subtle effect is worth further investigation.

Juror gender is an interesting variable. We found that there are some differences in the ways in which men and women participate in jury deliberations. We also found that women judge the offense of sexual abuse as more serious than men do. However, we found no significant difference in the vote cast by male and female jurors. It appears that one's vote is more closely related to one's views of the evidence than it is to one's attitude toward the crime, whether male or female. Given the structure the role of juror provides, men and women who have different reactions to an act and an alleged victim can still judge whether or not the defendant is guilty based on evidence introduced at the trial. Thus, it is not clearly better for the prosecution if more women are on the jury or better for the defense if more men are on the jury. Although their styles of participation may be different, both men and women seem able to perform the role of juror judiciously.

Having reported our results, we conclude our discussion with a caveat. Although the design was improved over much other work in this field (use of videotaped trials, emotionally toned content, deliberation, and jurors from the community), we are still dealing with a simulation, and that must be kept in mind. We also must note that this type of research is very expensive, and because of the expense, we were limited to one script and one actor in each of the roles. Our results may well be specific to the conditions of the study and may not generalize to other scripts and other actors. However, we did obtain some confirmation of our results by asking comparable persons to assess the credibility of child witnesses at different ages by means of a questionnaire format free of the limitations imposed by the videotape simulation method. We were able to confirm some of the results, suggesting that the child's age is indeed a salient factor. It is also interesting that we could use a very weak approach (written descriptions) to provide substantial confirmation for our experimental results. Paradoxically, the weak approach provided a strong control for external validity when used in this context. We suggest that others working with videotaped trials may wish to replicate their findings with the use of bare-bone sentences as a means of controlling for limitations resulting from the particular actors and the particular scripts employed in the jury study.

References

Ackerman, A.M., McMahon, P.M., & Fehr, L.A. (1984). Mock trial jury decisions as a function of adolescent juror guilt and hostility. *Journal of Genetic Psychology, 144,* 195–201.

Allen, V.L., & Newston, D. (1972). Development of conformity and independence. *Journal of Personality and Social Psychology, 22,* 18–30.

Allport, G.W., & Postman, L. (1947). *The psychology of rumor.* New York: Henry Holt. *American Jurisprudence Proof of Facts* (Vol. 6) (1960). San Francisco, CA: Bancroft-Whitney Co.

Arbuthnot, J. (1983). Attributions of responsibility by simulated jurors: Stage of moral reasoning and guilt by association. *Psychological Reports, 52,* 287–298.

Aubrey, M. (1986) Factors associated with victim credibility in rape cases. Unpublished manuscript, Department of Psychology, State University of New York at Buffalo.

Bahrick, H., Bahrick, P., & Wittlinger, R. (1975). Fifty years of memory for names and faces: A cross-sectional approach. *Journal of Experimental Psychology: General, 104,* 54–75.

Bales, R.F., & Cohen, S.P. (1979). *Symlog. A system for the multiple level observations of groups.* New York: Macmillan.

Bauer, H. (1983). Preparation of the sexually abused child for court testimony. *Bulletin of the American Academy of Psychiatry and Law, 11,* 287–289.

Berliner, L., & Barbieri, M.K. (1984). The testimony of the child victim of sexual assault. *Journal of Social Issues, 40,* 125–137.

Blaney, R.L., & Winograd, E. (1978). Developmental differences in children's recognition memory for faces. *Developmental Psychology, 14,* 441–442.

Brant, R.S.T., & Tisza, V.B. (1977). The sexually misused child. *American Journal of Orthopsychiatry, 47,* 80–90.

Bray, R.M. (eds.). *The psychology of the courtroom* (pp. 287–323). New York: Academic Press.

Bray, R.M., & Kerr, N.L. (1982). Methodological considerations in the study of the psychology of the courtroom. In N.L. Kerr, & R.M. Bray. *The Psychology of the Courtroom.* New York: Academic Press.

Browne, A., & Finkelhor, D. (1986). Impact of child sexual abuse: A review of the research. *Psychological Bulletin, 99,* 66–77.

Burgdorf, K. (1980). Recognition and reporting of child maltreatment. Findings from the *National Study of the Incidence and Severity of Child Abuse and Neglect.* Rockville, MD: Westat, Inc.

Burgess, A.W., Groth, A.N., Holmstrom, L.L., & Sgroi, S.M. (1978). *Sexual assault of children and adolescents*. Lexington, MA: D.C. Heath.

Burton, L. (1968). *Vulnerable children*. London: Routledge & Kegan Paul.

Burton, R.V. (1976). Honesty and dishonesty. In T. Lickona (ed.). *Moral development and behavior: Theory, research, and social issues* (pp. 173–197). New York: Holt, Rinehart, & Winston.

Carey, S., Diamond, R., & Woods, B. (1980). Development of face recognition— A maturational component? *Developmental Psychology*, *16*, 257–269.

Chance, J.E., & Goldstein, A.G. (1984). Face-recognition memory: Implications for children's eyewitness testimony. *Journal of Social Issues*, *40*, 69–85.

Chance, J.E., Goldstein, A.G., & Schicht, W. (1967). Effects of acquaintance and friendship on children's recognition of classmate's faces. *Psychonomic Science*, *7*, 223–224.

Chance, J.E., Turner, A.L., & Goldstein, A.G. (1982). Development of differential recognition for own- and other-race faces. *Journal of Psychology*, *112*, 29–37.

Chi, M.T.H. (1978). Knowledge structures and memory development. In R.S. Siegler (ed.). *Children's thinking: What develops?* (pp. 73–96). Hillsdale, NJ: Erlbaum.

Christiansen, R.E., Sweeney, J.D., & Ochalek, K. (1983). Influencing eyewitness descriptions. *Law and Human Behavior*, *7*, 59–65.

Cohen, R.L., & Harnick, M.A. (1980). The susceptibility of child witnesses to suggestion. *Law and Human Behavior*, *4*, 201–210.

Cook, T.D., & Flay, B.R. (1978). The persistence of experimentally induced attitude change. In L. Berkowitz (ed.). *Advances in experimental social psychology* (Vol. 2, pp. 2–59). New York: Academic Press.

Cross, J.F., Cross, J., & Daly, J. (1971). Sex, age, race, and beauty as factors in recognition of faces. *Perception and Psychophysics*, *10*, 393–396.

Dale, P.S., Loftus, E.F., & Rathbun, L. (1978). The influencing of the form of the question on the eyewitness testimony of preschool children. *Journal of Psycholinguistic Research*, *7*, 269–277.

Deffenbacher, K.A. (1980). Eyewitness accuracy and confidence: Can we infer anything about their relationship? *Law and Human Behavior*, *4*, 243–260.

DeFrancis, V. (1969). *Protecting the child victim of sex crimes committed by adults*. Denver, CO: American Humane Association.

Deitz, S.R., & Byrnes, L.E. (1981). Attribution of responsibility for sexual assault: The influence of observer empathy and defendant occupation and attractiveness. *Journal of Psychology*, *108*, 17–29.

De Jong, A.R., Hervada, A.R., & Emmett, G.A. (1983). Epidemiologic variations in childhood sexual abuse. *Child Abuse and Neglect*, *7*, 155–162.

deMause, L. (1974). The evolution of childhood. In L. deMause (ed.). *The history of childhood* (pp. 1–73). New York: Psychohistory Press.

Densen-Gerber, J., & Hutchinson, F.F. (1978). Medical-legal and societal problems involving children-child prostitution, child pornography and drug-related abuse; recommended legislation. In S.M. Smith (ed.). *The maltreatment of children*. Lancaster: MTP Press.

Diamond, R., & Carey, S. (1977). Developmental changes in the representation of faces. *Journal of Experimental Child Psychology*, *23*, 1–22.

Diamond, S.S., & Zeisel, H. (1974). A courtroom experiment on juror selection and decision-making. *Personality and Social Psychology Bulletin*, *1*, 276–277.

Doek, J.E. (1981). Sexual abuse of children: An examination of European criminal law. In P.B. Mrazek & C.H. Kempe (eds.). *Sexually abused children and their families* (pp. 75–84). New York: Pergamon Press.

Duggan, III, L.M. (1987). Jurors' perceptions of children in a child sexual abuse trial. Unpublished doctoral dissertation. SUNY Buffalo, Buffalo, NY.

Duncan, E.M., Whitney, P., & Kunen, S. (1982). Integration of visual and verbal information in children's memories. *Child Development, 53*, 1215–1223.

Ebbesen, E.B., & Konecni, V.J. (1982). Social psychology and the law: A decision-making approach to the criminal justice system. In V.J. Konecni & E.B. Ebbesen (eds.). *The criminal justice system: A social-psychological analysis* (pp. 3–24). San Francisco: W.H. Freeman.

Ellis, H., Shephard, J., & Bruce, A. (1973). The effects of age and sex upon adolescents' recognition of faces. *Journal of Genetic Psychology, 123*, 173–174.

Feild, H.S. (1979). Rape trials and jurors' decisions: A psycholegal analysis of the effects of victims, defendant, and case characteristics. *Law and Human Behavior, 3*, 261–284.

Finkelhor, D. (1979). *Sexually victimized children.* New York: The Free Press.

Finkelhor, D. (1983). Removing the child-prosecuting the offender in cases of sexual abuse: Evidence from the national reporting system for child abuse and neglect. *Child Abuse and Neglect, 7*, 195–205.

Flin, R.H. (1980). Age effects in children's memory for unfamiliar faces. *Developmental Psychology, 16*, 373–374.

Flin, R. H., Davies, G. M., & Stevenson, Y. (1987) Children as witnesses: Psycholegal aspects of the English and Scottish system. *Medicine and Law, 6*, 275–291.

Foss-Goodman, D. & Wright, L. M. (1987). Psycholegal issues in childhood sexual abuse: The credibility of the victim's testimony. Paper presented at the annual meeting of the Eastern Psychological Association, Alexandria, VA, April 10, 1987.

Fraser, B. G. (1981). Sexual child abuse: The legislation and the law in the United States. In P.B. Mrazek & C.H. Kempe (eds.). *Sexually abused children and their families* (pp. 55–74). New York: Pergamon Press.

Fritz, G.S., Stoll, K., & Wagner, N.N. (1981). A comparison of males and females who were sexually molested as children. *Journal of Sex and Marital Therapy, 7*, 54–59.

Gerbasi, K.C., Zuckerman, M., & Reis, H.T. (1977). Justice needs a new blindfold: A review of mock jury research. *Psychological Bulletin, 84*, 323–345.

Goldberg, J.A., & Goldberg, R.W. (1976). *Girls on city streets: A study of 1400 cases of rape.* New York: Arna Press.

Goodman, G.S. (1984). Children's testimony in historical perspective. *Journal of Social Issues, 40*, 139–156.

Goodman, G.S., Golding, J.M., & Haith, M.M. (1984). Jurors' reactions to child witnesses. *Journal of Social Issues, 40*, 9–31.

Goodman, G.S., Golding, J.M., & Helgeson, V.S., Haith, M.M., & Michelli, J. (1987). When a child takes the stand: Jurors' perceptions of children's eyewitness testimony. *Law and Human Behavior, 11*, 27–40.

Hastie, R., Penrod, S.D., Pennington, N. (1983). *Inside the jury.* Cambridge, MA: Harvard University Press.

Hoving, K.L., Hamm, J., & Galvin, P. (1969). Social influence as a function of stimulus ambiguity at three age levels. *Developmental Psychology, 1*, 631–636.

Johnson, M.K., Bransford, J.D., & Solomon, S.K. (1973). Memory for tacit implications and sentences. *Journal of Experimental Psychology, 98*, 203–205.

Johnson, M.K., & Foley, M.A. (1984). Differentiating fact from fantasy: The reliability of children's testimony. *Journal of Social Issues, 40*, 33–50.

Jones, R.J., Gruber, K.J., & Freeman, M.H. (1983). Reactions of adolescents to being interviewed about their sexual assault experiences. *Journal of Sex Research, 19*, 160–172.

Jorne, P.S. (1979). Treating sexually abused children. *Child Abuse and Neglect, 3*, 285–290.

Kaplan, S.J., & Pelcovitz, D. (1982). Child abuse and neglect and sexual abuse. *Psychiatric Clinics of North America, 5*, 321–332.

Kassin, S.M. (1983). Deposition testimony and the surrogate witness: Evidence for a "messenger effect" in persuasion. *Personality and Social Psychology Bulletin, 9*, 281–288.

Kelly, R.J. (1984). Gender and incest factors in reaction to adult-child sex. Unpublished doctoral dissertation, State University of New York at Buffalo, Buffalo, NY.

Kelly, R.J., & Tarran, M.J. (April 1983). Gender differences in childhood sexual experiences and subsequent attitudes toward child sexual abuse. Paper presented at the 54th Annual Convention of the Eastern Psychological Association, Philadelphia.

Kelly, R.J., & Tarran, M.J. (April 1984). Negative homosexuality bias in reactions to adult-child sex. Paper presented at the 64th Annual Convention of the Western Psychological Association, Los Angeles.

Kerr, N.L. (1978). Beautiful and blameless: Effects of victim attractiveness and responsibility on mock jurors' verdicts. *Personality and Social Psychology Bulletin, 4*, 479–482.

Khan, M., & Sexton, M. (1982). Sexual abuse of young children. *Clinical Pediatrics, 22*, 369–372.

Kinsey, A., Pomeroy, W., Martin, C., & Gebhard, P. (1948). *Sexual behavior in the human female*. Philadelphia: W.B. Saunders.

Knight, A. (December 29, 1980). A crime of scars. *Washington Post*, p. Bl.

Kulka, R.A., & Kessler, J.B. (1978). Is justice really blind? The influence of litigant physical attractiveness on judicial judgment. *Journal of Applied Social Psychology, 8*, 366–381.

Landis, J. (1956). Experiences of 500 children with adult sexual deviation. *Psychiatric Quarterly Supplement, 30*, 91–109.

Lindberg, M.A. (1980). Is knowledge base development a necessary and sufficient condition for memory development? *Journal of Experimental Child Psychology, 30*, 401–410.

Loftus, E.F. (1974). The incredible witness. *Psychology Today*, December.

Loftus, E.F. (1979). *Eyewitness testimony*. Cambridge: Harvard University Press.

Loftus, E.F., & Davies, G.M. (1984). Distortions in the memory of children. *Journal of Social Issues, 40*, 51–67.

Loftus, E.F., & Palmer, J.C. (1974). Reconstruction of automobile destruction: An example of the interaction between language and memory. *Journal of Verbal Learning and Verbal Behavior, 13*, 585–589.

Loh, W.D. (1981). Psycholegal research: Past and present. *Michigan Law Review, 79*, 659–707.

MacFarlane, K. (1978). Sexual abuse of children. In J. Chapman & M. Gates (eds.). *The victimization of women* (pp. 81–109). Hollywood: Sage Publications.

MacFarlane, K., & Bulkley, J. (1982). Treating child sexual abuse: An overview of current program models. In J. Conte & D. Shore (eds.). *Social work and child sexual abuse*. New York: Haworth Press.

Marin, B.V., Holmes, D.L., Guth, M., & Kovac, P. (1979). The potential of children as eyewitnesses: A comparison of children and adults on eyewitness tasks. *Law and Human Behavior, 3*, 295–306.

Melton, G.B. (1981). Children's competency to testify. *Law and Human Behavior, 5*, 73–85.

Meriwether, M.H. (1986). Child abuse reporting laws: Time for a change. *Family Law Quarterly, 20*, 141–171.

Messerschmidt, R. (1933). The suggestibility of boys and girls between the ages of six and sixteen years. *Journal of Genetic Psychology, 43*, 422–437.

Miller, G.R., Fontes, N.E., Boster, F.J., & Sunnafrank, M.J. (1983). Methodological issues in legal communication research: What can trial simulations tell us? *Communication Monographs, 50*, 33–46.

Mrazek, P.B. (1981). Definition and recognition of sexual child abuse: Historical and cultural perspectives. In P.B. Mrazek & C.H. Kempe (eds.). *Sexually abused children and their families* (pp. 5–16). New York: Pergamon Press.

Mrazek, P.B., & Mrazek, D.A. (1981). The effects of child sexual abuse: Methodological considerations. In P.B. Mrazek & C.M. Kempe (eds.). *Sexually abused children and their families* (pp. 223–245). New York: Pergamon Press.

Murray, S. (1983). The effect of post-event information on children's memory for an illustrated story. Unpublished paper, Aberdeen University, Scotland.

National Center on Child Abuse and Neglect (1981). Child sexual abuse: Incest, assault, and sexual exploitation. Department of Health and Human Services. DHHS Publication No. (OHDS) 81-30166. Washington, DC.

Neisser, V. (1979). The control of information pickup in selective looking. In A.D. Pick (ed.). *Perception and its development: A tribute to Eleanor Gibson* (pp. 201–229). Hillsdale, NJ: Erlbaum.

New York State Penal Law (1984), 130.00–130.60.

Powers, P.A., Andricks, J.L., & Loftus, E.F. (1979). Eyewitness accounts of females and males. *Journal of Applied Psychology, 64*, 339–347.

Pynoos, R.S., & Eth, S. (1984). The child as witness to homicide. *Journal of Social Issues, 40*, 87–108.

Quinsey, V.L. (1977). The assessment and treatment of child molesters: A review. *Canadian Psychological Review, 18*, 204–210.

Radzinowicz, L. (1948). *History of English criminal law*, Vol. 1. New York: Macmillan.

Rogers, C.M. (1982). Child sexual abuse and the courts: Preliminary findings. *Journal of Social Work and Human Sexuality, 1*, 145–153.

Ross, D.F., Miller, B.S., & Moran, P.B. (1987). The child in the eyes of the jury: Assessing mock jurors' perceptions of the child witness. In S.J. Ceci, M.P. Toglia, & D.F. Ross (eds.). *Children's eyewitness memeory*. New York: Springer-Verlag.

Russell, D.E.H. (1983). The incidence and prevalence of intrafamilial and extrafamilial sexual abuse of female children. *Child Abuse and Neglect, 7*, 133-146.

Sarafino, E.P. (1979). An estimate of nationwide incidence of sexual offenses against children. *Child Welfare, 58,* 127–134.

Schultz, L.G. (1982). Child sexual abuse in historical perspective. *Journal of Social Work and Human Sexuality, 1,* 21–35.

Sgroi, S.M. (1978). Child sexual assault: Some guidelines for intervention and assessment. In A.W. Burgess, A.N. Groth, L.L. Holmstrom, & S.M. Sgroi (eds.). *Sexual assault of children and adolescents* (pp. 129–142). Lexington, MA: D.C. Heath.

Strichartz, A.F. (1987). Lies and truth: A study opf the development of the concept. Unpublished manuscript. State University of New York at Buffalo, Buffalo, NY.

Strodtbeck, F.L., & Mann, R.D. (1956). Sex role differentiation in jury deliberations. *Sociometry, 19,* 3–11.

Villemur, N.K., & Hyde, J.S. (1983). Effects of sex of defense attorney, sex of juror, and age and attractiveness of the victim on mock juror decision making in a rape case. *Sex Roles, 9,* 879–889.

Visher, C.A. (1987). Juror decision making: The importance of evidence. *Law and Human Behavior, 11,* 1–18.

Weinberg, H.I., & Baron, R.S. (1982). The discredible eyewitness. *Personality and Social Psychology Bulletin, 8,* 60–67.

Weinberg, H.I., Wadsworth, J., & Baron, R.S. (1983). Demand and the impact of leading questions on eyewitness testimony. *Memory and Cognition, 11,* 101–104.

Wells, G.L., & Leippe, M.R. (1981). How do triers of fact infer the accuracy of eyewitness identifications? Using memory for peripheral detail can be misleading. *Journal of Applied Psychology, 66,* 682–687.

Wigmore, J.H. (1935/1976). *Evidence in trials at common law* (revised by J. Chadborn) (Vol. 6). Boston, MA: Little, Brown, & Co.

Yarmey, A.D., & Jones H.P.T. (1983). Is the psychology of eyewitness identification a matter of common sense? In S.M. Lloyd & B.R. Clifford (eds.). *Evaluating witness evidence* (pp. 13–40). New York: John Wiley & Sons.

6

The Opinions and Practices of Criminal Attorneys Regarding Child Eyewitnesses: A Survey

MICHAEL R. LEIPPE, JOHN C. BRIGHAM, CATHERINE COUSINS, and ANN ROMANCZYK

In the past decade, increasing numbers of young children have testified in court cases requiring their ability to identify others (e.g., in cases of sexual assault by a stranger) or to remember complex events (e.g., family violence cases, child custody hearings, sexual assualt by adults known to the child). Not surprisingly, a parallel increase has occurred in efforts by psycholegal researchers to asses the accuracy of young children's memories for faces and events. This research concerning the abilities of children to remember an event and to accurately report those memories to others has a relatively short history. Moreover, it has been conducted against a background of time-honored assumptions, by the legal system and developmental psychology, that children are unreliable witnesses—assumptions called into question by this new research.

The dominant belief in developmental psychology throughout this century has been that young children's memories are rather unreliable (see Ceci, Ross, & Toglia, 1987; Goodman, 1984). Evidence of this belief begins with the work of psychologists such as Whipple (1911) and Brown (1926), and it is still expressed today (e.g., Chance & Goldstein, 1984; Yarmey, 1984). In the legal realm, the belief that children are apt to be poor rememberers is reflected in such historically widespread legal procedures as requiring that children as old as fourteen undergo a competency examination by the court before their testimony is allowed (Goodman, 1984; Myers, 1987), requiring that a child's testimony be corroborated by additional evidence (e.g., another witness's testimony, physical evidence

John Brigham and Michael Leippe contributed equal efforts to the preparation of this chapter and the research described in it. Part or all of the work reported here occurred while Michael Leippe was supported by National Science Foundation grant SES-8711659 and John Brigham by National Science Foundation grant SES-8421030. The authors wish to thank Stacy Spier for assistance in data collection and Adelphi University for providing funds for mail costs.

of abuse) to be admissible (Myers, 1987), and suggesting that judges deliver special cautioning instructions to jurors about child witnesses (*American Jurisprudence*, 1976; Devitt & Blackman, 1977).

These traditional formal barriers to the use of child testimony have apparently contributed to additional, informal barriers, including practices that deter prosecution when the accuser is a child. For example, legal scholars (e.g., *Harvard Law Review*, 1985), eyewitness research psychologists (e.g., Goodman, 1984; Ross, Miller, & Moran, 1987), and clinicians involved with child victims of sexual assault (e.g., Berliner & Barbieri, 1984) have all suggested that prosecutors are reluctant to bring to court cases that rely primarily on a young child's eyewitness testimony, presumably because of burden-of-proof problems and a suspicion that jurors have negative stereotypes about children's memories. Given the entrenched institutional distrust of children's memory, this reticence is not surprising.

To be sure, developmental differences in recall of events and face recognition have been found in some recent studies (e.g., Brigham, Van Verst, & Bothwell, 1986; Chance & Goldstein, 1984; Yarmey, 1984), as has a greater susceptibility to suggestion among young children (Ceci, Ross, & Toglia, 1987; Cohen & Harnick, 1980). Yet a good deal of the research employing forensically relevant to-be-remembered events has observed little or no effects of age on memory (e.g., Goodman & Reed, 1986; List, 1986; Marin, Holmes, Guth, & Kovac, 1979) and suggestibility (Goodman, Hirschman, & Rudy, 1987). Importantly, research suggests that child–adult differences in memory performance are very much a function of task and context variables. Children as young as five years old may approach the memory performance of adults if, among other things, they are questioned in a simple, direct fashion with sensitivity to their language and conceptual skills, suggestive questioning is scrupulously avoided, and the events witnessed are familiar (see Berliner & Barbieri, 1984; Goodman & Reed, 1986; Melton, 1981; Melton & Thompson, 1987).

Growing awareness of these more positive research findings about children's memory skills, coupled with strong societal sentiment for bringing child abusers to justice, have produced calls for greater openness to child testimony (e.g., Altman & Lennon, 1986). Preliminary competency examinations are no longer routinely required of all children in many jurisdictions (Goodman, 1984; Melton, 1984). In most states, the requirement of corroborating witnesses or other evidence has been removed for cases of sexual abuse (Myers, 1987). Some states have even altered statutes to make testimony procedures more accommodating to what are perceived as children's special needs (e.g., allowing videotaped depositions in place of open court appearances to make testimony less traumatic for the child).

These developments are well-intentioned and, for the most part, are responses to the new research-based findings about young children. Interestingly, however, very little empirically derived information is available concerning the perception and treatment of child witnesses by important actors in the criminal justice system. For example, many psycholegal writers have assumed that prosecutors are hesitant to seek juried trials in child sex abuse cases, that defense attorneys treat child witnesses harshly on the witness stand, and that the experience of serving as a witness is traumatic to the average child. Yet no systematic attempts have been made to assess the validity of these assumptions. Empirical data on these and related issues are needed to clearly specify the frequency and consequences of current procedures involving child witnesses, to identify any apparent problems inherent in these procedures, and to suggest possible avenues for resolving these problems.

With these purposes in mind, we conducted a systematic survey of the beliefs and self-reported behaviors toward children of a crucial group of participants in the justice system: prosecuting and defense attorneys. Attorneys' impressions of the accuracy of children's testimony and the credibility of children as perceived by jurors are likely to affect attorneys' decisions about going to trial as well as the strategies they employ at trial. Since a child's accuracy and credibility may depend largely on the questioning technique used to elicit answers from the child, and since attorneys are in a position to determine how questions are posed to the child, the beliefs an attorney holds about child witnesses can directly influence the accuracy of the child's responses. In addition, methods of questioning are likely to determine whether or not the child's testimony is presented in a way that can be appropriately evaluated by the jury (see Melton & Thompson, 1987).

Beyond the powerful influence of lawyers on how the child witness fares in the justice system, the opinions of a representative sample of attorneys can provide important, "inside" estimates and impressions about factors of interest to criminal justice scientists (Brigham & WolfsKeil, 1983). Accordingly, we sought estimates about such matters as how often child (versus adult) eyewitnesses make false identifications, what factors influence those errors, the extent of use of special procedures such as videotaped testimony, and the prevalence of certain prosecution and defense strategies for enhancing or denigrating the statements of a child.

Finally, if past surveys of attorneys and of adults in general can serve as clues, we can expect some inaccuracy in the overall beliefs of attorneys about the recall and recognition skills of young eyewitnesses. For purposes of survey research, a belief is considered inaccurate if it does not correspond to prevailing psychological research conclusions. Yet the extent and direction of attorneys' inaccuracies are not readily predictable. The distribution of answers to questions about specific memory and related cognitive skills, compared to relevant research results, will help determine whether there is a need for educating lawyers about psycholegal research with children.

Past Surveys

Since the early 1980s, several surveys have inquired about the views on and knowledge about eyewitness testimony among prominent actors in the legal system. Surveys of eligible jurors have produced compelling evidence that jurors have misconceptions about how certain, forensically relevant factors influence memory (Deffenbacher & Loftus, 1982; Yarmey & Jones, 1983) and that they typically overestimate the accuracy of adult eyewitnesses (Brigham & Bothwell, 1983). Of special concern here, though, are those surveys that include attorney respondents and/or items assessing perceptions of children's testimony.

Brigham and WolfsKeil (1983) obtained the responses of 166 defense attorneys and 69 prosecuting attorneys (as well as 186 police officers) in the state of Florida to questionnaire items dealing with various aspects of eyewitness evidence. The most striking characteristic of the results was the marked differences in the responses of defense and prosecuting attorneys. Whereas most defense attorneys estimated that 50 to 75 percent of the eyewitness identifications they had observed were accurate, the large majority of prosecutors believed almost all (90 percent or more) of the identifications had been correct. As might be expected from these opposing perceptions, defense lawyers generally felt that jurors and judges placed too much emphasis on eyewitness evidence whereas most prosecutors thought they gave eyewitness evidence the right amount of emphasis. In turn, most defense attorneys were very receptive to the inclusion of courtroom expert testimony by psychologists about eyewitness reliability, but prosecutors were unanimously opposed to it. Finally, despite substantial agreement on how various viewing conditions influence accuracy, prosecutors were more likely than defenders to believe in a positive relationship between eyewitness accuracy and the confidence with which testimony is delivered and between the accuracy and arousal of witnesses. Defense attorneys generally expected a negative accuracy–arousal relationship.

Brigham and WolfsKeil suggested these differences in perceptions and beliefs could reflect the fact that, in the typical eyewitness case, the defense attorney's job (defending the object of eyewitness identification) requires skepticism about eyewitnesses whereas the prosecutor's job (using the identification to get a conviction) requires confidence in the eyewitness; that is, the defense attorney and prosecutor have opposing motives. Under these circumstances, research in social psychology leads us to expect the opposing attorneys to come to genuinely different conclusions about the same information (i.e., the eyewitness's testimony and corroborative evidence). Through a process known as biased assimilation (Lord, Ross, & Lepper, 1979), defense attorneys may attend more closely to the weak aspects of the eyewitness testimony and interpret neutral or ambiguous aspects as consistent with their argument that the witness is inaccurate.

Prosecutors, in contrast, may more readily perceive the strong aspects of the testimony and interpret objectively ambiguous statements as supporting their presumption that the witness is accurate.

Brigham and WolfsKeil also suggested the possibility that defense attorneys, "because of their direct involvement with the suspect, may be in the best position to estimate the reliability of eyewitness identifications of their client" (p. 347). In other words, defenders' perceptions actually may be more accurate, rather than simply different, because of the different way they (compared with prosecutors) have processed eyewitness information. Indeed, defenders' opinions about the diagnostic value of eyewitness confidence and arousal, as well as their more jaundiced views of eyewitness reliability in general, seem more in line with the current research findings of psychologists (e.g., see Bothwell, Deffenbacher, & Brigham, 1987; Loftus, 1979; Wells & Loftus, 1984; Yarmey, 1979, for reviews of the research evidence).

Beliefs about factors affecting the accuracy of eyewitness testimony were addressed in the Yarmey and Jones (1983) survey involving criminal lawyers, judges, and law students, as well as college students, private citizens, and eyewitness researchers (psychology "experts"). The survey questionnaire contained sixteen questions in which a brief eyewitness scenario was presented along with four possible eyewitness outcome choices. The questions covered many factors, including eyewitness arousal, eyewitness confidence, same-race bias in face recognition, leading questions, elderly witnesses, and children's testimony. The authors looked primarily at the frequency with which the various groups of respondents answered the items "correctly." The "correctness" of the outcome choice was determined by the authors' "understanding of the current literature in the field, and its subsequent confirmation by the foremost professionals in that area of research" (p. 16). Given this criterion, substantial inaccuracies were present among all nonpsychologist groups, leading Yarmey and Jones to conclude that eyewitness identification is *not* a matter of "common sense." Given our present focus on attorneys, it is noteworthy that the lawyers, judges, and law students fared no better than college students and private citizens in selecting the correct outcomes; this suggests that attorneys, in Yarmey and Jones' words, "would not be in any better position than the jurors themselves to question witnesses effectively, and direct and guide the jury on relevant eyewitness issues" (p. 37).

The question about child witnesses asked: "If a young child (about 8 years old) is questioned by police or in court, which statement best reflects your view of the type of replies the child might give?" The authors and the polled psychologists (82 percent) considered the correct answer to be that the "child is likely to reply the way he/she thinks the questioner wants him/her to." Half of the legal professionals chose this answer while 40 percent chose "The child is likely to reply accurately." Given the mixed findings of recent research, however, it is not clear today which prediction should be considered as most accurate. As noted earlier, a crucial determinant of children's accuracy is questioning style. The questioning situation was not described in sufficient detail to identify a "correct" answer to this question. At the same time, the bimodal pattern of the responses may reflect disagreement among attorneys and judges about children's testimony. A casual analysis of quotes by attorneys in media coverage of child sexual abuse cases suggests the same bimodal distribution of attitudes, with some attorneys viewing children as accurate witnesses and others viewing them as highly suggestible and therefore inaccurate. These discrepant beliefs usually fall along partisan prosecution/defense lines in a manner similar to that found by Brigham and WolfsKeil.

Reactions to Child Witnesses in Trial Simulations

The similarity of the responses of legal professionals and adults in general in the Yarmey and Jones survey suggests that the attitudes toward child eyewitnesses expressed by mock jurors in trial simulation studies could be indicative of attorneys' perceptions as well. In mock jury studies, verdicts are rendered following presentation of a case in which the age of a crucial eyewitness is varied for different groups of mock jurors while other features of the case are kept constant. A number of these studies have found that child eyewitnesses are perceived as less credible than adult eyewitnesses (Goodman, Golding, Helgeson, Haith, & Michelli, 1987, Experiments 1, 2, and 3) and that the position children represent can be weakened by this perception (Leippe & Romanczyk, 1989, Studies 2 and 3). This bias, though, has been absent in some mock trials (Johnson & Grisso, 1986; Ross, Miller, & Moran, 1987). In an attempt to reconcile these different findings, Leippe and Romanczyk (1989, Studies 4 and 5) suggested, with some supportive evidence, that the bias may be removed or even reversed (i.e., children are seen as more credible) if the child comes across as particularly competent and articulate. Thus, at present it seems that, unless given reason to believe otherwise, adults consider a young child witness a problematic witness.

This conclusion is supported by a modest survey of parents of elementary school children (Leippe & Romanczyk, 1987). The parents saw five- to nine-year-olds as highly suggestible to adult influence and gave an average age of 11.03 years in response to the query "At what age does a child become as believable as an adult as an eyewitness in a criminal court case?" Attorneys, of course, may have different views from lay adults, given their greater exposure to legal precedent and procedure regarding children (and the attitudes these reflect) and to children actually giving testimony. But another aspect of the overall picture, if Leippe and Romanczyk's (1989) notion is correct, is that attorneys, regardless of whether their own beliefs resemble those of jurors, can influence jurors' impressions of child witnesses by using their courtroom skills to manipulate the witness' apparent competence.

The Present Survey: Overview

There seems, then, ample need to poll lawyers about child eyewitnesses. To this end, we surveyed both defense and prosecuting attorneys, seeking information in five broad categories. First, we sought attorneys' input on the prevalence of children in witness roles. Just how often and in what types of cases are children involved as key witnesses? And do these cases often fail to reach the courtroom because of burden-of-proof problems, as some legal scholars have suggested? Second, we asked questions about the lawyers' beliefs regarding children's memory and communication skills. A third general area assessed was lawyers' beliefs about how jurors view child witnesses. Attorneys, of course, are in a unique position to judge jurors' assumptions and perceptions, and attorneys' judgments about jurors will certainly affect their behavior in and out of the courtroom. A fourth topic was attorneys' views on the prevalence and acceptability of alternative methods for obtaining and presenting children's testimony (videotape, hearsay evidence of teacher or psychologist, etc.). Finally, we asked the attorneys about how they themselves behave toward child eyewitnesses. Children's courtroom performance apparently depends on questioning formats, and jurors seem to be susceptible to variations in apparent competence of a child witness. It seems clear, therefore, that the ways attorneys coach and question children and talk about them in arguments directed to the jury are extremely important determinants of how children—and justice—fare in the courtroom.

Method

Procedure

In February 1987, packets of six questionnaires were sent to the central Public Defender's Office and to the central State Attorney's Office in each of Florida's twenty Judicial Circuits. Follow-up letters were mailed approximately six weeks after the original mailing to those offices from which no reply had been received or which had misplaced the original mailing. About four weeks after the second mailing, phone calls were made to those offices that had not yet responded, encouraging them to complete and return the questionnaires. All respondents were informed that their responses would remain anonymous and would be evaluated only by respondent number.

Instrument

Questionnaire items were designed to elicit experience-based knowledge and impressions about child witnesses from practicing criminal attorneys. Several types of questions (e.g., frequency estimates, forced-choice options, Likert-type scales) were employed to gather information from the respondents in each of the following five general categories: (1) estimated frequency with which children are involved as key eyewitnesses to various crimes and the likely disposition of cases involving a key child witness, (2) estimates of children's memory and communication skills, (3) beliefs about jurors' reactions to child witnesses, (4) frequency and acceptability of various alternative formats for eliciting and presenting children's testimony, and (5) courtroom strategies employed in dealing with a child witness. Additional items assessed respondents' age, race, sex, and amount and type of legal experience. In total, thirty-one questions were asked.

Subjects

Packets of questionnaires were returned by 85 percent (17/20) of the Public Defender's offices and 50 percent (10/20) of the State Attorney's offices. These returns consisted of completed questionnaires from a total of seventy-four defense attorneys and forty-seven prosecutors. The two groups of participants did not differ significantly in demographic characteristics. The defense attorneys averaged 34.4 years of age, 68 percent were male, and they had been working as defense attorneys for an average of 6.6 years. The prosecutors averaged 35.2 years of age, 76 percent were male, and they had an average of 5.7 years experience as prosecutors. Ninety-eight percent of the defense attorneys and 93 percent of the prosecutors were white. Attorneys in both samples reported handling an average of thirteen cases during the previous year that were tried before a jury. The state prosecutors reported a heavier overall caseload, averaging 312 cases each year that were settled without a jury trial, while the defense attorneys reported an average of 234 such cases.

Results

Prevalence and Types of Child Witness Testimony

We first asked attorney respondents about several eyewitness-relevant aspects of their caseloads. Most attorneys reported that fewer than 10 percent of the cases they handled involved disputed eyewitness identifications by a child aged nine years or younger. For defense attorneys the average was 6 percent, and for prosecutors, 9 percent. In contrast, 26 percent (prosecutors) to 30 percent (defense attorneys) of their cases involved disputed

TABLE 6.1 Child eyewitness cases: Defense and prosecuting attorneys' estimates of the number of cases of each type they had handled within the past two years in which a child was an important eyewitness.

Type of Case	Defense Attorneys	Prosecuting Attorneys
Sexual abuse by parent	6.6	20.0
Sexual abuse by nonparent	6.3	26.0
Physical abuse by parent	3.5	17.9
Family violence	7.8	17.2
Murder or attempted murder of family member	0.8	0.8
Murder or attempted murder of non-family member	1.5	1.1
Assault	7.7	10.8
Robbery/shoplifting	10.6	10.0
Vehicular homicide or injury	0.5	0.3

eyewitness testimony by adults. Analysis of variance (ANOVA) involving age of witness (child or adult) and type of attorney (defense or prosecution) as independent variables revealed that the percentages of cases involving disputed children's testimony were significantly lower than the percentages of cases involving disputed adult eyewitness testimony. Interestingly, contrary to what some observers have suggested (e.g., *Harvard Law Review*, 1985), neither type of attorney expressed reluctance to bring to trial cases relying on a young child witness. Indeed, attorneys estimated that a significantly (by ANOVA) higher percentage of their cases that involve a pivotal child eyewitness (23 percent) reach the courtroom than their cases involving a pivotal adult eyewitness (18 percent). This surprising difference was particularly pronounced among prosecutors (32 vs. 19 percent) compared with defense attorneys (19 vs. 17 percent), as evidenced by a significant Attorney Type × Witness Age interaction.

Are child witnesses (nine years or younger) usually victims rather than bystanders, as current newspaper coverage of child witness cases would suggest? Both defense and prosecuting state attorneys agreed, based on their personal trial experience. On the average, they estimated that the child was the victim in 80 percent of child witness cases. To see more specifically what kinds of cases involve child witnesses, we presented attorneys with several crimes and asked how many times within the preceding two years they had handled a child witness case involving each type of crime. Table 6.1 lists the mean estimates made by defenders and prosecutors. A chi-square test indicated that the relative frequencies of various types of cases were not significantly different for defense and prosecuting attorneys. The differences in raw frequencies in Table 6.1 reflect the generally greater caseload carried by state prosecutors. Sexual abuse, physical abuse, and family violence cases are by far the most prevalent, accounting for 53 per-

TABLE 6.2 Perceived eyewitness accuracy: Defense and prosecuting attorneys'
estimates of the percentage of disputed eyewitness identifications that were
"probably correct" in cases with which the attorney was familiar.

	Defense Attorneys (%)	Prosecuting Attorneys (%)
Disputed IDs made by adults (age 18 or older)	67	83*
Disputed IDs made by older children (ages 10–17)	61	84***
Disputed IDs made by younger children (ages 9 or younger)	46	83***

*Prosecutor and defense attorneys' estimates differ according to a *t*-test at $p < .05$ (two-tailed); *** at $p < .001$.

cent of the public defenders' and 78 percent of the state prosecutors' cases
that involve children. These kinds of cases, of course, are precisely the
ones that have aroused the interest and controversy currently surrounding
children's witness testimony. If one multiplies the average frequencies of
these cases by the sample sizes of, for example, prosecutors, it becomes
clear that abuse and violence cases involving young children as witnesses
(and predominantly victims) are far from rare in Florida.

Perceptions of Children's Memory and Communication Skills

Accuracy of Identifications

Table 6.2 presents the mean percentages given by public defenders and
state prosecutors when asked to estimate the percentage of disputed
eyewitness identifications by adults, older children (ten to seventeen years),
and younger children (nine years or younger) that, in the attorneys' experience, were probably correct. Attorney Type × Witness Age ANOVA on
the reported percentages indicated, first, that, across age groups, prosecutors gave a significantly higher mean accuracy estimate (83 percent) than
did defenders (58 percent). The higher estimates for adult accuracy among
prosecutors replicates Brigham and WolfsKeil's (1983) findings for Florida
attorneys. Of special interest here, however, is a second ANOVA outcome—a significant interaction between attorney type and witness age.
As can be seen in Table 6.2, prosecutors, on average, gave the same high
estimates of accuracy (83 to 84 percent) for adults, older children, *and*
younger children, whereas defense attorneys perceived a definite age–
accuracy relationship, with accuracy increasing with age, from 46 to 67
percent. Defense attorneys, on average, felt that more than half of disputed identifications made by younger children were *inaccurate*.

Comparison of Child and Adult Responses to an Eyewitness Episode

We asked respondents to imagine an assault of an eyewitness' acquaintance by a stranger that lasted fifteen seconds, and then to contrast the recall and lineup recognition accuracy of five- to nine-year-old witnesses to this event with that of adult witnesses. The attorneys were also asked to compare child witnesses to adult witnesses on likely overall suggestibility, sincerity, and consistency of eyewitness accounts. All comparisons were made on five-level scales, with the options being much less, less, about the same, more, and much more (than adults). For statistical analyses, responses were grouped into three categories—less or much less than adults, about the same, and more or much more than adults—and the distributions of responses were subjected to two chi-square tests of proportions. First, to determine whether the attorneys expected children to differ from adults, the obtained distributions for defense attorneys and prosecuting attorneys were separately contrasted with the null expectation of equal proportions in each category. Second, to gauge differences in expectations between types of attorneys, the frequency distributions of defense and prosecuting attorneys were compared.

Table 6.3 presents the distribution of responses to each comparative question. Significantly greater than chance proportions of both defenders and prosecutors expected five- to nine-year-old witnesses to recall fewer details of the event than their adult counterparts, to be less likely to identify the assailant, to be more suggestible to the influence of authority figures, and to include more inconsistencies in their eyewitness accounts. A majority of attorneys had each of these expectations. In contrast, significantly more than chance numbers of prosecutors, but not of public defenders, expected greater sincerity from a child (versus an adult) communicating an eyewitness account to police, lawyers, or juries.

The greater suggestibility and (among state prosecutors) greater sincerity ascribed to children concurs with the views held by the small group of lay respondents (parents and college students) surveyed by Leippe and Romanczyk (1989). However, the poor recall, recognition, and consistency expected of children by the attorneys contrasts with this earlier survey, in which the lay respondents had shown no dominant tendency to see children as either inferior or superior on these dimensions. Perhaps the greater familiarity of criminal lawyers with actual child eyewitness cases accounts for this difference. Alternatively, or in addition, the fact that a specific scenario was provided in the present survey, but not in Leippe and Romanczyk's, may have contributed to the differing estimates.

Turning to between-attorney differences, defense attorneys saw significantly greater child–adult differences, all favoring adults, than did prosecutors. As can be seen in Table 6.3, a significantly greater proportion of defense attorneys than prosecutors perceived child witnesses as recalling less, less able to identify the assailant from a lineup, more suggestible, and

TABLE 6.3 Percentage of ratings of five- to nine-year-old children's characteristics compared to those of adults among defense and prosecuting attorneys.[a]

Compared to adults, child witnesses are:		Defense Attorneys (%)	Prosecuting Attorneys (%)
likely to recall	less/much less	96	57
——.	about the same	4	36
	more/much more	0	7
—— likely to identify an assailant who is present in the lineup.	less/much less	83	41
	about equally	14	50
	more/much more	3	9
—— suggestible.	less/much less	3	11
	about as	6	19
	more/much more	91	70
—— sincere when communicating to a police officer, attorney, or jury.	less/much less	22	4
	just as	39	33
	more/much more	39	63
apt to give accounts of a witnessed criminal event that include —— inconsistencies.	fewer/many fewer	4	9
	about the same number	9	35
	more/many more	87	56

[a] Prosecutors' and defense attorneys' percentage distributions differ significantly at $p < .05$ for all five characteristics according to chi-square tests. Only the defense attorneys' distribution of perceived sincerity did not differ from a chance, equal probability distribution according to a chi-square goodness-of-fit test; everywhere else, $p < .001$.

more prone to inconsistency in their eyewitness accounts. Significantly more defenders saw child witnesses as *less* or equally sincere compared with adults. The magnitude of the response differences between the two groups of attorneys was considerable, as can be seen by taking a close look at Table 6.3 and by the computed eta^2 values of .10 to .29. The latter indicate that roughly 10 to 30 percent of the variance in responses to each of the five questions was accounted for by attorneys' task—defense or prosecution.

Accuracy of Accounts of Sexual Abuse by Children

Another question asked specifically about the testimony accuracy of five- to nine-year-old children who report having been sexually abused. Here again we see differences depending on attorney type, depicted in Table 6.4. On average, prosecutors estimated that these accounts were "quite an accurate description of what happened" 63 percent of the time, while de-

TABLE 6.4 Perceived inaccuracy in cases of alleged sexual abuse.[a]

Outcome[b]	Estimated Percentage (%) of Time Where the Child's Description Is Likely To Be:			
	Quite an accurate description	Significantly distorted or exaggerated though sexual abuse did take place	Completely inaccurate/ fabricated, no sexual abuse took place	Inaccurate because child under-estimated extent of sexual abuse
Defense attorneys	44	44	19	10
Prosecutors	63	12	18	20

[a] Attorneys' evaluations of "instances in which a five- to nine-year-old child reports that she or he was sexually abused and the situation comes to the attention of law enforcement personnel and/or an attorney."
[b] Attorneys made percentage estimates for each outcome, and often the percentages given totaled more than 100%.

fenders estimated that a child's account is accurate in only 44 percent of the cases. Defense attorneys saw more than 40 percent of sex abuse accounts as being significantly distorted or exaggerated, in contrast to only 12 percent by prosecutors. Prosecutors asserted that the extent of sexual abuse is *underestimated* about one-fifth of the time; defense attorneys believe this occurs only one-tenth of the time. Finally, despite such decidedly greater skepticism about children's accounts among defense attorneys, both sets of attorneys agreed on the frequency of *completely* fabricated sexual abuse allegations, estimating that, on average, roughly one in every six reports to law enforcement agencies by five- to nine-year-olds is a total fabrication. This consensual estimate deserves further attention; it is higher than one would expect based on the opinions of many child abuse experts, who suggest that young children seldom have either the motivation or knowledge (of sexual acts) to completely fabricate sexual abuse (see Faller, 1984; Goodman & Helgeson, 1985).

Respondents were also asked to consider situations in which a child retracts his or her report of sexual abuse. They were asked to estimate the percentage of reports that are later retracted and to rate (on a five-point scale ranging from "never" to "very often") how often the retractions result from each of the reasons listed Table 6.5. Both sets of attorneys responded that a child who reports sexual abuse later retracts the statement in about 20 percent of the cases. And both saw pressure from parents or other family members as the dominant reason for retraction. This latter perception concurs with clinical research observations (Berliner & Barbieri, 1984; Goodman & Helgeson, 1985). When the accused abuser is a parent (e.g., the father), for example, other members of the child's family (e.g., the mother) may believe a trial and a possible prison term for the

TABLE 6.5 Reasons for retraction of testimony: Percentages of attorneys reporting each is "often" or "very often" a reason why a child reports sexual abuse and later retracts the statement.

	Defense Attorneys (%)	Prosecuting Attorneys (%)
Pressure from parent or family member	65	82***
Embarrassment about the incident (s)	45	31*
Feeling responsible for, or guilty about, the incident	34	43
Fear of retaliation or harm	29	45
Fear of being on the witness stand	26	16
Knowledge that the previous testimony was false	25	2**

*Prosecutor and defense attorney percent distributions differ by a chi-square test at $p < .05$; **at $p < .01$; ***at $p < .001$.

alleged abusive parent would be devastating to the family's financial situation and/or community standing. In other cases, the nonabusive parent may not believe the accusation of his or her child. These clinical observations may also be related to the perception among both sets of attorneys that feelings of embarrassment, responsibility, and fear of retaliation or harm often figure prominently in retractions of testimony (see Table 6.5). The survey question did not probe into what people these feelings are directed at, but it is likely that they include family members.

Defenders and prosecutors differed in their estimates of the frequencies of several reasons for retraction. To analyze these differences, for each reason, both defense and prosecuting attorneys were further categorized into two groups: those who indicated the reason was a cause of a retraction "often" or "very often" and those who indicated the reason was a cause of a retraction "never," "seldom," or "occasionally." These frequencies were then subjected to a Reasons × Attorney Type log linear analysis. This analysis revealed a significant interaction between reasons and attorney type. As can be seen in Table 6.5, whereas significantly (by a chi-square test) more prosecutors than defense attorneys perceived retractions as often stemming from pressure from a parent or family member, significantly more defense attorneys than prosecutors perceived retractions as often resulting from the child's embarrassment about the incident and from the child's knowledge that the previous testimony had been false. One-quarter of the defenders (versus only 2 percent of the prosecutors) estimated that deception (knowingly giving false testimony) occurs often with child witnesses. This underscores saliently the distrust of young children among defense attorneys that was evident throughout this survey. On the other hand, prosecutors typically may have more first-hand experience with recanting child witnesses, and hence be more aware of reasons for the retraction other than that previous testimony was false.

Perceptions of Jurors' Reactions to Child Witnesses

In this section of the survey, attorneys were asked, first, to judge whether jurors would be as likely to convict a defendant in a case involving a five- to nine-year-old child as the sole prosecution eyewitness as they would be to convict if the sole eyewitness was an adult. Table 6.6 presents the percent-

TABLE 6.6 Attorneys' perceptions of jurors' reactions to child eyewitnesses: Percentage choosing a given option to characterize jurors' comparisons of adults and children.[a]

Question	Option	Defense Attorneys (%)	Prosecuting Attorneys (%)
Compared to when the prosecution eyewitness is an adult, a jury is _____ likely to *convict* if the eyewitness is 5 to 9 years old.	less/much less	44	58[a]
	about equally	18	20
	more/much more	38	22
Inconsistencies in a person's courtroom testimony lower a child's credibility _____ an adult's.	less than	66	35[a,b]
	equally as much as	23	37
	more than	11	28
Jurors believe 5- to 9-year-olds' ability to *remember* events is _____ to adults'.	inferior/much inferior	68	77
	equal	26	23
	superior/much superior	6	0
Jurors see 5- to 9-year-olds as _____ *suggestible* than (as) adults.	less/much less	15	2
	equally	10	17
	more/much more	75	81
Jurors see 5- to 9-year-olds as _____ *sincere* than (as) adults.	less/much less	8	15
	equally	25	32
	more/much more	67	53

[a] Prosecutors' and defense attorneys' distributions differ on the dimension of juror perception at $p < .05$ according to a chi-square test.
[b] Prosecutors' distribution on inconsistencies question did not differ significantly from an equal probability distribution, according to a chi-square goodness-of-fit test; everywhere else they differ at least at $p < .02$.

ages of each type of lawyer predicting that jurors faced with a child eyewitness would be less, equally, or more likely to convict. Applying the equal probability analysis employed earlier on lawyers' perceptions of children, it was found that a significant majority of prosecutors (59 percent) felt jurors would be less likely to convict when the sole eyewitness was a child. Public defenders, on the other hand, were more sharply split on the matter. A greater than chance number (44 percent) agreed with the prosecutors, but almost as many (38 percent) felt a child eyewitness was more likely to sway a jury to convict. This difference in the distributions of expectations by type of attorney was significant according to a chi-square test and accounted for 26 percent of the variance in responses to the conviction likelihood question.

When asked how inconsistencies in the witness' courtroom testimony is likely to affect jurors' impressions of a child versus an adult witness, prosecutors were evenly divided into those who believed it would lower the child's credibility more, those who believed it would lower the child's and adult's credibility equally, and those who believed inconsistency would lower an adult's credibility more (see Table 6.6). In contrast, a statistically significant two-thirds of the defense attorneys expected inconsistencies to be more damaging to an adult's credibility. Based on these responses and the fact that defenders were split over whether a child witness inhibits or facilitates jury convictions, it appears that, even though they themselves are highly skeptical of children's testimony, many public defenders perceive jurors as decidedly *un*skeptical about child witnesses.

Three additional questions about jurors asked the lawyers to indicate how jurors generally would rate five- to nine-year-old children, compared with adults, on the dimensions of ability to remember events, suggestibility, and sincerity, using the same five-point comparison scales on which they had rated their own impressions of child witnesses. Interestingly, the distributions of defenders' and prosecutors' ratings of jurors' impressions did not differ for any of these three dimensions. Both attorney types significantly leaned toward beliefs that jurors see five- to nine-year-olds as less likely to remember, more suggestible, and more sincere. These data appear in Table 6.6.

When asked to estimate the age at which a child becomes as believable an eyewitness as an adult to the average juror, defenders gave a mean age of 12.86 years and prosecutors a mean age of 11.58. This difference approaches significance by t-test ($p = .08$) and seems a bit inconsistent with the fact that defenders are more likely than prosecutors to believe jurors will more readily accept children's (versus adults') eyewitness testimony. Perhaps the attorneys were responding to this question in terms of the age at which *they* believed children should be equally believable. If this is so, the responses of the two types of lawyers concurs with the general pattern of greater distrust of child witnesses on the part of public defenders. It is noteworthy, though, that, despite the trend of differences between attorney types, substantial variation in opinion exists *within* each attorney group. A substantial number of prosecutors (42 percent) and defenders (24 percent) felt that children ten years old and younger were as believable as adults among jurors, and similarly large numbers of prosecutors (24 percent) and defenders (37 percent) opined that a child had to be at least fifteen years old to be perceived as equally believable to an adult!

Alternative Methods of Presenting Children's Testimony

We listed eight alternative methods of obtaining and presenting the testimony of children who are victim or bystander witnesses in alleged crimes of sexual abuse (Table 6.7). For each method, attorneys were asked to (1) estimate the percentage of relevant cases that currently employ the method and (2) indicate on a five-point scale how acceptable they found the method "in principle" from "Completely Unacceptable" to "Completely Acceptable." Defenders and prosecutors showed considerable agreement in their estimates of current frequencies of method use. Most notably, the attorneys saw the use of anatomically correct dolls and hearsay evidence of

TABLE 6.7 Frequency and acceptability of alternative ways of obtaining and presenting the testimony of children who are witnesses or victims in alleged crimes of sexual abuse.

Method	Attorneys' combined mean estimate of how frequently (% of the time) this method is currently used	Percentage (%) of attorneys responding that "In principle, this method is *somewhat acceptable* or *completely acceptable* to me"[a]	
		Defense Attorneys	Prosecuting Attorneys
Hearsay evidence of medical doctor	53	19	93
Testimony with aid of anatomically correct dolls and other props	48	51	98
Hearsay evidence of parents	46	7	86
Hearsay evidence of psychologist	38	16	84
Hearsay evidence of teacher	27	10	81
Hearsay evidence of other children	22	5	71
Videotaped testimony	18	13	77
Written testimony of child's account	3	1	31

[a] The percentage of prosecutors exceeded the percentage of defense attorneys for all eight methods at $p < .001$, according to chi-square tests.

medical doctors and parents as most common among the methods, with each being used in about half the cases. However, while agreeing on frequency of current use, attorneys on separate sides of the bench disagreed markedly about the acceptability of the methods. Chi-square comparisons of defenders' and prosecutors' distributions of acceptability ratings revealed highly significant ($p < .001$) differences for all eight methods, with prosecutors finding every method more acceptable than defenders. Moreover, eta^2's illustrate that the magnitude of these differences between attorney types dwarf differences within the groups, because from 24 to 64 percent of the variance in responses was accounted for by the attorney's role. As can be seen in Table 6.7, the only alternative method that even a small majority of defense attorneys accepted was testimony aided by anatomically correct dolls and other props. In contrast, the prosecutors' modal response to seven of the eight procedures was "completely acceptable." The only procedure that prosecutors tended to dislike was written testimony of the child's account.

Attorneys' Self-Reported Behavior in Child Witness Cases

We asked attorneys to consider a trial in which *their opponent's* case included a child eyewitness as an important component and then presented them with several possible ways (listed in Table 6.8) that a trial lawyer might call into question the child's testimony. The attorneys indicated the extent to which they would employ each strategy, using a five-point scale (never, seldom, occasionally, often, always). The prosecutors reported significantly less use of the strategies than did defense attorneys. Almost all of the defenders responded "often" or "always" to two of the strategies: pointing out reasons to distrust children's testimony in closing arguments and pointing out weaknesses of children's testimonies—inconsistencies, memory lapses, and apparent compliance—during the trial. More than two-thirds of defense attorneys said they would also often or always highlight the youth of an eyewitness in opening arguments and "use to advantage the child's vulnerabilities" during their cross-examination. About half as many prosecutors said they would use these two techniques. Thus, the public defenders, who probably most often have to "oppose" child witnesses in court, apparently are especially likely to attempt to use any juror misgivings about children and any weaknesses of children to their advantage in the courtroom.

Interestingly, two "academic" strategies—bringing in an expert witness such as a psychologist to testify about children's memory abilities and citing relevant psycholegal research—are seldom used by either defenders or prosecutors. In fact, the modal response from both was "never" to these possible actions. Despite a large body of empirical literature on eyewitness testimony contributed by psychologists in the last decade, most of our Florida attorney respondents seem either unaware of it or unimpressed with its

TABLE 6.8 Attorneys' preferred techniques for dealing with opposing testimony by child witnesses: Percent of attorneys responding that they use a technique "often" or "always."

Strategy	Defense Attorneys (%)	Prosecuting Attorneys (%)
Point out instances of child's inconsistencies, memory lapses, apparent compliance with others' expectations, etc.	97	76***
In closing arguments, stress the youth of the witness and reasons to distrust child's testimony.	91	51***
Use to advantage the child's vulnerabilities (e.g., confusion, inarticulateness, fear, suggestibility) during cross-examination.	67	34***
In opening arguments, stress the youth of the witness and reasons to distrust child's testimony.	65	31***
In opening or closing arguments, cite psycholegal research that children are highly suggestible and prone to memory failure.	13	10*
Bring in an expert witness such as a psychologist to testify about children's memory abilities.	12	13

*** Percentage of defense attorneys exceeds the percentage of prosecutors according to chi-square analysis at $p < .001$; * at $p < .05$.

usefulness in their practice. In a later section, we analyze possible reasons for this lack of enthusiasm for psychologist expert witnesses.

When asked next about strategies to *support* a child witness' testimony for *their own side*, differences between prosecutors and defense attorneys disappeared. Eliciting the sympathy of the jury toward the child, extensively coaching the child's testimony before the trial, imploring the jury to excuse mistakes made by the child, and stressing the child's sincerity, were strategies reportedly used "often" or "always" by 50 to 70 percent of both kinds of attorneys (all statistical contrasts between lawyer types were nonsignificant). Once again, bringing in a psychologist as an expert witness and citing psycholegal research were decidedly unpopular options. Fewer than 15 percent of the respondents said they used these strategies often or always.

Effects of Personal Characteristics of Attorneys

Attorneys' Age and Experience

Correlational analyses carried out separately for each set of attorneys yielded few significant relationships between the responses discussed here and attorneys' age or years of professional experience as courtroom lawyers. For state attorneys and for public defenders, neither age nor years of experience correlated significantly with general evaluations of children, opinions about jurors' perceptions of child witnesses, or preferred strategies for dealing with child witnesses.

Attorney Gender

Gender was not strongly associated with responses to most items. The only area yielding consistent significant gender differences concerned the perceived reasons that children might retract their previous testimony. Although male and female attorneys did not differ significantly in the perceived likelihood that children would retract their testimony, they did differ in the reasons they endorsed. As Table 6.9 indicates, female attorneys were more likely to see each of the six reasons as more often involved in children's retractions. The gender differences were particularly pronounced for two factors: fear of retaliation or harm and embarrassment about the incident(s). For some reasons, gender differences were located mainly within an attorney set. Female public defenders were more likely to cite fear of retaliation and embarrassment than were their male counterparts. Female prosecutors were significantly more likely than their male counterparts to cite fear of retaliation, a child's feelings of guilt or responsibility, and the possibility that the previous testimony was false. Finally, moving to a different question, female prosecutors saw conviction solely on

TABLE 6.9 Gender differences in attorneys' perceived reasons why a child witness might retract earlier allegations of sexual abuse.[a]

	Male[b] Attorneys (%)	Female[c] Attorneys (%)
Pressure from a parent or family member	66	89
Feeling responsible for, or guilty about, what happened	34	43
Embarrassment about the incident (s)	33	50*
Fear of retaliation or harm	26	57**
Fear of being on the witness stand in front of many people	17	36
Knowledge that his/her previous testimony was false	14	18

[a]Defense and prosecuting attorney samples are combined. Figures represent the percentage of respondent attorneys who responded that a child's retraction is "often" or "very often" due to these reasons.
[b]$N = 85$
[c]$N = 34$
**Percentage of females exceeds percentage of males by chi-square test at $p < .01$; *at $p < .05$.

the basis of a child's testimony as significantly less likely than did male prosecutors.

The reasons for these gender differences are not clear. In particular, we can offer no account of why female lawyers see jurors as less likely to be swayed by children's testimony than male lawyers do. The differences in estimated frequencies of reasons for recanting testimony, though, do invite at least brief speculation. Perhaps, consistent with overall gender differences in Western culture (see Eagly, 1987), female attorneys have a warmer, more empathic style of working with witnesses than their male counterparts. As a result, they may evoke more self-disclosure from child witnesses who retract testimony that reveals a more complete picture of the reasons for the retractions. It is also possible that female attorneys, like women in general (see Hall, 1984), typically read nonverbal cues better than male attorneys and are therefore more likely to infer fear and embarrassment from the nonverbal behavior of recanting child witnesses.

Discussion

The survey results indicate that defense and prosecuting attorneys in Florida view five- to nine-year-old eyewitnesses as having poorer memories and as being more suggestible than adults. Further, these attorneys believe that jurors view child witnesses in the same way. The impression that children's testimony is inferior to that of adults was especially strong among public defenders. Interestingly, despite their apparent distrust of children's memories and of their ability to convince jurors, only slightly more than half of the attorneys believed juries convict less often when the prosecution case rests on a young child's testimony than on an adult's. Almost 30 percent believed conviction is *more* common in such cases. Attorneys also estimated that, despite the perceived relative inferiority of children's testimony, cases that rely on a child's word are slightly *more* likely to end in a juried trial than those that rest on adult testimony.

Our discussion focuses on four aspects of the survey results and their implications for practice and research in the area of children's testimony. We will look more closely at attorneys' perceptions of children, at their perceptions of jurors' reactions to children, at differences in opinions between prosecuting and defense attorneys, and, finally, at the important question of attorneys' courtroom behavior toward child witnesses.

Perceptions of Child Witnesses

The overall belief that children are less trustworthy eyewitnesses concurs with the traditional view of children that has been the basis of legal practices like competency tests even for children considerably older than five to nine years, special cautioning instructions to jurors, and so on. These views conflict, however, with growing research evidence that, if properly questioned and safeguarded against stressful or memory-distorting experiences while they participate in the criminal justice system, children even younger than five years of age can recall and recount episodes they have witnessed with a level of accuracy approaching that of adults (e.g., Goodman & Helgeson, 1985; Goodman & Reed, 1986; List, 1986; Melton & Thompson, 1987). There is also evidence that past research has overestimated the suggestibility of children who witness or experience sexual and other abuse (Goodman, Hirschman, & Rudy, 1987).

It is unclear where lawyers' perceptions of children's testimony fit into this larger research framework. One reason we surveyed attorneys is that they have far more exposure to real child eyewitnesses than do researchers and therefore are in a unique position to appraise children's skills as witnesses. Nevertheless, there are reasons to question the validity of the attorneys' judgments, or at least to suspect them of being somewhat biased. One factor is the considerable difference in the judgments of defense and prosecuting attorneys. Defense attorneys echoed the traditional view of extreme skepticism about children's testimony. In contrast, prosecutors, as a group, saw five- to nine-year-olds as only somewhat less adept than adults at memory and communication. They viewed them as just as accurate as adults on the crucial issue of identification accuracy. Who is correct, if either? Beyond this problem of disagreement, to which we will return, there is survey evidence (Yarmey & Jones, 1983) of considerable ignorance among lawyers about factors that generally affect memory. This suggests caution in accepting the accuracy of our own sample's estimates. But, as we discuss later, what lawyers believe may have important consequences for how child witnesses fare, whether or not their beliefs are accurate.

When attorneys (especially public defenders) are in disagreement with new research viewpoints on child witnesses, it could be because they are unaware of the research or because they are unconvinced by it. Even those attorneys who are aware of the early research on child witnesses may disregard it because, until recently, most psychological research on children's memory and suggestibility involved memory tasks and situations low in mundane realism. Caution in generalization was appropriate. Yet much recent research employs realistic situations and would seem applicable to the judicial realm (e.g., Brigham, VanVerst, & Bothwell, 1986; Goodman, Hirschman, & Rudy, 1987; Goodman & Reed, 1986). Hopefully, greater dissemination of this work will lead to increasing forensic usage. Undoubtedly, many attorneys are simply unaware of psycholegal research on child witnesses. This high level of unawareness may be illustrated by the extremely low rate at which attorneys reported relying on psychological research and expert appraisal in cases involving child witnesses.

Use of Psychological Expertise

The marked lack of enthusiasm for a psychologist expert witness expressed by attorneys in our sample is noteworthy in its own right. We suspect it may result in part from the attorneys' experience with the negative evaluation of expert witnesses on eyewitness identification prevalent in the Florida courts. Although such expert testimony has been admitted in a handful of cases in Florida, it is usually excluded by the trial judge (probably more than 90 percent of the time, in the second author's experience). The Florida Supreme Court has been notably unenthusiastic about admitting expert testimony about eyewitness memory (*M.E. Johnson v. State*, 1981; *P.B. Johnson v. State*, 1983). There has not yet been a court decision reversed in Florida for failure to admit psychologists' expert testimony on eyewitness identification. In contrast, there has been a growing trend nationwide to admit this testimony at the discretion of the trial judge (e.g., *People v. Brooks*, 1985; *State v. Buell*, 1986; *US v. Downing*, 1985; *US v. Moore*, 1986; *US v. Smith*, 1984). Further, in at least three states—Arizona, California, and Washington—appeals courts have reversed convictions for failure to admit psychological expert testimony concerning eyewitness identification (*State v. Chapple*, 1983; *People v. McDonald*, 1984; *State v. Moon*, 1986). Attorneys' evaluations of the usefulness of eyewitness expert witnesses may be more positive in these three states and in other jurisdictions in which such expert testimony has received more favorable judicial treatment than it has in Florida.

In the specific case of expert witnesses brought to court to aid the jury in evaluating the testimony of an allegedly sexually abused child, there is likewise considerable controversy, in Florida and elsewhere. Some state courts have ruled that an expert may not give an opinion on the credibility of a particular child complainant (e.g., *State v. Moran*, 1986). Other courts have refused to permit an expert to give background information on characteristics typically observed in sexually abused children or to offer explanations for recantations or delays in reporting abuse (e.g., *Commonwealth v. Seese*, 1986). The central arguments for rejecting such testimony are that in invades the province of the jury to decide the victim's credibility or that it involves information that is already part of the typical juror's "common knowledge."

In two recent cases, however, the Minnesota (*State v. Meyers*, 1984) and Montana (*State v. Geyman*, 1986) supreme courts ruled that expert testimony can be a valuable aid to jurors. These courts maintained the nature of child sexual abuse "places lay jurors at a disadvantage" because they are unlikely to be aware of either the dynamics inherent in situations of abuse or the postabuse behavioral and psychological symptoms that characterize many victims. In essence, this argument acknowledges that jurors may need to be apprised of what psychologists have identified as the "sexually abused child syndrome" if they are to appropriately evaluate the behavior of child witnesses who claim to have been abused (Myers, 1987; Summit, 1983). The Minnesota Supreme Court noted that, "Background data providing a relevant insight into the puzzling aspects of the child's conduct and demeanor which the jury could not otherwise bring to its evaluation of her credibility is helpful and appropriate in cases of sexual abuse of children . . . ." The court saw no infringement on the jury's role as long as jurors remained free to accept or reject the expert testimony.

We can expect to see continued judicial controversy as the courts struggle to find the most appropriate ways to evaluate the credibility of child witnesses. If, in fact, greater openness to expert testimony becomes the rule, and frameworks are established for deciding its admissibility, it seems likely that attorneys will begin to use expert testimony more and perhaps also acquire a more positive view of psychological research than our respondents reported.

Perceptions of Jurors' Beliefs

The two sets of attorneys showed great agreement in believing that jurors see children as less able than adults to remember events, as more suggestible, and as more sincere. These perceptions concur with research indicating that jury-age adults do indeed have a stereotype of children consisting of these three qualities (Leippe & Romanczyk, 1987; 1989; Wells, Turtle, & Luus, this volume). Interestingly, however, both attorney types (but especially defenders) were split on whether defense cases that rely heavily on elementary-school children's testimony are less or more likely to eventuate in convictions than those that rely on an adult eyewitness. A substantial number of both types (50 percent) saw convictions as less likely when a child's testimony was crucial to the defense, but many others (31 percent) saw conviction as more likely under these circumstances. Moreover, many attorneys (54 percent overall) expected jurors to overlook the inconsistencies of a child more readily than those of an adult. Some attorneys (again, especially among the public defender group) seem to be well aware that, as research with mock jurors suggests, the negative stereotype of children (regarding memory and suggestibility) can sometimes work to confer *greater credibility* on a child's testimony. This occurs, for example, when the child appears more competent than the stereotype (Leippe & Romanczyk, 1989), when the child's stereotypic sincerity or naivete rules out revenge or complicity (Goodman, Bottoms, Herscovici, & Shaver, this volume), when inconsistencies are seen as attributable to age and not to poor memory (Leippe & Romanczyk, 1987, 1989), or perhaps when the child elicits jurors' sympathy. The apparent insights of attorneys into how young witnesses will appear to juries thus lend credence to empirical findings with mock juries. Few people, of course, know juries as well as lawyers; their job is to persuade jurors and, like politicians or advertisers, they study the habits of their influence targets, albeit subjectively. At the same time, attorneys' beliefs about jurors' perceptions appear to directly influence their attempts to present children in the courtroom in a fashion that supports their case. Depending on whether the child witness was theirs or their opponents', the same attorneys reported playing either to the positive aspects of the child stereotype (sincerity, discounting/excusing of errors) or to the negative aspects.

Attorney Differences

The finding that defense attorneys were significantly more skeptical of eyewitness testimony than prosecutors is a striking replication of Brigham and WolfsKeil's (1983) survey findings based on a sample drawn from the same attorney population. In the present sample, this difference of opinion between the two sets of attorneys was largest in their respective estimates of the accuracy of eyewitness identifications made by five- to nine-year-olds, as opposed to estimates given for older children and adults (see Table 6.2). Defense attorneys estimated that, among the disputed eyewitness identifications by five- to nine-year-olds they were familiar with, a little less than one out of two (46 percent) was probably accurate. Prosecutors estimated that five of every six (83 percent) five- to nine-year-olds were likely to be correct. This greater distrust of child witnesses by defense attorneys extended to views on recall and recognition skills, suggestibility, and level of inconsistency in testimony. Defense attorneys even begrudged children the one positive witness-relevant characteristic that prosecutors (in the present survey) and lay people (in Leippe & Romanczyk's 1987 survey) believed is more prevalent in children than adults—the majority of defense attorneys *did not* see children as more sincere than adults.

Brigham and WolfsKeil suggested that the different perceptions of public defenders and state prosecutors could result from either the different job demands or the actual experience afforded by those jobs. Regarding the former explanation, defense attorneys most often defend alleged perpetrators against the incriminating accounts of eyewitnesses. Perhaps the skepticism necessary for this role generalizes to impressions of eyewitness memory. In contrast, the need to believe the witnesses for one's own case may lead prosecutors to a greater generalized trust in eyewitness testimony. Selective perception and memory may also play a part in the development of these role-driven beliefs. Social psychological research offers much support for the general idea that both people's behavior and their goals can exert powerful influences on their attitudes, beliefs, and memories (for general reviews, see Chaiken & Stangor, 1987; Fiske & Taylor, 1984).[1]

---

[1] Given the absence of significant relations between perceptions and years of experience in their professional roles among the attorneys we sampled, it would seem that these role-consistent beliefs develop fairly quickly. It is not inconceivable,

Perhaps, alternatively, role demands compelled the two attorney types to give responses that "toed the party line," so to speak, even though they might actually have agreed privately with each other in their beliefs about child and adult eyewitnesses. That is, perhaps both sets of attorneys responded in a way that would outwardly justify to readers of the survey their professional behaviors of condemning or selling (to jurors) eyewitness testimony. Impression management of this sort cannot be ruled out entirely, given that attorneys were asked to identify whether they were prosecutors or defense attorneys and may have felt a strong association with their professional roles. However, we consider it highly unlikely that many of these accomplished professionals would fail to give genuine personal appraisals when explicitly asked to participate in a scientific research study.

The other possibility proposed by Brigham and WolfsKeil is that, via job experiences, one attorney groups has a more veridical perception of eyewitness testimony. These researchers suggested, specifically, that defense attorneys could conceivably be more accurate than prosecutors because thay have more direct involvement with defendants and hence may have the better feel for the likely behavior of those defendants and their alleged presence at crime scenes. This differential accuracy account is, of course, not testable with the present data. The notion of an accuracy edge for public defenders, however, can be challenged on at least two grounds. First, the defense attorneys' mean estimated rate of identification inaccuracy (54 percent) among five- to nine-year-olds and their estimated rate at which sex abuse testimony (63 percent) is totally or partially distorted by five- to nine-year-olds are higher than the most recent realistic children's memory studies would suggest (e.g., Goodman et al., 1987). Second, it can perhaps as readily be argued that prosecutors would be in the better position to assess witness accuracy because they typically have more contact with the witnesses themselves.

What is clearly needed is more research on this interesting discrepancy in the opinions of prosecutors and defenders regarding adult and, particularly, child eyewitness testimony. At this point, it is most important to recognize that, if (as is perhaps most plausible) attorneys' behaviors and roles shape their opinions toward child witnesses, these opinions in turn will likely influence how the attorneys behave toward both witnesses and jurors, which may affect the performance and believability of a child

---

however, that role-consistent beliefs about eyewitnesses are correlated with decisions to *become* a defense or prosecuting attorney. Young attorneys, that is, may select the side of the bench they wish to work on, to an extent, and their selection may be influenced by beliefs relevants to the perceived veracity of eyewitness testimony (e.g., "Most criminal defendants are guilty." "The courts are biased against the accused—too many innocent people are wrongly convicted."). Caution, of course, is advised in considering these explanations without further research, particularly since the Brigham and WolfsKeil (1983) survey did uncover some significant correlations between experience and perceptions of eyewitness testimony.

eyewitness. Thus, skeptics (defense attorneys) may vigorously pursue the discrediting of an accusing child eyewitness, perhaps with both a zeal for their professional role *and* the passion of their convictions that children are untrustworthy memory sources. Prosecutors are also somewhat skeptical, as we have seen in their comparisons of children with adults, and thus may, in subtle ways, less agressively argue cases that rely on a small child's word. On the other hand, prosecutors may actually overbelieve children who appear particularly competent. Recall that prosecutors estimated that, on average, five- to nine-year-olds' disputed identifications are accurate as often as adults' identifications.

Attorney Courtroom Behavior

Attorneys seem most capable of influencing the outcomes of cases involving child witnesses by the way they question children in the courtroom. Unfortunately, what attorneys told us about their courtroom tactics concerning child witnesses suggests a real danger of reducing the veracity of the child's account and the ability of jurors to validly judge that veracity. To begin with, attorneys reported questioning children with an eye toward building on either the negative or positive aspects of the stereotype of children's memory, depending on whether the child witness was theirs or their opponent's. Second, and perhaps more troubling, two-thirds of the defense attorneys and one-third of the prosecutors told us they would often or always focus cross-examination questioning on an opposing child witness' special vulnerabilities, such as inarticulateness, fear, and suggestibility. Goodman and Helgeson (1985) have reviewed compelling evidence from children's memory research that cross-examinations of this sort will reduce the likelihood of obtaining the completeness and accuracy of which a child is otherwise capable. Heightened stress, for example, is a likely consequence for the child subjected to questions designed to confuse. Stress, in turn, reduces the short-term memory capacity necessary to comprehend an attorney's sentences and promotes memory retrieval failures that may lead to suggestibility. As another example, it is known that children connect events less fully than adults in their verbal reports. The alert attorney can point out this habit to the jury and attribute it to poor recall, and can also confront the child with queries of why he or she is so inconsistent. The results are predictable. Indeed, Wells, Turtle, and Luus (this volume) have demonstrated that the memory accuracy of eight-year-old eyewitnesses (to a videotaped crime) is significantly more worsened by cross-examination than is the accuracy of twelve-year-olds and adults. Jurors, then, may get fewer accurate facts as a consequence to attorney tactics as well as unnecessary "noise" (heightened emotion, errors of omission and commission, irrelevant statements about unrelated matters, etc.) that cloud the cues that might allow a fair assessment of the truth of children's statements. Quite often, this results in underbelief of the child witness (Goodman & Rosenberg, 1987). But it could work otherwise. In the Wells et al. study, there was greater inaccuracy in the testimony of the eight-year-old eyewitnesses who were subjected to cross-examination than in the testimony of those who were not. Yet the accuracy estimates of adult "mock jurors" who watched videotapes of their testimony were the same whether or not the child witnesses had been cross-examined. As a result, the less accurate cross-examined eight-year-olds were overbelieved by the adult evaluators.

Our attorneys' candid admissions of commonly manipulating jurors' impressions of children on the witness stand are relevant to growing concerns that adversarial methods like rigorous cross-examinations may be ill-suited to truth-gathering in the case of young child witnesses (e.g., Goodman & Helgeson, 1985). Another approach that is sensitive to the special needs of children may be called for, although public defenders, judging from their low ratings of the acceptability of various alternative forms of gathering testimony, are likely to strongly resist reform in this area. For the first time we have survey evidence of extensive use of courtroom strategies that are known to affect both witness performance and reactions to that performance. If past informal reports of attorneys, psychologists, and other observers have been enough to arouse concern, the present systematic survey data indicate that more definitive research on how these strategies influence child witnesses in forensically relevant settings would be most valuable and that determined efforts at making changes based on current evidence may be warranted.

Conclusion

We have learned much from the Florida lawyers who completed our questionnaire. Their judgments of the prevalence of pivotal child witnesses in the criminal justice system, the likely identification accuracy of these children, and some of the reasons child witnesses may err in or even retract their testimony provide important insights that are not available elsewhere. Their responses along these lines add to the clarity of our picture of children's actual experiences as witnesses. They also suggest where research is needed. Perhaps most important, we have argued, are attorneys' reports of their impressions and behaviors regarding child witnesses in the courtroom and other legal settings that require verbal memory reports from children. We can fully understand, and try to improve if need be, the process of gathering justice-relevant information from young children only if, in addition to understanding children's behavior, we know the beliefs and behaviors of those who children will encounter in the criminal justice system.

References

Altman, M.J., & Lennon, D. (1986). Child witnesses in felony trials—Competency and protection. *New York Law Journal*, 1–3.

American Jurisprudence, 2nd ed. (1976). Rochester, NY: Lawyers Co-Operative Publishing Company.

Berliner, L., & Barbieri, M.K. (1984). The testimony of the child victim of sexual assault. *Journal of Social Issues, 40 (2)*, 125–137.

Bothwell, R.K., Deffenbacher, K.A., & Brigham, J.C. (1987). Correlation of eyewitness accuracy and confidence: The optimality hypothesis revisited. *Journal of Applied Psychology, 72*, 691–695.

Brigham, J.C., & Bothwell, R.K. (1983). The ability of prospective jurors to estimate the accuracy of eyewitness identifications. *Law and Human Behavior, 7*, 19–30.

Brigham, J.C., VanVerst, M., & Bothwell, R.K. (1986). Accuracy of children's eyewitness identifications in a field setting. *Basic and Applied Social Psychology, 7*, 295–306.

Brigham, J.C., & WolfsKeil, M.P. (1983). Opinions of attorneys and law enforcement personnel on the accuracy of eyewitness identifications. *Law and Human Behavior, 7(4)*, 337–349.

Brown, M.R. (1926). *Legal psychology*. Indianapolis: Bobbs-Merrill Co.

Ceci, S.J., Ross, D.F., & Toglia, M.P. (1987). Age differences in suggestibility: Narrowing the uncertainties. In S.J. Ceci, M.P. Toglia, & D.F. Ross, eds. *Children's eyewitness memory*, New York: Springer-Verlag.

Chaiken, S., & Stangor, C. (1987). Attitudes and attitude change. *Annual Review of Psychology, 38*, 575–630.

Chance, J.E., & Goldstein, A.G. (1984). Face recognition memory: Implications for children's eyewitness testimony. *Journal of Social Issues, 40*, 69–86.

Cohen, R.L., & Harnick, M.A. (1980). The susceptibility of child witnesses to suggestion: An empirical study. *Law and Human Behavior, 4*, 201–210.

Commonwealth v. *Seese*, 40 Crl. 2196 (Pa. 1986).

Deffenbacher, K., & Loftus, E. (1982). Do jurors share a common understanding concerning eyewitness behavior? *Law and Human Behavior, 6*, 15–30.

Devitt, E.J., & Blackman, C.B. (1977). *Federal jury practice and instruction* (Vol. 1). St. Paul, MN: West Publishing Co.

Eagly, A.H. (1987). *Sex differences in social behavior: A social role interpretation*. Hillsdale, NJ: Erlbum.

Faller, K.C. (1984). Is the child victim of sexual abuse telling the truth? *Child Abuse and Neglect, 8*, 473–481.

Fiske, S.T., & Taylor, S.E. (1984). *Social cognition*. Reading, MA: Addison-Wesley.

Goodman, G.S. (1984). Children's testimony in historical perspective. *Journal of Social Issues, 40*, 9–32.

Goodman, G.S., Bottoms, B.L., Herscovici, B.B., & Shaver, P. (In this volume). Determinants of the child victim's perceived credibility.

Goodman, G.S., Golding, J.M., Helgeson, V., Haith, M.M., & Michelli, J. (1987). When a child takes the stand: Jurors' perceptions of children's eyewitness testimony. *Law and Human Behavior, 11*, 27–40.

Goodman, G.S., & Helgeson, V.S. (1985). Child sexual assault: Children's memory and the law. *University of Miami Law Review, 40*, 181–208.

Goodman, G.S., Hirschman, J. & Rudy, L. (1987, April). Children's testimony: Research and policy implications. In S. Ceci (Chair). *Children as witnesses: Research and social policy implications*. Symposium conducted at the meeting of the Society for Research in Child Development, Baltimore, MD.

Goodman, G.S., & Reed, R.S. (1986). Age differences in eyewitness testimony. *Law and Human Behavior, 10*, 317–332.

Goodman, G.S., & Rosenberg, M.S. (1987). The witness to family violence: Clinical and legal considerations. In D. Sonkin (ed.). *Domestic violence on trial.* New York: Springer.

Hall, J.A. (1984). *Nonverbal sex differences: Communication accuracy and expressive style.* Baltimore: Johns Hopkins University Press.

Harvard Law Review. (1985). The testimony of child victims in sex abuse prosecutions: Two legislative innovations. *98*, 806–827.

Johnson, M.K., & Grisso, T.J. (1986, August). *On the credibility of child eyewitnesses: The jury is still out.* Symposium paper presented at the meeting of the American Psychological Association, Washington, DC.

Leippe, M.R., & Romanczyk, A. (1987). Children on the witness stand: A communication/persuasion analysis of jurors' reactions to child witnesses. In S.J. Ceci, M.P. Toglia, & D.F. Ross (eds.). *Children's eyewitness memory.* New York: Springer-Verlag.

Leippe, M.R., & Romanczyk, A. (1989) Reactions to child (versus adult) eyewitnesses: The influence of jurors' preconceptions and witness behavior. *Law and Human Behavior, 13*, in press.

List, J.A. (1986). Age and schematic differences in the reliability of eyewitness testimony. *Developmental Psychology, 22*, 50–57.

Loftus, E.F. (1979). *Eyewitness testimony.* Cambridge, MA: Harvard University.

Lord, C.G., Ross, L., & Lepper, M.R. (1979). Biased assimilation and attitude polarization: The effects of prior theories on subsequently considered evidence. *Journal of Personality and Social Psychology, 37*, 2098–2109.

Marin, B.V., Holmes, D.L., Guth, M., & Kovac, P. (1979). The potential of children as eyewitnesses: A comparison of children and adults on eyewitness tasks. *Law and Human Behavior, 3*, 295–306.

M.E. Johnson v. State. Fla. 393 So. 2d 1069 (1981).

Melton, G.B. (1981). Children's competency to testify. *Law and Human Behavior, 5*, 73–85.

Melton, G.B. (1984). Child witnesses and the First Amendment: A psychological dilemma. *Journal of Social Issues, 40*, 109–125.

Melton, G.B., & Thompson, R.A. (1987). Getting out of a rut: Detours to less traveled paths in child-witness research. In S.J. Ceci, M.P. Toglia, & D.F. Ross, eds. *Children's eyewitness memory.* New York: Springer-Verlag.

Myers, J.E.B. (1987). The child witness: Techniques for direct examination, cross-examination, and impeachment. *Pacific Law Journal, 18(3)*, 801–942.

P.B. Johnson v. State, 438 So. 2d 774 (Fla, 1983).

People v. Brooks, 490 N.Y.S. 2d 692 (Co. Ct. 1985).

People v. McDonald, 37 Cal. 3d 351, 208 Cal. Rptr. 236, 690 P. 2d 709, (Cal. 1984).

Ross, D.F., Miller, B.S., & Moran, P.B. (1987). The child in the eyes of the jury: What's the verdict on jurors' perceptions of the child witness? In S.J. Ceci, M.P. Toglia, & D.F. Ross, eds. *Children's eyewitness memory.* New York: Springer-Verlag.

State v. Buell, 489 N.E. 2d 795 (Ohio, 1986).

State v. Chapple, 135 Ariz. 281, 660 P. 2d 1208, 1222–24 (1983).

State v. Geyman, 729 P. 2d 475 (Mont., 1986).

State v. Moon, 726 P. 2d 1263 (Wash. App., 1986).

State v. Moran, 40 Crl. 2198 (Ariz., 1986).

State v. *Myers*, 359 N.W. 2d 604 (Minn., 1984).

Summit, R.C. (1983). The child sexual abuse accommodation syndrome. *Child Abuse and Neglect*, 7, 177–193.

US v. *Downing*, 753 F. 2d 1224 (3rd Cir., 1985), 609 F. Supp. 784 (D.C. Pa., 1985).

US v. *Moore*, 786 F. 2d 1308 (5th Cir., 1986).

US v. *Smith*, 736 F. 2d 1103 (6th Cir.), *cert. denied*, 469 U.S. 868, 105 S. Ct. 213, 83 L. Ed. 2d 143 (1984).

Wells, G.L., & Loftus, E.F., eds. (1984). *Eyewitness testimony: Psychological perspectives*. Cambridge: Cambridge University Press.

Wells, G.L., Turtle, J.W., & Luus, C.A.E. (1989). The perceived credibility of child eyewitnesses: What happens when they use their own words? In S.J. Ceci, D.F. Ross, & M.P. Toglia, eds. *Perspectives in children's testimony*. New York: Springer-Verlag.

Whipple, G.M. (1911). The psychology of testimony. *Psychological Bulletin*, 8, 307-309.

Yarmey, A.D. (1979). *The psychology of eyewitness testimony*. New York: Free Press.

Yarmey, A.D. (1984). Age as a factor in eyewitness memory. In G.L. Wells & E.F. Loftus, eds. *Eyewitness testimony: Psychological perspectives*. New York: Cambridge University Press.

Yarmey, A.D., & Jones, H.P.T. (1983). Is the psychology of eyewitness identification a matter of common sense? In S.M.A. Lloyd-Bostock & B.R. Clifford, eds. *Evaluating witness evidence: Recent psychological research and new perspectives*. Chichester, England: Wiley.

7
Children's Conceptions of the Legal System: "Court Is a Place to Play Basketball"

KAREN J. SAYWITZ

Children are participating in legal investigations and litigation more frequently than ever before. They become involved with the legal system as victims of abuse, neglect, or kidnapping; as witnesses to burglary or to a parent's murder; or as the foci of custody disputes and civil injury cases. When children come in contact with the legal system, they often become involuntary participants in a complex web of repeated contacts with strangers, in unknown situations, governed by a set of unfamiliar rules that are admittedly difficult even for adult witnesses to comprehend.

Very little is known about children's perceptions of the system. Authors from both the legal and mental health fields have called for research on this issue (Macaulay, 1987; Melton & Thompson, 1987). A better understanding of the development of children's conceptualization of the legal system is needed to understand fully the factors that affect children's behavior in the courtroom. Such information would be valuable to judges, jurors, attorneys, and policymakers who must assess children's competence to testify and credibility as witnesses. In addition, such research findings would clarify our understanding of children's subjective experience of participation. This information is critical to the efforts of parents, mental health professionals, and children's advocates who work to ensure that children are not revictimized, this time by the court system that is supposed to protect them.

A negligible amount is known about the way in which children's legal knowledge contributes to the effectiveness of their testimony or their credibility in the eyes of the jury. However, there is reason to believe that it does. The literature on discourse processes suggests that the effectiveness

This study was supported in part by a grant from the Harbor-UCLA Collegium to Karen Saywitz and a grant from the Hasbro Children's Foundation to the Kids in the Court System Project at the Children's Institute International. The author expresses appreciation to Kee MacFarlane, Toni Johnson, and Patricia Leuhrs for their collaboration. The author also wishes to thank Lorinda Camparo, Peter Mundy, and Richard Romanoff for their efforts and suggestions.

of communicative acts, such as testimony, rest on the interaction between the unspoken expectations, attitudes, and knowledge of both the listener (e.g., juror) and the speaker (e.g., witness). The literature on perspective-taking and referential communication skills suggests that children's ability to infer what others think, feel, or intend does influence the effectiveness of their communications (Dickson, 1981).

When children's understandings of the people and procedures in court are not well developed, it is likely to effect their performance on the stand. For example, children who believe the judge is the sole decision maker in a case, may try vigorously to communicate their view to the judge, but fail even to make eye contact with the jurors who are seen as mere spectators. If we hope to converge on a comprehensive understanding of the factors that affect a child's credibility as a witness, much more must be known about children's perceptions of the people, places, and procedures that constitute our legal system.

There is growing national concern regarding the potential for revictimization by a legal system that is insensitive to children's needs and limitations. Consider the following vignette. A frightened young child sat in the back of the courtroom anxiously awaiting the judge's decision. Will she be allowed to go home, sent to a stranger's house, or sent to a children's hall? She listened intently while a decision was made about where she would be placed for the next six months as the civil and criminal cases unfold. The hearing was over and she was still bewildered. She started to cry. She asked her caseworker where she was going to live. The caseworker responded with a puzzled look "Didn't you listen to what the judge said? He said the minor will live with her grandmother."

The child responded, "I heard him say the minor was gonna live with grandma, but where am *I* gonna live?" Children's misunderstandings of legal proceedings are all too common. What effect might their misconceptions have on their experience of the process? Had the judge recognized that many children under ten think of minors as people who dig coal (Saywitz & Jaenicke, 1987), this child's fear and anxiety about her future could have been reduced.

Recent research suggests that while some child witnesses perceive the process of investigation and litigation as helpful, others report that it was a harmful experience (Tedesco & Schnell, 1987). At the very least, testifying can be a distressing and confusing experience for witnesses of any age. When children face equally unfamiliar and frightening medical procedures, their anxiety is reduced by preparation techniques that involve desensitization and anticipatory coping strategies based on increased knowledge of what will happen to them (Jay, 1984). It follows that sensitive and age-appropriate preparation of child witnesses before court appearance could alleviate much of their confusion, fear, and anxiety, as well. Yet, to develop age-appropriate preparation procedures, one must consider what knowledge, prior experience, expectations, and fears children of different age groups bring to the situation.

The study of children's perceptions is important to understand fully the factors that effect children's competence and credibility as witnesses and the potential for preventing revictimization by the system. This chapter focuses on children's conceptions of the legal system at different age levels and the sources from which they acquire such knowledge. The first section reviews existing literature on children's knowledge of social institutions, including the legal system. The second section describes a study, based in part on the findings of past studies, designed to compare the perceptions of different aged children with varying amounts of experience in the legal system.

Review of the Literature

Children's Knowledge of Social Institutions

In the past, there have been studies of children's conceptions of content areas related to the judicial system, such as children's understanding of political systems (Greenstein, 1965) and laws (Adelson, Green, & O'Neil, 1969). However, the primary focus of this research was on adolescence, not early childhood. During the 1970s, there were many studies of young children's moral reasoning (Kohlberg & Gilligan, 1975), political socialization (Tapp & Kohlberg, 1971), and some interest in young children's conceptions of social institutions from a Piagetian framework (Furth, Baur, & Smith, 1976). More recently, several trends have contributed to an increased interest in young children's understanding of sociolegal institutions:

1. An inability of subsequent research to validate Piaget's structures-of-the-whole notion across different domains of development (Fischer, 1983; Saltzstein; 1983).
2. Theoretical advances in the domain of social-cognitive development, moving away from "hard-stage" theories toward models of gradual, context-sensitive transformations (Damon, 1977; Snyder & Feldman, 1984; Turiel, 1978).
3. Efforts of the child advocacy and children's rights movements.
4. Increased public awareness of legal cases concerning child abuse, as well as genuine increases in the number of cases reported for legal investigation resulting from new statutes mandating reports from various professional groups.
5. A growing awareness of the powerful influences of television on social-cognitive development.[1]

---

[1] In particular, the 1986–87 American television season involved an explosion of series related to the legal system during after school hours, including Divorce Court, People's Court, Superior Court, and The Judge to list the daytime schedule alone.

All of these trends have contributed to renewed interest in the general study of young children's conceptions of sociolegal systems.

Among the researchers who have studied factors closely related to children's conceptions of the judicial system are Tapp and Levine (1974). They postulated a stagelike model of legal reasoning that was an adaptation of Kohlberg's model of moral reasoning. They reported significant age-related differences similar to those found by Piaget (1960). According to Tapp and Levine, the preconventional level, common in five- to eight-year-olds, involves a "sanction-oriented deference stance," in which legal reasoning is based on the fear of being punished by an authority figure. The conventional level, emerging in ten- to fourteen-year-olds, is a "law and order conformity posture," focusing on the maintenance of law by means of obedience. The postconventional level, the highest stage, is "a law-creating, principled perspective," involving conceptions of the legislative process and universal ethics. Tapp and Levine concluded that the cross-cultural literature supports the notion of a universal age-related sequence of the development of ideas related to law and justice, despite cultural differences (Gallantin & Adelson, 1971; Hess & Tapp, 1969; Minturn & Tapp, 1970). They concluded that the conventional (law and order) level is the modal level in most societies.

Melton (1980) modified Tapp and Levine's model in a study of first, third, fifth, and seventh graders' concepts of rights. He found that both developmental factors (reflected in school grade) and socioeconomic status (SES, reflecting the opportunity to exercise one's rights) affect children's conceptions of their rights. Most children had some idea of the nature of rights by third grade, regardless of SES level. Older children viewed rights as based on a criteria of fairness and self-determination. Younger children possessed a more egocentric view; rights were based on the whim of an authority figure who decides what children are allowed to do.

Melton also found a significant interaction between SES and school grade, suggesting that cognitive–maturational advances are necessary, but not sufficient, for a mature view of rights. Higher SES (reflecting opportunity and experience in exercising one's rights) was associated with a higher level of understanding rights for older, but not for younger, children. Consistent with the age-related findings of Kohlberg and Gilligan (1975) and Tapp and Levine (1974), Melton (1980) found that the vast majority of his oldest subjects (seventh graders) did not reach the highest level of reasoning.

Children's Conceptions of the Legal System

Recently, a few descriptive studies of children's understanding of legal concepts have emerged. In a study of children's conceptions of the French penal system, Pierre-Puysegur (1985) reported significant age-related effects on legal knowledge in six- to ten-year-old French children but few effects of SES on knowledge. Although she did not test this hypothesis, Pierre-Puysegur speculated that the effects of SES were attenuated by the equal access to television of all groups.

From her results, Pierre-Puysegur postulated a developmental model of conceptualizing the French penal system. At the initial phase, children believed that an offense could go unpunished or that the accused could be arrested, condemned, and punished by the police. In a second phase, children began to understand that arrest leads to an intermediary stage where a judge, rather than the police, makes a decision about guilt and punishment. Yet, there was still no sense of the possibility of an appeal process. In the final phase, children came to understand that the judgment was made through the process of a trial, with attorneys, witnesses, and laws playing apart, rather than at the whim of the judge. Finally, the possibility of an appeal process was conceptualized.

Flin, Stevenson, and Davies (1987) interviewed six-, eight-, and ten-year-olds to examine developmental trends in the ability to describe and define legal concepts. Overall, the children adequately comprehended concepts of police, court, breaking the law, criminals, and being guilty or not guilty. Knowledge of witnesses and judges appeared to be acquired later. The authors reported that children of all ages were unfamiliar with the role of sheriff, lawyer, jury, what it means to be prosecuted, what a trial involves, and what is evidence and why it is needed in court.

Flin et al. (1987) also asked children how they felt about going to court. Only two children (both six years old) felt positive about going to court as a witness or victim. Most children felt it was a place for bad people, although by age ten some realized that anyone may be called to court, not only criminals. All of the children felt it was important to tell the truth in court. They thought it was important because they feared punishement, not because they viewed the trial as a fact-finding, truth-seeking process.

Saywitz and Jaenicke (1987) studied grade-related trends in kindergartners, third-graders', and sixth graders' understanding of thirty-five legal terms selected from transcripts of actual court proceedings when child witnesses were present. Some of the terms showed significant grade-related trends (*fact*, *witness*, *case*, *truth*, *date*, *lawyer*, *denied*, *hearing*, *attorney*, *identify*, *oath*, *parties*, *evidence*, *objection*, *jury*, *swear*, and *testify*). Other terms were too difficult, no matter what the child's age, since their legally relevant definitions were understood by virtually none of the children (*allegation*, *petition*, *minor*, *motion*, *competent*, *hearsay*, *strike*, *charges*, and *defendant*). Still other terms were relatively easy and understood by all the children (*judge*, *lie*, *police*, *remember*, and *promise*).

The younger children in this study frequently assumed that an unfamiliar word, such as jury, was in fact a similar sounding familiar word, such as jewelry. The authors hypothesized that child witnesses may frequently be operating under the false impression that they understand a term that they have, in fact, misconstrued.

Another frequent error showing grade-related trends involved younger children assuming that the adult was referring not to the legally relevant definition but to an alternative definition:

"Court is a place to play basketball"
"Charges are what you do with your credit card"
"Hearing is what you do with your ears"
"Date is what you do with a boyfriend"
"Case is what you carry papers in"
"Minor is someone who digs coal"
"Parties are for getting presents"
"Swear is like cursing"
"Strike is when you hit somebody"

When asked if these words could mean anything else in the context of court, the children answered no.

Warren-Leubecker, Tate, Hinton, and Ozbek investigated the legal knowledge of the largest sample of children to date, 563 children from three to fourteen years of age. Their results are described in this volume. Overall, the results of all of these studies do not differ greatly, considering the different age groups, methodologies, and scoring systems used by different investigators. Young children repeatedly demonstrated limited knowledge of the people, places, and procedures that make up our legal system. Very young children did not simply demonstrate a paucity of knowledge, but also misunderstandings and inaccuracies. None of these studies, however, involved actual witnesses with first-hand experience in the legal system. The role of experience in the development of legal knowledge remains unexplored.

Sources of Knowledge about the Legal System

The study that follows explores not only age-related trends in knowledge of the legal system, but also factors that affect the development of legal knowledge, such as first-hand experience as a witness in the legal system and television viewing of court-related dramas.

The Role of Experience

In a series of studies of juveniles' competence to waive their rights, Grisso (1981) assessed the abilities of 600 juvenile court wards to understand the Miranda warnings and their implications. He found that juveniles' understanding of their rights were not related to the amount of prior experience with the courts or police nor to race or SES. The majority of juveniles fourteen years of age and under did not grasp the meaning of the warnings sufficiently to understand their implications.

In the field of cognitive science, researchers have investigated the effect of experience as it is reflected in the memory skills of adults and children who are experts or novices in certain areas (e.g., chess) (Chi, 1978; Chi and Ceci, 1987; Chi and Koeske, 1983; Gobbo and Chi, 1986). Subjects with expert knowledge were found to be superior to novice subjects in their ability to employ and access their knowledge, possibly because it is more cohesive and integrated. To the extent that this is also the case in the development of legal knowledge, children with significantly more legal experience should have a more cohesive, well-integrated conceptualization of the legal system based on more experience with the system. However, Grisso (1981) did not find this to be the case with juvenile court wards. Melton (1980) did find a relation among understanding of one's rights, SES, and age, the latter two variables reflecting opportunity and experience with exercising one's rights. Pierre-Puysegur (1985) failed to find effects of SES on legal knowledge, but postulated that the availability of television attenuated the effects of SES. It is not yet clear what role direct and indirect experience play in the acquisition of knowledge about the legal system.

The Role of Television

Gerbner, Gross, Signorielli, Morgan, and Jackson-Beeck (1979) have studied extensively the role of television in children's developing views of social reality. Their work suggests that crime and law enforcement play a key role in television's portrayal of social order and that the television version differs from reality in many respects. In a comprehensive series of studies, Gerbner et al. (1979) found that among children from seven years to adolescence, heavy viewers perceived social reality differently from light viewers, even when other factors (e.g., sex, age, ethnicity, vocabulary, and the child's own report of victimization) were held constant. For example, heavy-viewing adolescents saw the world as more violent and were more likely to overestimate the number of people who commit serious crimes than light viewers.

Although exposure to television programs about the legal system is likely to influence children's knowledge base, it is not clear whether it will lead to more accurate knowledge. Macaulay (1987) has stated that, as a source of information about the legal system, television misrepresents reality. Macaulay believes that viewers who rely on television are "badly misled" about the roles of professionals in the legal system. For example, he points out that lawyers are portrayed atypically, in Perry Mason style. "Mason doesn't get his client acquitted by showing that the prosecutor failed to carry the burden of proof. Instead, he proves his client's innocence by exposing the real killer" (1987, p. 198). The role of television and experience in children's conceptualizations of the legal system require further study.

③ Concept Acquisition

How do children develop conceptions of the legal system? Perhaps, it is not unlike the development of other concepts. Investigators have demonstrated support for the use of weighted features (attributes) to define a given concept (Clark, 1973; Hampton, 1979; Rips, Shoben, & Smith, 1973; Rosch & Mervis, 1983). Thus, a concept is represented mentally by a set of features or attributes that are variously weighted on the degree to which they enable individuals to make accurate decisions about that concept. Some of the features are weighted more heavily (defining features), and some are weighted less heavily (characteristic features). For example, the concept *judge* is defined by a list of attirbutes, some of which are defining features (in charge of the courtroom, decides the sentence) and some of which are characteristic features (wears a robe, bangs a gavel). The terms "defining" and "characteristic" are used loosely and may best be understood as representing the ends of a continuum of definition (McCloskey & Glucksberg, 1978).

Keil and Batterman (1984) found evidence for a developmental shift from a phase where children make judgments about concepts based on many characteristic features to a phase where defining features are most prevalent. Applying this data to the topic at hand, young children may not be aware of defining features (e.g., the jury is part of the decision-making process) but may have knowledge of characteristic features (e.g., jurors watch the trial). Gradually, children come to use defining features in evaluating a concept. Keil and Batterman (1984) suggest that the characteristic-to-defining shift occurs at different points in development for different concepts, depending on the domain of knowledge.

A Study of Children's Conceptions of the Legal System

The goal of the present study was to describe developmental differences in children's conceptualizations of the legal system and to begin to identify factors that contribute to the acquisition of legal knowledge and competence. Based on the studies just reviewed, a group of researchers (present investigator included) designed an experiment to examine developmental differences in conceptualizing the judicial system among children with varied amounts of direct legal experience and varied television-viewing habits. The data presented are observations from semistructured interviews with forty-eight children from four to fourteen years of age divided into three age groups. Half of them were actively involved in legal cases as victim-witnesses and half were not.

While age and first-hand experience were expected to be associated with accuracy and completeness of knowledge about the legal system based on many of the research findings reviewed earlier, it is important to recall that

Grisso (1981) did not find a relation between experience and knowledge of Miranda warnings and Pierre-Puysegur (1985) did not find a relation between socioeconomic status and knowledge of the French penal system. Based on current views of cognitive development, it also seemed reasonable to expect an interaction between age and experience such that inherent cognitive limitations could attenuate the effects of experience with younger children. Although television has been found to influence children's knowledge of their social world (Gerbner et al., 1979), Macaulay (1987) and others have pointed out that although television could be educational, it also could provide children with a distorted view of the legal process. Thus, the following study is designed to investigate associations between legal knowledge, maturational factors—reflected in age groupings, and direct and indirect experiential factors—reflected in witness status and watching television programs about the legal system.

Method

Subjects

Forty-eight children from Los Angeles County, ranging in age from four to fourteen years, participated. Twenty-four had been actively involved in legal cases as witnesses for at least three months (high-legal-experience group). These children had been referred to the "Kids in the Court System" project for an educational/supportive intervention program to assist them and their parents with the legal process. The children were interviewed at intake before they participated in the intervention program. Another twenty-four children who had not been involved in a legal case were recruited through local schools and scout troops (low-legal-experience group). Each of these children was matched to one of the high-experience subjects on the basis of age (within one year).

Subjects within each experience group were divided into three age groups: four-to-seven year olds (M = 5.6 years), eight-to-eleven year olds (M = 9.9 years), and twelve-to-fourteen year olds (M = 13.0 years). There were sixteen boys and thirty-two girls in the sample. Preliminary analyses showed no effects of sex. Both of the experience groups contained at least 25 percent children from low-income and 50 percent from middle-income families. Subjects were excluded if they showed any signs of a psychotic process, delayed language development, or mental retardation or were enrolled in special education.

All of the subjects were interviewed about their past legal experience. Responses were rated on a seven-point scale (7 = testifying in open court; 1 = no legal experience), allowing for the characterization of the legal experiences of "normal" children. The distribution of the low-experience group past legal experience was as follows: 63 percent received their legal knowledge solely from TV, parents, peers and school, while 21 percent had visited a court either with a parent (e.g., traffic violation) or on a school field trip. For the more experienced group (all of whom were witnesses), 58 percent had been interviewed by attorneys and police and had appeared in the courtroom during the proceedings, although they did not testify. Thirty-three percent had testified, but only one child had testified publicly in open court. Thus, amount of exposure to the courtroom varied within both groups. All of the experienced children were victims of abuse and one-third were simultaneously involved in custody disputes that arose subsequent to the allegations of abuse.

Instrumentation

In choosing the particular concepts to be investigated, this investigator visited courtrooms during proceedings and selected concepts that were associated with visually salient attributes of the court that could be represented pictorially as prompts. Thus, the interview focused on eight concepts related to the court itself and the people involved in the judicial process:

court	*jury*	*judge*	*witness*
lawyer	*baliff*	*court clerk*	*court reporter*

Children were told that the interviewer was interested in what they thought about court. They were asked the same set of questions about these eight judicial concepts and provided with illustrations of each concept. In general, the questions elicited the concept's meaning, appearance, function, why we have the concept in court, what would happen if we did not have the concept, and the child's source of information (direct experience, television, through another person). Some concepts were followed with additional questions (e.g., Question 11, following). For example, these were the questions asked about the term *jury*:

1. "Do you know what a JURY is?"
2. "What is a JURY?"
3. "What does a JURY look like? (picture introduced after this prompt)
4. "Who is in a JURY? How does somebody get to be in a JURY?"
5. "What is the job of the JURY in court?"
6. "Why do we have JURY in court?"
7. "What would happen if we didn't have a JURY in court?"
8. "Have you ever seen a JURY in person? Tell me about it."
9. "Have you ever seen a JURY on TV? Tell me about it."
10. "Did you ever know anybody that was on a JURY?" Tell me about it."
11. "What makes a person in the JURY believe a witness?" (Subjects understanding of *witness* was assessed prior to this question.)

After the eight concepts were discussed, questions about additional concepts were introduced to assess children's understanding of the following:

a. Witness credibility: "What makes a judge (or jury) believe a witness?"
b. The decision-making process: "How do they decide who wins in court?"
c. The fact-finding, truth-seeking process: "What happens when people tell the truth in court? What happens when people tell a lie in court? Why is it important that people tell the truth in court?"
d. The differentiation between subsystems, such as, police, penal and judicial systems: "What does a policeman have to do with court?"

Procedure

Children were interviewed individually for approximately 45 to 60 minutes by a licensed social worker or a psychology graduate student, each of whom was trained in the clinical interview method. They followed up the children's leads to uncover the reasoning behind in their answers. The individualized, semistructured interview led to questions that were not completely standardized across all subjects. This method was employed to reveal subtleties in conceptualization that would have been lost with the restraints imposed by a forced-choice method or structured interview.

Scoring the Data

When children's discussions of the concept demonstrated comprehension of defining features, they were considered to possess accurate concept knowledge. Importance of features was determined by a task modeled after one developed for adults by McNamara and Sternberg (1983) and for children by Schwanenflugel, Guth, and Bjorklund (1986).[2] The children's correct responses to the interview were separated into a comprehensive list of features for each concept. A feature had to be mentioned by at least two of the subjects to be included in the list.

These features were then presented in random order to twenty-five college students in a physics class at California State University, Dominguez Hills, who rated each feature on a three-point scale describing how important the feature was to accurate understanding of the concept (1 = not very important, 2 = important, 3 = very important). They were instructed to leave a feature blank if they felt is was not related to the concept. Features were referred to as defining if endorsed as very important by two-thirds or more of the adults. The rest were considered to be characteristic.

Concepts were scored in two ways. First, a completeness score for each

---

[2]These studies have shown that children's ratings of feature importance do not necessarily coincide with adult ratings. However, for our purposes we used adult ratings of feature importance to determine whether children had mastered an understanding of a concept, because in the legal environment it is the adult definition that sets the standard, which is expected to be understood by all. However, we also took the child's viewpoint into consideration by asking adults to rate only features that were generated previously by the children.

concept reflected the number of true features (both defining and characteristic) mentioned about that concept. In devising a total completion score, features were summed across five concepts. Only five of the concepts were used because subjects proved to be unfamiliar with the minor courtroom personnel of bailiff, court clerk, and court reporter. Thus, total completion score reflects the sum of features about the five major concepts.

Accuracy scores were also computed for each concept, using the following four-point qualitative scale:

0 = I don't know, irrelevant, in accurate response
1 = Characteristic response
2 = At least one defining feature
3 = The concept was defined uniquely; More than one defining feature.

Both 2 and 3 on this scale were considered an accurate response. An example at each level for the concept of *jury* may serve to clarify the accuracy scoring system:

0 = "The stuff you wear on your neck and finger like a ring" (i.e., jewelry).
1 = "People who sit there and watch, I don't know why they are there."
2 = "They listen to the case and then make a decision about it."
3 = "When there are both a jury and a judge in the case, the jury listens to the case, they discuss it with each other and then give a verdict about the guilt or innocence of the accused and the judge gives the sentence."

These scores were summed for each child across concepts to yield a total accuracy score.

Results

Interrater Reliability

There were two graduate student coders who were bline to subjects' age, sex, legal experience, and the hypotheses of the study. They coded twenty-eight randomly selected children's protocols. Mean percentage agreement for completion scores was 85 percent and for the accuracy scores was 90 percent. Disagreements were resolved through discussion.

Age Group and Experience Level

The means and standard deviations of total accuracy and total completeness scores by age group and experience level are presented in Table 7.1.[3]

---

[3] Relative to the means, the standard deviations of the accuracy and completion scores were quite large. This indicates that there was considerable variability on these scores. The breadth of variability in the children's responses reduced the power of the analyses. Nevertheless, a number of significant findings were obtained. Possible explanations for the differences in children's scores include variability in attention span or measurement imprecision.

TABLE 7.1 Means, standard deviations, and ranges for total accuracy and total completeness scores by age group and experience group.

	Age					
	4-to-7 years $N = 18$		8-to-11 years $N = 19$		12-to-14 years $N = 11$	
	Experience		Experience		Experience	
	Low $n = 10$	High $n = 8$	Low $n = 9$	High $n = 10$	Low $n = 5$	High $n = 6$
Total Accuracy Score	0.40[a] (0.69) [0–2]	0.125 (0.35) [0–1]	4.11 (0.93) [0–6]	2.51 (2.50) [0–6]	6.00 (1.41) [5–8]	5.17 (0.98) [4–6]
Total Completion Score	3.4 (4.20) [0–10]	3.25 (3.41) [0–9]	23.75 (5.99) [15–31]	17.70 (13.12) [3–36]	38.20 (2.77) [34–41]	25.67 (7.00) [15–31]

[a] Mean (SD) [Range].

These scores were treated as interval data and subjected to two-way analyses of variance (age group × experience level). Hypotheses concerning age effects on accuracy and completeness were confirmed ($F(2, 42) = 46.08$, $p < .0001$; $F(2, 42) = 53.02$, $p < .0001$, respectively). Older subjects demonstrated more accurate and more complete knowledge. Multiple comparisons using the Bonferroni Method ($p < .01$) resulted in significant differences among all comparisons.

Group effects of experience on total accuracy and total completeness scores were also significant ($F(1, 42) = 4.13$, $p < .049$; $F(1, 42) = 7.60$, $p < .009$, respectively). As can be seen in Table 7.1, and contrary to expectation, children with more experience demonstrated less accurate and less complete knowledge than children with less experience. Age group by experience level interactions were not significant.

The effects of experience are difficult to interpret. The results lend themselves to two possible interpretations. First, children with more experience, who are witnesses in abuse cases, may also come from more dysfunctional families, possessing emotional difficulties that interfere with their cognitive abilities. This raises a methodological issue with regard to the prospect of measuring legal experience independent of emotional or cognitive abilites in children. Second, actual court experience may, in fact, be chaotic and confusing, making acquisition of knowledge about the legal system a more arduous task. As a result of the difficulty in interpreting experience effects, these effects was excluded from the remainder of the analyses.

Data for each individual legal concept are presented in Table 7.2. Age effects on completeness and accuracy of all five major concepts were highly significant. Age effects on accurate conceptions of two of the minor courtroom personnel did not reach significance.

TABLE 7.2 Means, standard deviations, significant age effects for the judicial concepts. [a]

Concept	4-to-7 years N = 18		8-to-11 years N = 19		12-to-14 years N = 11		Age Effects
	Mean (SD)	[range]	Mean (SD)	[range]	Mean (SD)	[range]	
Age Effects on Accuracy Scores (Scale = 0–3)							
Court	0.61 (0.77)	[0–3] [b]	2.26 (0.99)	[1–3]	2.82 (0.40)	[2–3]	$H = 26.38$ df = 2, $p < .001$
Jury	0.0		0.79 (0.91)	[0–3]	1.91 (1.30)	[0–3]	$H = 19.81$ df = 2, $p < .001$
Judge	0.56 (0.61)	[0–2]	1.77 (0.94)	[0–3]	2.36 (0.67)	[1–3]	$H = 23.11$ df = 2, $p < .001$
Witness	0.33 (0.68)	[0–2]	1.74 (1.14)	[0–3]	2.46 (0.52)	[2–3]	$H = 23.24$ df = 2, $p < .001$
Lawyer	0.12 (0.32)	[0–1]	1.58 (1.07)	[0–3]	2.55 (0.52)	[2–3]	$H = 29.32$ df = 2, $p < .001$
Bailiff	0.11 (0.47)	[0–2]	0.05 (0.22)	[0–1]	0.36 (0.67)	[0–2]	$H = 4.10$ df = 2, $p < .13$
Court clerk	0.0		0.05 (0.22)	[0–1]	0.36 (0.81)	[0–2]	$H = 4.00$ df = 2, $p < .14$
Court reporter	0.0		0.68 (1.05)	[0–3]	1.45 (1.21)	[0–3]	$H = 14.11$ df = 2, $p < .001$
Age Effects on Completion scores							
Court	1.39 (1.85)	[0–6]	8.42 (4.42)	[0–16]	10.27 (2.49)	[5–15]	$F(2,45) = 32.95, p < .001$
Jury	0.0		1.79 (2.14)	[0–6]	4.46 (3.23)	[0–9]	$F(2,45) = 16.24, p < .001$
Judge	1.06 (1.39)	[0–4]	4.28 (2.13)	[0–8]	6.55 (1.63)	[4–10]	$F(2,45) = 35.29, p < .001$
Witness	0.78 (1.59)	[0–5]	3.21 (2.20)	[0–6]	5.18 (1.47)	[3–7]	$F(2,45) = 20.60, p < .001$
Lawyer	0.11 (0.32)	[0–1]	2.95 (2.36)	[0–8]	4.91 (2.07)	[2–8]	$F(2,45) = 26.12, p < .001$

[a] Individual accuracy scores were treated as ordinal data using nonparametric tests, Kruskal-Wallis (H). Completion scores were treated as interval data using analyses of variance.
[b] Mean (SD) [range].

TABLE 7.3 Percentage of subjects with accurate responses, by age.

Age group (years)	N	Percentages (%)							
		Court	Jury	Judge	Witness	Lawyer	Bailiff	Court Clerk	Court Reporter
4–7	18	0.06	0	0.06	0.11	0	0.06	0	0
8–11	19	74	21	93	86	93	0	0	50
12–14	11	100	73	91	100	100	0.09	0.18	64
Total	48								

The percentage of subjects showing accurate concepts at each age level are presented in Table 7.3. Across the concepts, it appeared that the concept of *jury* consolidated at a later age than the other concepts. The difference was most pronounced in the eight- to eleven-year-olds. That is, many children in this age range had an adequate understanding of *court*, *judge*, *witness*, and *lawyer*, but few appeared to have mastered the concept of *jury*. This assumption was tested with pairwise chi-square analyses. The results indicated that significantly more children between the age of eight and eleven years ($N = 19$) presented evidence of understanding defining features of *court* than *jury* ($\chi^2 = 17.96$, $p < .001$), *judge* than *jury* ($\chi^2 = 15.03$, $p < .001$), *witness* than *jury* ($\chi^2 = 12.06$, $p < .001$), and *lawyer* than *jury* ($\chi^2 = 17.96$, $p < .001$). Mean completion scores by age displayed in Table 7.2 also supported the notion that *jury* is a later-developing concept, than *judge*, *witness*, *lawyer*, and *court*.

Mean completion scores indicated that, although the very young children did not demonstrate knowledge of the defining features of *court*, *judge*, *lawyer*, and *witness* (criteria for accuracy), they were providing correct information about these legal concepts in the form of characteristic features.

The Role of Watching Court-Related Television Programs

It was also hypothesized that, in addition to age and direct experience, frequency of watching court-related television programs would contribute to development of legal knowledge. Children were asked what programs they watch that have courts in them and how frequently they watch each program. Responses were rated on a three-point scale:

0 = Doesn't watch shows with courts in them or has only seen TV court once.

1 = Watches only one or two of these shows once in a while.

2 = Watches any of these shows every time it is on or watches two or more of these shows regularly.

There was a significant positive correlation between scores on watching court-related television shows and accuracy ($r = .70$, $p < .01$) and completion ($r = .72$, $p < .01$). Furthermore, the television-watching score was also significantly correlated with age ($r = .69$, $p < .01$). This raised the issue of whether the effects of age on accuracy and completion were confounded with the effects of television watching. Therefore, partial correlations were computed to assess the association between age and accuracy or completion while holding variance associated with television-watching habits constant.

The correlation between age and accuracy fell (from $r = .86$ $p < .01$ to $r = .44$, $p < .01$) when the effects of television-watching scores were held constant and the correlation between age and completion fell (from $r = .85$, $p < .01$ to $r = .41$, $p < .01$) when the effects of television-watching scores were held constant. These partial correlations indicate that the correlations between age and accuracy as well as age and completion are sharply reduced by controlling for variance associated with television watching, but nevertheless remained significant. These two aspects of the data suggest that both television watching of court-related series and age are important and partially independent correlates of accuracy and completion of understanding the judicial system in children.

Conversely, the correlation between television-watching scores and accuracy fell (from $r = .70$, $p < .01$ to $r = .29$, $p < .05$) when the effects of age were held constant, as did the correlation between television-watching scores and completeness (from $r = .72$ $p < .01$ to $r = .34$, $p < .02$). Thus, in this particular sample, age was the more powerful variable, although there seemed to be a reliable television effect independent of age that is worthy of further investigation.

Additional Concepts

Each child's entire protocol was scored for four additional conceptualizations, rated on a four-point scale (0 to 3). Means, standard deviations, and significant age effects for three of them appear in Table 7.4. (Interrater reliabilities ranged from 72 to 98 percent for these four variables.)

First, responses to two questions were scored for understanding of witness credibility ("What makes a jury (or judge) believe a witness?"). Responses to the jury and judge questions were combined for analysis. The number of times children mentioned the following were summed:

a. Witness factors ("If he always tells the truth; If he doesn't stutter or look guilty.")
b. Judge/jury factors ("They are smart; They concentrate; They just trust the witness.")
c. Evidence factors ("If what they say is believable; If other people said the same thing, too.").

TABLE 7.4 Mean, standard deviations, and significant age effects for additional concepts.

	Age Groups			
	4–7 years	8–11 years	12–14 years	Age effects
Witness credibility[a]	0.06[d] (.25) [0–1]	0.77 (0.75) [0–2]	1.60 (0.51) [1–2]	$F(2,37) = 22.14$, $p < .0001$
Awareness of decision-making process[b]	0.0	1.00 (0.74) [0–2]	2.00 (0.94) [0–3]	$H = 26.45$ (df = 2) $p < .0001$
Awareness of truth-seeking process[c]	1.15 (0.35) [0–1]	1.86 (0.63) [1–3]	1.85 (0.47) [1–3]	$H = 14.25$ (df = 2) $p < .001$

[a] Scores were number of factors mentioned and were treated as interval data using analyses of variance.

[b,c] Scores treated as ordinal data (scale = 0–3), using nonparametric tests, Kruskal-Wallis (H).

[d] Mean (SD) [range].

As can be seen in Table 7.4, a two-way ANOVA (age group × experience level) revealed a significant effect of age group. The data show a linear effect with comparable increments between group means. The effect of experience and the age by experience interaction were not significant. The data indicate that, although older children began to consider factors that a judge or jury could use in determining the credibility of a witness, children in the youngest age group did not. Many four- to seven-year-olds simply assumed that witnesses tell the truth and they are believed.

Second, the entire protocol was scored for understanding of the decision-making process used to reach a verdict and the child's ability to distinguish between the role of the judge and the role of the jury in that process[4] ("How do they decide who wins the case in court?"). Again, the effect of age group was significant, but not that of experience level. The data revealed a linear effect with equal increments between group means. The majority of eight- to fourteen-year-olds believed that the judge's and jury's decisions are dependent on each other in some significant manner, but their understanding was inaccurate. For example, children suggested that the judge and jury go into a room and discuss the case together, and that

[4] This variable was scored on the following four-point scale: 0 = I don't know, irrelevant or idiosyncratic response; 1 = judge alone decides the case; 2 = judge and jury's decision are dependent on each other in some way; 3 = judge and jury's decisions are independent.

the judge can change the jury's verdict if he doesn't like it. Only three children (all in the twelve- to fourteen-year-old range) understood that the judge and jury make relatively independent decisions, even though the judge's determination of a sentence depends on the jury's verdict.

Third, protocols were scored for understanding the fact-finding, truth-seeking process.[5] This type of awareness showed a significant effect of age group, but not of experience group. As can be seen in Table 7.4, means show a nonlinear effect, with children from eight to fourteen years of age performing comparably. The majority of four- to seven-year-olds demonstrated no awareness that a goal of the court process is to gather evidence and determine whether or not it is truth. Their responses indicated that the goal was to accomplish an act (e.g., punish the criminal or give the child to one of his parents), but they did not understand that evidence must be collected, presented, and evaluated. Instead, they had a naive view, assuming that the evidence almost magically presented itself and was, of course, true and believed.

Fourth, protocols were scored for the child's ability to distinguish among the police, penal, and judicial systems, a finding suggested by the work of Pierre-Puysegur (1985). One-third of the four- to seven-year-olds in this study demonstrated evidence of this type of confusion. Some thought that the policeman decided if someone did something wrong and could be put in prison for life with no appeal. Some thought that court was just a room you pass through on your way to jail. Most of the remaining four- to seven-year-olds simply said they did not know. None of the eight- to fourteen-year-olds evidenced this misperception.

Discussion

These data affirm that children of different ages and varying amounts of experience bring different expectations to the courtroom. The findings are generally consistent with the age-related trends reported by Piaget (1960), Tapp and Levine (1974), Melton (1980), Pierre-Puysegur (1985), and Warren-Leubecker et al. (this volume). As Grisso (1981) found, direct experience with the legal system did not lead to enhanced knowledge of the system. Consistent with the findings of Gerbner et al. (1979), heavy watching of court-specific television programs did appear to influence children's conceptions of the legal system. The findings support Keil and Batterman's (1984) notion of a characteristic-to-defining shift in concept acquistion. The fact that the age of the shift for *jury* differed significantly from that of

---

[5]This variable was scored on the following four-point scale: 0 = I don't know, irrelevant, idiosyncratic response; 1 = no evidence of awareness of truth-seeking process; 2 = evidence of awareness of truth-seeking process; 3 = aware that truth may be independent of what the judge/jury decide.

the other legal concepts supports their hypothesis that shifts occur at varying points in time for different concepts rather than a hard-stage model.

Age-Related Trends in Conceptualizing the Legal System

The importance of maturational processes in the development of legal knowledge was strongly supported by the observations presented. A description of the developmental progression follows.

Four- to Seven-Year-Olds

For the most part, children in this age group reasoned on the basis of what they saw and their own egocentric view of the world. They understood observable characteristics of the legal system, but not the defining features. As a result, the four- and five-year-olds were unable to meet the criteria of accuracy on any of the five major concepts. This may have been a result of the verbal nature of the interview. Overall, four- to seven-year-olds described how legal personnel behaved in global terms, such as talking, sitting, and helping. There was little differentiation among the roles of different personnel. The children knew many visually salient aspects of the system existed but treated them as rituals and could not explain their purpose further. For example, "The judge is there to talk and listen, nothing else, he sits in a high desk and bangs a hammer, I don't know why." They did not know that the judge is in charge of the courtroom or determines the sentence—features rated as defining by the adults.

The lack of differentiation within and between people and their social roles was pervasive. For example, they were confused about whether judges continue to be judges when they go home at night. One-third of the four- to seven-year-olds confused the roles of the police, prison, and court process. Some said, "Court is a room you pass through on your way to jail." Others said, "The policeman decides if somebody did it or not and whether they should go to jail for the rest of their life." Pierre-Puysegur (1985) reported a similar misunderstanding. The children tended to generalize from personal experience across social systems, reasoning about court personnel on the basis of their own experiences at home and school where infractions are responded to by a single parent or teacher who makes the arrest, judges, and sets the punishment, so to speak.

To their credit, the four- to seven-year-olds demonstrated a sense of a social institution that is "out there" beyond home and school. This is contrary to the Piagetian notion that very young children have little direct experience with intangible social systems, and thus are severely limited in their ability to develop mental representations of social institutions. Children growing up in the age of television are regularly exposed to social systems beyond the family and school.

Four- to seven-year-olds' responses revealed coceptualizations consistent with the early phases described by Piaget (1960) and Tapp and Levine (1974) in which a fear of punishment by authority figures underlies reasoning processes. For example, they knew witnesses had to tell the truth, but thought it was because they would be punished if they did not. They did not understand that evidence had to be presented and evaluated. They naively believed that all evidence presented is true. Although legal personnel were viewed as benign and helpful, the court process was seen as treacherous and potentially leading to jail. They described court from the point of view of someone who has done something wrong. Even one nine-year-old who was aware of the alternative roles one might have in the court process feared that "if the witness gives the wrong answer, he'll go to jail." One can speculate that this level of reasoning feeds into children's fears about going to court. They may begin to think they did something wrong and as a result of the court process they themselves will somehow end up in jail.

Eight- to Eleven-Year-Olds

By the age of eight to nine years, typically third grade, accurate concepts of court and the roles of judges, witnesses, and attorneys began to emerge. For example, court was seen as a place you go to work out disagreements. Melton (1980) found that by third grade children also had a concept of rights. However, for the concept of jury, the shift from knowledge based on characteristic to defining features began to emerge substantially later, within the ten- to eleven-year-old level. Pierre-Puysegur (1985) found the same age-related pattern for the concepts of judge versus jury in a different culture.

Not surprisingly, the vast majority of children in our sample were completely unfamiliar with the roles of the bailiff and court clerk. The court reporter was frequently assumed to be a reporter from the news media, even when a picture was shown of her typing court.

Although the younger children could not say what court reminded them of, many eight- to eleven-year-olds responded, "Church, because you have to be quiet and its serious." In this age group, lawyers were seen in a positive light as someone who is there to help. These children demonstrated an emergent understanding of the adversarial nature of the process ("The lawyer is on your side.") and the representational aspect of the lawyer–client relationship ("He stands up for you in court."). The eight- to eleven-year-olds viewed witnesses as people who answer a lot of questions, tell the truth, and help the judge and lawyer by telling what happened. Gradually, the judge's role in determining guilt or innocence and in deciding the punishment were realized within this age group.

Generally, children in the eight- to eleven-year-old group showed substantial increases in differentiating between people, social roles, processes, and functions. For example, they no longer confused the judiciary with the role of the police. They were aware that the court is a fact-finding process that seeks to uncover the truth but did not understand that sometimes the truth (reality) differs from the judge's or jury's decision about what happened because the evidence on which they based their decision was flawed. The "law and order mentality" described by Tapp and Levine (1974) was evident in responses of children at this phase, although this was not tested.

Twelve- to Fourteen-Year-Olds

Only this oldest age group demonstrated a sense of societal role for the legal system beyond the one-to-one relationships of the individuals they described, for example, discussing the court as a subsystem of an overriding government. They began to become aware of the function of the jury. Five children understood that although the process seeks to uncover the truth, this is not necessarily always the case. They understood that decisions may, in fact, be based on inaccurate information, and that winning the case is not always synonymous with finding truth. The oldest age group appeared to demonstrate reasoning commensurae with the conventional level described by Tapp & Levine (1974) and Melton (1980), although this hypothesis was not tested. None of the subjects described the "law-creating, principled perspective" characteristic of the highest level of reasoning in Tapp and Levine's (1974) model.

Credibility in the Eyes of the Jury

Credibility is a function of the interaction among the listeners (jurors), the speakers (witnesses), and the context (courtroom) in which the testimony occurs. A thorough understanding of children's credibility requires not only comprehension of jurors' perceptions of children but also children's perceptions of juries. In this sample, the concept of jury appeared to develop in three phases. Children under ten years of age did not know what jury meant. Responses showed auditory discrimination errors confusing the word jury with jewelry.

A second phase was reflected by the eight- to eleven-year-olds' perceptions that jurors are indistinguishable from other spectators ("They sit there and watch, I don't know why."). Most of these children did not realize that the jury was an impartial group, but thought that victims, witnesses, and defendants ask their friends to come be on the jury. For the most part, these children said that the judge was the only one who decides the case and were unaware of the jury's role in determining the verdict.

An indication of a third phase is that a few eleven-year-olds and the children in the twelve- to fourteen-year-old group understood that the jury had a role in deciding the verdict. However, most of these children were extremely confused about the nature of the jury's role in the decision-making process. They still believed that it is the judge's opinion that counts. Some children believed that the judge could change the verdict if he did not agree with the jury. Several children even suggested that the judge and jury go off during recess into a room together to discuss the case.

Only the three oldest children understood that the judge and jury make an independent decision. Even older children's reasoning about why we have juries in court was limited. For example, "The jury is there to second the judge's opinion," "so the judge does not have to stay up all night thinking about it," or "so the judge does not get blamed for the decisions." These data support the notion that some children who testify may be unaware of the need to convey their message not only to the judge but also to the jury. In this way, their credibility may be affected by their level of knowledge of the concept of jury.

Children's understanding of witness credibility was assessed by asking "What makes a judge (or jury) believe a witness?" The four- to seven-year-olds' responses reflected the bias that judges want to believe witnesses indiscriminately because "judges think witnesses are nice," "they are just trying to help," "judges feel sorry for witnesses," or simply because "witnesses always tell the truth." Their responses could be characterized more as blind faith ("They hope that the witness is telling the truth," "They like the witness and want to believe him.") or an omniscient view of the judge ("He's so smart he can tell if they are telling the truth or not."). Not only were they unaware of the adversarial nature of the system, but there was no doubt that as witnesses they would be quite surprised by the disbelief confronting them in cross-examinations and repeated interviews.

Eight- to eleven-year-olds began to understand that judges and jurors evaluate a witness' credibility and could consider a limited number of realistic factors. However, it was the twelve- to fourteen-year-olds who distinguished themselves by discussing a wide range of factors that jurors could take into consideration, including whether the witness hesitates, the witness's facial expressions, witness's personality and reputation for telling the truth in the past, the believability of the evidence, the amount of corroborating evidence, and factors associated with the jurors' interactions with each other.

Sources of Knowledge about the Legal System

The Role of First-Hand Experience

As in Grisso's (1981) report, these findings call into question the assumption that experience in the legal system helps children develop a more accurate, complete, and cohesive understanding of the system in which they are participating. Contrary to expectations, the child witnesses demonstrated significantly less accurate and less complete knowledge of the legal system than age-mates without legal experience. A subjective reading of their responses indicated that they were more confused. One can only speculate as to why.

As previously mentioned, the more experienced children were not only more experienced in court, but also victims of abuse and at high risk for emotional difficulties that could interfere with their ability to absorb legal knowledge from the experience or to perform on the interview task. Although children with overt signs of delay and psychopathology were excluded, an objective measure of psychopathology was not employed, and the victim-witnesses probably came from more dysfunctional families. It is also possible that variables such as SES or verbal ability accounted for this phenomenon. To evaluate the role of experience, researchers will need to choose comparison groups that are matched to the victim-witness group on variables such as psychopathology, SES, verbal fluency, or other cognitive skills. For example, a group of depressed or conduct-disordered children may be more appropriate than normal controls.

On the other hand, it is also probable that the development of legal knowledge depends on the context in which the information is learned. Therefore, since the inexperienced subjects gained their knowledge primarily from television or school and parent involvement, they may have been presented with a view that is in actuality on oversimplification of the legal process, but simple enough for them to extract the main points. Children who participate in the legal system as a victim-witness experience numerous delays and continuances, a variety of meetings (depositions, preliminary hearings, placement decisions, trials), as well as the retelling of their story over and over again in diverse situations. To these children the legal system may appear to be a far more confusing and chaotic concept to master. It may be far more difficult to extract a consistent schema or frame for conceptualization from these experiences than from a lesson plan presented at an age-appropriate level or from a half-hour situation comedy. Court may be a confusing place regardless of the level of emotional disturbance in the sample.

Both interpretations lead to a similar conclusion. Child witnesses have a limited and at times faulty understanding of the system in which they are participating. Often, they do not accurately understand what is happening around them. They require age-appropriate preparation regarding the people, places, and procedures of the legal system.

Anecdotally, when asked "What does the judge's robe remind you of?," the inexperienced children tended to give neutral answers such as "a priest" or "somebody graduating." However, the experienced children's responses took on a morbid and frightening connotation, such as, "a priest at a funeral," "a witch," and "Dracula." Additional study of the relation between the emotions and cognitions of child witnesses may shed further light on the role of experience in acquiring legal knowledge. It is possible such research will reveal that some current practices are actually detrimental.

The Role of Television Viewing in Conceptualizing the Legal System

In this sample, there was a reliable effect of watching court-related television programs on accuracy and completeness of knowledge about legal system that merits replication. Heavy viewers of television programs about court demonstrated more accurate and complete legal knowledge, despite Macaulay's speculations regarding the extent to which television misleads the public about the legal system. Further investigation is needed to determine whether television also perpetuates or creates common childhood misperceptions regarding the legal system.

Implications for Future Research

These data suggest the child witnesses possess misunderstandings and limited knowledge of the legal system. Future research is needed to determine how this affects their performance, credibility, and subjective experience of the process.

Thus far studies have relied primarily on verbal interviews or written questionnaires, which may underestimate children's true conceptual knowledge. Children are likely to know more about a concept than they can express in verbal statements. Additional knowledge can be inferred from the way children use a word or make judgments about a concept. Therefore, one goal of future research would be to replicate the results of these initial descriptive studies with true/false verification, picture sorting, and/or response to vignettes or video tape methodologies.

The fact that child witnesses in this sample demonstrated less accurate and less complete knowledge of the legal system than age mates strongly supports the need to allocate resources to develop techniques to prepare children for participation in legal proceedings. Further research is needed to understand the relative contributions of innate maturational limitations on legal competence and the degree to which experience through education, television, or participating as a witness can modify the development of legal knowledge. Empirical findings are necessary to determine whether interventions to enhance children's legal competence can be effective in maximizing the accuracy of the children's accounts, minimizing distortion, and reducing stress. Studies of pediatric psychology certainly suggest that children's stress can be reduced by increasing their knowledge of what will happen to them in the system, including anticipatory coping strategies and desensitizing visits to the unfamiliar surroundings of the courtroom (Jay, 1984).

One such program of research could build on the available descriptive data to develop an assessment tool that would evaluate children's knowledge, past experiences, attitudes, and feelings regarding the legal system.

This tool could be used to identify gaps in a child witness' legal knowledge, as well as his or her misperceptions and fears about testifying. An educational-therapeutic intervention program could be developed to remediate the identified gaps in knowledge, correct the misperceptions, and reduce identified fears to whatever degree possible.

From example, consider the following line of reasoning. Young children typically interact with safe adults whom they know well and can trust. They may be frightened by unfamiliar places and strangers. Anxiety associated with strangers, and strange situations in the courtroom can interfere with their ability to perform at their highest level of cognitive and verbal ability when testifying. Admittedly, the experience of testifying is stressful even for adult victims. In addition to their anxiety, the extent to which young children's thinking is bound by their immediate surroundings has profound implications for their performance on the stand. Initially, they are likely to spend a great deal of mental energy taking in and adapting to the new and distracting environment in which questioning will take place. They are not likely to be listening carefully to the questions at hand.

An intervention program that increases children's knowledge of what will happen to them in the system and familiarizes children with the surroundings, rules, and roles of the various strangers can reduce their anxiety and stress, increasing the potential for accurate reporting. Research is needed to determine what kinds of interventions can be developed that allow children to perform optimally on the stand; how children might be inoculated in this way against the stress of testifying; and how accuracy and completeness could increase as a result of such interventions without generating increased distortions.

At present, one can only speculate as to whether children's paucity of knowledge and misunderstandings are due to a lack familiarity with the content, emotional factors, or to some inherent cognitive maturational constraint that will limit the effect of any educational attempt to alter the acquisition of legal concepts. The study of children's conceptions of the legal system is critical to fully understanding the factors that affect children's competence and credibility as witnesses and the potential for protecting children from undue stress through preparation. Understanding the interplay between children's knowledge of and performance in the legal system will be a rich and rewarding area for future research endeavors.

References

Adelson, J., Green, B., & O'Neil, R. (1969). Growth of the idea of law in adolescence. *Developmental Psychology*, *1*, 327–332.

Chi, M. (1978). Knowledge structures and memory development. In R. Siegler, ed. *Children's thinking: What develops?* Hillsdale NJ: Erlbaum, 73–96.

Chi, M., & Ceci, S. (1987). Content knowledge and the reorganization of memory. *Advances in Child Development and Behavior*, *20*, 1–37.

156   Karen J. Saywitz

Chi, M., & Koeske, R. (1983). Network representation of a child's dinosaur knowledge. *Developmental Psychology, 19(1)*, 29–39.

Clark, E. (1973). What's in a word? On the child's acquisition of semantics in his first language. In. T. Moore, ed. *Cognitive development and the acquisition of language*. New York: Academic Press, 65–110.

Damon, W. (1977). *The social world of the child*. San Francisco: Jossey-Bass.

Dickson, P.W., ed. (1981). *Children's Oral Communication Skills*. New York: Academic Press.

Fischer, K. (1983). Illuminating the processes of moral development. *Monographs of the Society for Research on Child Development, 48(1–2)*.

Flin, R., Stevenson, Y., & Davies, G. (1987). Children's knowledge of the Law. Submitted for publication.

Furth, H., Baur, M., & Smith, J. (1976). Children's conception of social institutions: A Piagetian framework. *Human Development, 19*, 351–374.

Gallantin, J. & Adelson, J. (1971). Legal guarantees of individual freedom: A cross-national study of the development of political thought. *Journal of Social Issues, 27(2)*, 93.

Gerbner, G., Gross, L., Signorielli, N., Morgan, M., & Jackson-Beeck, M. (1979). The demonstration of power: Violence profile No. 10. *Journal of Communication, 48*, 177–196.

Gobbo, C., & Chi, M. (1986). How knowledge is structured and used by expert and novice children. *Cognitive Development, 1(3)*, 221–238.

Greenstein, F. (1965). *Children and politics*. New Haven: Yale University Press.

Grisso, T. (1981). *Juveniles' waiver of rights*. New York: Plenum Press.

Hampton, J. (1979). Polymorphous concepts in semantic memory. *Journal of Verbal Learning and Verbal Behavior, 18*, 237–254.

Hess, R., & Tapp, J. (1969). *Authority, rules, and aggression: A cross national study of socialization into complicance systems* (Part I). (Project No. 2947), Washington, DC: U.S. Office of Education.

Jay, S. (1984). Pain in children: An overview of psychological assessment and intervention. In A. Zener, D. Bendell & C. Walker, eds. *Health psychology treatment and research issues*. New York: Plenum Press, 167–196.

Keil, F., & Batterman, N. (1984). A characteristic-to-defining shift in the development of word meaning. *Journal of Verbal Learning and Verbal Behavior, 27*, 221–236.

Kohlberg, L., & Gilligan, C. (1975). The adolescent as philosopher: The discovery of the self in a postconventional world. In P. Mussen, J. Conger, & J. Kagan, eds. *Basic and contemporary issues in developmental psychology*. New York: Harper & Row, 18–33.

Macaulay, S. (1987). Images of law in everyday life: The lessons of school, entertainment, and spectator sports. *Law and Society Review, 21(2)*, 185–218.

McCloskey, M., & Glucksberg, S. (1978). Natural categories: Well defined or fuzzy sets? *Memory and Cognition, 6*, 462–472.

McNamara, T., & Sternberg, R. (1983). Mental models of word meaning. *Journal of Verbal Learning and Verbal Behavior, 22*, 449–474.

Melton, G. (1980). Children's concepts of their rights. *Journal of Clinical Child Psychology, 9(3)*, 186–190.

Melton, G., & Thompson, R. (1987). Getting out of a rut: Detours to less traveled paths in child-witness research. In S. Ceci, M. Toglia, & D. Ross, eds. *Children's eyewitness memory*. New York: Springer-Verlag.

Minturn, L., & Tapp, J. (1970). *Authority, rules, and aggression: A cross-national study of children's judgments of the justice of aggressive confrontations.* (Part II). (Project No. 2974), Washington, DC: U.S. Office of Education.

Piaget, J. (1960). *The moral judgement of the child.* New York: The Free Press.

Pierre-Puysegur, M. (1985, July). The representations of the penal system among children from six to ten years. Presented at the 8th biennial meetings of the International Society for the Study of Behavioral Development, Tours, France.

Rips, L., Shoben, E., & Smith, E. (1973). Semantic distance and the verification of semantic relations. *Journal of Verbal Learning and Verbal Behavior, 12,* 1–20.

Rosch, E., & Mervis, C. (1983). Fuzzy set theory and class inclusion relations in semantic categories. *Journal of Verbal Learning and Verbal Behavior, 22,* 509–525.

Saltzstein, H. (1983). Critical issues in Kohlberg's theory of moral reasoning. *Monographs of the Society for Research on Child Development, 48(1–2),* 108–119.

Saywitz, K., & Jaenicke, C. (1987, April). *Children's understanding of legal terminology: Preliminary findings.* Presented at the annual meeting of the Society for Research on Child Development, Baltimore, Md.

Schwanenflugel, P., Guth, M., & Bjorklund, D. (1986). A developmental trend in the understanding of concept attribute importance. *Child Development, 57(2),* 421–430.

Snyder, S., & Fledman, D. (1984). Phases of transition in cognitive development: Evidence from the domain of spatial representation. *Child Development, 55,* 981–989.

Tapp, J., & Kohlberg, L. (1971). Developing senses of law and legal justice. *Journal of Social Issues, 27(2),* 65–91.

Tapp, J., & Levine, F. (1974). Legal socialization: Strategies for an ethical legality. *Stanford Law Review, 27,* 1–72.

Tedesco, J., & Schnell, S. (1987). Children's reactions to sex abuse investigation and litigation. *Child Abuse and Neglect, 11,* 267–272.

Turiel, E. (1978). Social regulations and domains of social concepts. In W. Damon, ed. *Social cognition: New directions for child development.* San Fransisco: Jossey-Bass, Inc., 45–74.

Warren-Leubecker, A., Tate, C., Hinton I., & Ozbek, N. (In this volume). What do children know about the legal system and when do they know it?

8
What Do Children Know about the Legal System and When Do They Know It?* First Steps Down a Less Traveled Path in Child Witness Research

AMYE WARREN-LEUBECKER, CAROL S. TATE,
IVORA D. HINTON, and I. NICKY OZBEK

The likelihood that an American child will participate in the legal system in some fashion has increased exponentially in recent years. From 1955 to 1975, juvenile crime rose in the United States by 1600 percent (Footlick, 1977). During those same years, more than half of all crimes were committed by juveniles (Uniform Crime Reports for the United States, 1975). Divorce increased 700 percent between 1900 and 1977, to the point that half of the children born in the 1970s have spent at least part of their childhood in a one-parent home (Keniston, 1977). Reports of child physical abuse increased 142 percent between 1976 and 1983, and an estimated 71, 961 American children were reported to be sexually abused in 1983 (American Association for Protecting Children, 1985). These statistics serve to highlight the fact that American children are more likely than ever to be confronted with the legal system; either as witnesses in abuse or custody cases, defendants in juvenile crime cases, or perhaps even plaintiffs in actions against their own parents or guardians (Westman, 1979).

The Context of Courtroom Testimony: Task Demands

Although a great deal of current research on children as witnesses focuses on memory skills or suggestibility, much less is known about the context in which the child witness is asked to recall information (namely, the legal

---

* Adapted from "What did the President know and when did he know it?" Our apologies to Howard Baker, Senate Watergate Investigation Committee, 1974.

The authors would like to thank the many students, teachers, parents, and children who made these studies possible. In addition, we wish to thank Sarah Byrd for inspiring the idea, and Glyndora Munday, Carolyn Boyd, and Ernest Tubbs for their many and varied contributions to this project. These studies were supported in part by a University of Chattanooga Foundation Instructional Excellence Grant to the first and fourth authors.

system and possibly the courtroom itself) and how it may affect their testimony as well as their emotional health. As Melton and Thompson (1987) point out, task demands and age by task interactions are possibly more important than age effects per se in eyewitness testimony research. For example, young children may perform as well as adults on simpler tasks (e.g., recognition as opposed to recall) or in familiar settings (e.g., home versus the laboratory), but do poorly in comparison to older children or adults in unfamiliar tasks requiring complex reasoning (Ceci, Ross, & Toglia, 1987). Any memory task, even a supposedly "pure" or "isolated" laboratory task, includes a plethora of linguistic, cognitive, social, and emotional demands. Different tasks place differing social and cognitive processing "loads" on children who may or may not have less total information processing resources than adults (Evans & Carr, 1984). As yet, we know very little about the unique set of demands imposed by the legal system, and even less about how children of various ages interpret and respond to those demands (e.g., Goodman, 1984). Thus, to accurately predict children's credibility and competency within the legal system, and to best adapt the court system to child participants, we should understand what children know, feel, and think about the legal system itself (Melton & Thompson, 1987).

Several psychologists and legal professionals have provided anecdotal support for the notion that children lack knowledge of legal procedures and terminology, which hinders their participation in the system (e.g., Goodman, 1984; Saywitz, this volume). For example, Goodman (1984) reports that one boy falsely accused of arson believed that this job was to convince the judge that the fire did not occur, not that he did not start it. Considering the overwhelming evidence that the fire *did* occur, the boy's testimony totally lacked credibility and he was convicted. Whitcomb, Shapiro, and Stellwagen (1985) gathered such anecdotes more systematically by surveying attorneys and professionals involved with child witnesses. The results of their report suggest that children may fear many aspects of the legal system because of lack of knowledge or experience with it. They may be scared of confronting the suspected abuser, overwhelmed by the size and other physical attributes of the courtroom, afraid of the audience, the judge, and the jury. Children may be particularly frightened of the defense attorney and cross-examination, as they have little understanding of legal actors' roles and duties. Moreover, since they do not understand these numerous and varied legal roles, they may be afraid or uncertain as to why they must tell their story over and over again to different strangers. They may see the judge as a big man in a black robe with the power to punish, yet not understand that they will not be the objects of such punishment.

Given this bleak picture painted by professionals who deal with child witnesses, it is not surprising that participation in the legal system in general and courtroom testimony in particular are assumed to be traumatizing to young children. Indeed, this assumption has resulted in a variety of techniques designed to improve or prevent open court testimony altogether (Whitcomb et al., 1985). Not only does the assumption on which such techniques are based remain untested, it is also unknown whether the techniques now used to avoid such trauma actually have the desired effects. It is possible that children are less traumatized than we suppose; or they may even feel empowered by the courtroom testimony experience. Unfortunately, at this point we lack even *unsystematic* data on most of these issues (Melton & Thompson, 1987).

The Development of Moral and Legal Reasoning

Considering the dearth of research on children's legal knowledge and attitudes, we have been forced to look elsewhere for information that might bear on the issue. The best sources to date have been the literature on political socialization and moral development, although these are only indirectly relevant to our present concerns. The seminal works of Piaget (1932/1965) and Kohlberg (1963) have been most influential in this area.

In both theories, very young children are considered to be premoral because they lack internal standards or concern for rules, and abide by them only as a result of external enforcement or to satisfy their own needs. Once an awareness of rules is attained, children may view them as unalterable, believing that all violations will be punished (even if no one is around to see the violation, i.e., immanent justice). Children may also judge rule violations primarily by the consequences of the action (e.g., amount of damage) rather than by the intentions of the person who committed the violation (although there is some argument on this point; see Nelson, 1980). Along this line, the punishments that children this age would mete out seem to have no relation to the rule violation (e.g., eating a cookie without permission and breaking your sister's arm would both deserve a jail sentence). Finally, older children and adolescents realize that social rules are indeed changeable and can be violated for good reasons. They also begin to favor "reciprocal punishments," which "fit the crime."

The possible connection of legal reasoning to moral reasoning, and the process of legal socialization was a topic of great interest in many subsequent investigations (e.g., Hogan & Mills, 1976; Tapp & Kohlberg, 1971). For example, several researchers asked grade-school children and adolescents questions such as "What are laws?," "Are laws fair, and why or why not?," "Are there times when it is right to break a rule?," "Should laws be permanent or changeable?," and the like (e.g., Adelson, Green, & O'Neil, 1969; Hess & Torney, 1967; Tapp & Kohlberg, 1971; Torney, 1971). Not surprisingly, older children were more likely to view laws as changeable, and not necessarily fair. Their legal reasoning was more abstract and less conformist or based on external authority (Tapp & Kohlberg, 1971).

What, if anything, do these studies suggest about a child's competency to participate in the legal system? Clearly, a child who does not appreciate rules or consider intentions or the nature of the "crime" in deciding a punishment would make a poor judge or lawmaker. The results may have implications for their understanding of a judge's role, although the child's decision may be quite different from those they think a true judge might impose. But would this hinder their involvement as a witness-victim? Unfortunately, these results have limited applicability to the child witness in a courtroom setting for several reasons. First, the moral dilemmas and the questions typically posed are extremely abstract. Not only are younger children automatically excluded when such abstract reasoning is called for, but research indicates that subjects of any age reason at lower levels about more practical, everyday, or concrete moral dilemmas that could have negative consequences for themselves (Leming, 1978). Second, the primary if not exclusive emphasis has been placed on the development of children's reasoning about the legal system rather than on their development of knowledge about it. Certainly these two achievements are linked, but the direction and strength of such a relation is unknown. One might assume that children must reach a certain level of moral reasoning before they could acquire relevant conceptual knowledge about the legal system. For example, a child who does not differentiate between accidental and intentional actions would not understand our legal concept of differentiating punishment based on intent. Conversely, perhaps a child must have some knowledge of the concept to successfully reason about it (e.g., knowing what a law *is* is essential to deciding whether it is fair). Thus, the link between these two domains of achievement is unclear, and inferring knowledge from reasoning becomes dangerous, particularly in application.

The Development of Legal Knowledge

Fortunately, some researchers have more directly assessed legal knowledge, although such studies are scarce and have largely involved adolescents. For example, Grisso (1981) found that adolescents are unlikely to fully understand the role and obligations of their attorneys, and possibly as a result, hold largely negative attitudes toward them. Grisso and Lovinguth (1982) suggested that knowledge of younger children's concepts of attorneys is virtually nonexistent.

Recently, however, three studies concerning legal knowledge in younger children have emerged. Flin, Stevenson-Robb, and Davies (1987) investigated forty-five lower socioeconomic status, Scottish six-, eight-, and ten-year-olds' familiarity with and ability to describe some commonly used legal terms, as well as their understandings of the terms and feelings about various aspects of court. Their responses in the first three knowledge segments of the interview were scored for accuracy (a 0 score reflecting complete lack of knowledge or a wrong answer, a 1 score a poor but correct answer, and a 2 score a more detailed correct answer), and compared with responses of ten adults. As expected, across age groups, subjects performed best on vocabulary, slightly worse in descriptions, and worse yet in understanding of legal concepts. Developmental trends were noted for all three segments, in that ten-year-olds achieved a level of 62 percent of adult performance, eight-year-olds only 41 percent, and six-year-olds 30 percent. Overall, children were slightly more knowledgeable about police, criminals, and description of a court, and more familiar with breaking the law, with rules, criminals, and being guilty or not guilty than about judges or witnesses. They were even less knowledgeable about what it means to go to court, what one means by the law, the role of the lawyer and the jury, the concept of prosecution, evidence and why it is needed, and the concept of an oath. In the segment of the interview regarding feelings about court, most young children believed only bad people went to court, and felt very negatively about court because of fear of not being believed, not being able to understand or answer questions correctly, having to speak in front of a large audience, and fear of retribution by the accused. Interestingly, although the children reported the greatest fear of court, they also were more likely to think they would be treated kindly there.

Saywitz and her colleagues (Saywitz & Jaenicke, 1987; Saywitz, this volume) have also investigated children's understanding of legal terms and their ability to describe them. Saywitz & Jaenicke (1987) compared eighteen kindergartners, twenty third-grade, and twenty sixth-grade children on their abilities to define thirty-five terms commonly used in court proceedings. The terms *judge*, *lie*, *police*, *remember*, and *promise*, among others, were accurately defined by all age groups, whereas the terms *allegation*, *petition*, *minor*, *motion*, *competent*, *hearsay*, and *defendant* were not well understood by even the oldest children. Significant age differences were observed for the terms *witness*, *lawyer*, *attorney*, *oath*, *swear*, *evidence*, *jury*, and *testify*. Saywitz (this volume) reports further data indicating that young children (ages four to eight in her study) are limited in comparison with older children and adults in their understandings of even the most basic legal concepts. Using a scoring system similar to that of Flin, et al. (described earlier, a continuum of inaccurate to accurate answers), Saywitz finds that by age eight, many children have an adequate understanding of court, judge, witness, and lawyer, but few have mastered the concept of jury or seem aware of minor court personnel such as bailiffs and court reporters.

Although these studies represent a much needed advance in an area in which little or no information exists, they share at least two characteristics that limit their practical applicability at present. First, the small number of children interviewed reduces the probability that the sample is representative of the population. Second, only a small number of age groups and ranges have been used. Of course, these are problems common to all preliminary studies which are easily resolved through subsequent research. Another possibly more problematic aspect of these studies, however, concerns the coding system used and the assumptions behind it. Both Flin et al., and Saywitz and her colleagues conceive of children's legal knowledge as developing in a continuous fashion, from less accurate to more accurate, or toward incorporating more and more defining features of legal concepts. This approach is advantageous in many respects. First and rather obviously, such an ordinal scale allows the use of a wider array of statistical techniques, because the variables may be considered continuous rather than discrete. Second, and more important, recent theoretical approaches to cognitive development are moving farther away from stage theories and focusing more on quantitative differences in information-processing capacity or strategies (e.g., Flavell, 1985; Pascual-Leone, 1970) or the gradual acquisition of domain-specific knowledge (e.g., Chi, 1983), as qualitative changes in development past infancy become more difficult to demonstrate (e.g., Flavell, 1982).

In contrast, our recent work (Tate, Hinton, Boyd, Tubbs, & Warren-Leubecker, 1987; Warren-Leubecker, Tate, & Munday, 1986) has led us to take a different and somewhat Piagetian approach, not in looking for possible stages, but in focusing on children's errors rather than correct answers in our attempts to characterize the development of legal knowledge. Combining lack of an answer ("I don't know") with incorrect and seemingly irrelevant answers is potentially misleading, as it is possible that there are regressions of sorts, and changes from one type of misperception to another, in addition to changes from less well-formed to accurate perceptions as development proceeds. Saywitz & Jaenicke (1987) noted in their study of legal vocabulary acquisition that several children provided alternative (nonlegal) definitions for many of the terms, suggesting that children may think they understand a term, but their definition is qualitatively different from adults'. Such misperceptions are potentially more damaging than lack of knowledge to a child's ability to testify or participate meaningfully in the legal system.

The Present Studies

The present series of studies was designed to investigate developmental trends in children's perceptions of several aspects of the legal system, including the courtroom itself, significant courtroom personnel (e.g., judge, jury, lawyer), reasons for going to court and the types of people who go there, and how decisions are made. In addition to factual legal knowledge, we also were interested in social/cognitive perceptions such as how to tell if someone is lying, and if it is ever acceptable not to tell the truth.

Study 1

Method

Subjects

Participants in study 1 were 563 children from the Chattanooga, Tennessee, area who were obtained through public and private schools, church groups, clubs, day care centers and private families. The children ranged in age from two years, nine months to fourteen years. Forty-eight percent of the overall sample was male. The sample was largely, though not exclusively, white and middle-class. All the children participated voluntarily. Because of the large number of subjects and our desire not to pool subjects across broad age groups arbitrarily, the children were divided into discrete age groups by years (i.e., $4;0$ to $4;11$, $5;0$ to $5;11$ and so on), with the exception of children aged $2;9$ to $3;11$ and children $13;0$ to $14;0$ who were grouped together. A complete breakdown of the number of subjects by age group is provided in Table 8.1. For the second part of our study, three subgroups were randomly selected from the appropriate age groups in the total sample: 21 subjects (11 girls, 10 boys) became the "young" group (ages 3 years; 1 month to $6;6$, mean $= 5;3$, $SD = 10.9$ months), 25 children (15 girls, 10 boys) made up the "middle" group (ages $7;6$ to $9;5$, $M = 8;8$, $SD = 6.7$ months), and another 25 (13 girls, 12 boys) were in the "older" group (ages $11;1$ to $12;10$, $M = 11;9$, $SD = 7.4$ months).

Procedure

All children were administered a questionnaire containing at least twenty-three common questions, although some children received two additional questions (see Table 8.1). A random subgroup of children (from which the seventy-one described previously were randomly selected) was also read a

TABLE 8.1 Number of subjects by age group.

Age in Years	Total Number of Subjects	Number for Last Two Questions
3	11	2
4	28	4
5	39	18
6	23	13
7	26	16
8	39	29
9	124	69
10	100	73
11	116	87
12	47	30
13	10	9

legal concept story with questions, which essentially concretized some of the information we had requested previously. These questions and the story are presented, verbatim, in the results section.

Children under the age of eight were individually interviewed, whereas children eight years old and over were tested either individually or in groups. If group tested, children read the questions silently and wrote their own answers, to avoid the possibility of peer influence. Each child was informed that participation was voluntary and confidential. To minimize irrelevant responses, the children were also told that "some of the questions are hard, if you don't know the answer it's okay to say you don't know." The children were given as much time as they needed to complete the questions.

After all data collection was completed, fifteen of the twenty-three questions were selected for analysis on the basis of distinctiveness (redundant questions were discarded). Each is identified in the results section; the responses to each question were then categorized. To qualify as a separate category, the response had to be mentioned by at least 10 of the 557 children. All categories were determined post hoc and are explained in detail in the results section. Ten percent of the protocols were independently scored by two of the experimenters. Intercoder reliability was calculated as percentage agreement over all categories and averaged 97 percent for the total sample. Perfect intercoder consistency was achieved on half of the questions, and 94 percent agreement or greater was obtained for all but one of the remaining questions (disagreements on this question are fully addressed in the results section following). The frequency of responding in each category at each age was tallied, and then converted to percentages of the total number of children within each age group.

Results and Discussion

For the questions, "Do you know what a courtroom is?" and "Have you ever seen a courtroom on TV?," the number of affirmative answers was calculated for each age group. Only 18 percent of the three-year-olds said yes to question 1, but this number steadily increased with age (approximately 40 percent at age six, 85 percent at age seven, and over 90 percent for all age groups past nine years) up to 100 percent affirmative by age 13. Interestingly, the pattern of answers was different for question 2. Only 9 percent of the three-year-olds and 46 percent of the four-year-olds responded that they had seen a courtroom on TV. This is lower than the number who said they did know what a courtroom was, for both these age groups. At age five, more children said that they had seen a courtroom on TV (64 percent) than had answered that they knew what one was (36 percent). The same pattern, though not as marked, was observed for the six-, seven-, and eight-year-olds as well. By age nine, approximately equal numbers (90 percent) of the children reported knowing what a courtroom was *and* that they had seen one on TV. The one-way chi-square analyses for both questions revealed significant ($p < .001$) age differences [$\chi^2(10, N = 553, 506) = 125.76$ and 112.93, for questions 1 and 2, respectively]. Thus, it appears that the majority of children past age seven years know about courtrooms, at least through the medium of television. Younger children, however, appeared to be confused, reporting either not seeing a courtroom on TV, yet knowing what it was (we could speculate on how they might have acquired such information, but doubt that they actually knew what a courtroom was considering their answers to subsequent questions), or not knowing what a courtroom was yet having seen it on TV. This merely serves to highlight the problem with a verbal survey such as this. The younger children may have much more knowledge than they are capable of demonstrating verbally, in the absence of visual recognition aids.

For the question "Who is in charge of a courtroom?," we divided the responses into three categories, *I don't know/No answer*, *A Judge*, and *Other/Wrong & Unrelated*. Fully 82 percent of the 3-year-olds did not know, the remaining 18 percent answered incorrectly (e.g., a doctor). Fifteen percent of the four-year-olds answered *A judge*, for the five-, six-, seven-, and eight-year-olds, the percentage of like answers were 25, 56, 73, and 92, respectively. Age eight was also the point at which wrong answers dropped tremendously (in fact, to 0). An average of 20 percent of all the younger children answered incorrectly (e.g., a teacher, a manager, "The guy who owns it," and "The court man"). One five-year-old obviously influenced by TV stated "Judge Wapner!" The two-way chi-square was significant [$\chi^2(20, N = 563) = 666.9, p < .001$].

We then asked "What does the judge look like and wear?" After reviewing the protocols, we devised a list of commonly mentioned features. For the three most often mentioned characteristics (wearing black, being male, wearing a robe), separate one-way chi-square analyses were conducted, and all were significant at $p < .01$. Ninety-one percent of the three-year-olds did not know anything about a judge (hardly surprising, given their answers to the previous question). By age four, children began mentioning that a judge "dresses in black" (for ages four, five, six, seven, and eight, for example, the percentages were 21, 31, 43, 50, and 69, respectively). They did not, however, necessarily mention that it was a black robe (although we gave credit for long dress, cape, cloak, "graduation costume," and even blanket), with several children suggesting that a judge wears a suit or "tocseto" (tuxedo). Several children across age groups mentioned white or gray hair or a wig and, accordingly, suggested that judges were "old" (one indicated that a judge has to have experience as a lawyer first, and thus will be older on average). Other children mentioned wearing glasses, being bald, and being big. Older children occasionally indicated that it does not really matter what a judge looks like, its the ability that counts. Finally, a few older children (over eight years) mentioned person-

TABLE 8.2 "Who else is in the courtroom (besides the judge)?" Percent subjects answering by category.

Category	Age, in years										
	3	4	5	6	7	8	9	10	11	12	13
Jury	0	0	3	4	8	13	19	28	38	38	40
Lawyer	0	0	3	0	8	15	31	44	36	40	20
Witness	0	11	3	0	0	28	23	20	16	19	30
Police	0	11	0	26	15	36	26	17	23	34	30
Defendant	0	7	0	0	8	15	19	28	27	21	20
Plaintiff	0	0	0	0	4	8	10	15	19	17	20
Audience	9	0	0	4	4	3	2	4	7	2	20
Bailiff	0	0	0	4	4	0	4	6	9	15	0
Court clerk or reporter	0	0	0	0	0	3	3	14	15	9	0

ality characteristics, with equal numbers suggesting that judges are nice, mean, and wise.

When asked "Who else is in a courtroom," the children gave a variety of answers, so we again devised a list reflecting this variety and calculated the percentage of children at each age who mentioned the personnel on the list. These figures are displayed in Table 8.2. Because any one child's response might include more than one category, separate one-way chi-squares were conducted for categories with no 0 cells, or using only age groups who mentioned the particular legal actor. With the exception of bailiff and court reporter, these analyses were all significant at $p > .01$. In general, children under the age of seven did not mention any court personnel except for "police." The frequency with which children mentioned the jury, lawyers, witnesses, and "criminals" or defendants became nonnegligible at age eight. Plaintiffs were increasingly mentioned after age ten. Minor court personnel (bailiff, court clerk, and court reporter) did not appear at all until age six, and never reached high levels (only 15 percent ever mentioned the court reporter). Older children were more likely to mention important court figures such as attorneys and juries, but it is important to note that only 40 percent of even the oldest group mentioned a jury, and the highest rate of mentioning attorneys was 44 percent, in the ten-year-old group. It should also be noted that our interpretation of their responses was fairly liberal. For example, we considered the following to be descriptions of a witness: "a man who sits in a chair and tells who hit him or killed him" (age five); "people who sit beside the judge" (age eight). Other interesting responses included "the people in the cages" (jury?); "the sewers" (sue-ers?); "the servant," and "a judges helper" (bailiff, court clerk?); "person who tapes the words down"; and last, "the contestants and coaches."

The majority of the children also had only vague impressions about

TABLE 8.3 "What does a lawyer do?" Percent subjects answering by category.

Category	Age, in years										
	3	4	5	6	7	8	9	10	11	12	13
Don't know	82	57	72	57	54	28	25	9	7	9	10
Wrong/unrelated	18	21	15	17	15	21	10	8	4	4	0
Talks/preaches	0	11	8	13	0	0	3	5	8	6	0
Helps	0	11	5	4	15	13	22	16	9	15	10
Asks questions	0	0	0	4	8	13	9	5	6	4	10
Defends	0	0	0	4	0	5	17	33	32	43	50
Wins case/sticks up for client	0	0	0	0	8	21	14	24	32	19	20

"What do lawyers do?" We divided the children's answers into the following categories: *Don't know/no answer*; *Wrong/unrelated*; *Helps people*; *Talks or presents the story*; *Defends people*; *Asks questions*; and a final broad category including these types of responses, *Prosecutes and defends*; *Stricks up for one side*; *Tries to wins the case for his client* (see Table 8.3). Reliability for this question was only 82 percent because of a problem differentiating between *Defends*, which implied the presence of only the defense attorney, and the last broad category, *wins the case for his client*, which was interpreted as involving either a plaintiff or a defendent. Disagreements were resolved through discussion. We still believe the distinction is a viable one, in that so many television shows mainly depict defense attorneys and many children seem to believe that lawyers are only for "getting people off." They appear to have little understanding that the other person attempting to prove responsibility or guilt is also a lawyer. At this point, however, the distinction between the two categories is more blurry than it appears.

The children under age seven years simply had no idea of what a lawyer does and another 15 to 20 percent had incorrect notions such as "loans money," "writes down everybody who's bad," and "makes sure nobody gets in a fight" or "decides who's guilty," indicating they have attorneys confused with the bailiff or jury. (They also mentioned "plays golf," "lies," and "sits around," although these impressions may be realistic.) Again the influence of TV was evidenced by one five-year-old who said, "they just get together and talk together because I watch *L.A. Law* with my dad." Not until age ten do the children who say an attorney prosecutes or defends outnumber those who do not know or answer incorrectly. The chi-square analysis of age by response type proved to be significant $[\chi^2(60, N = 563) = 697.25, p < .001]$.

The next question was "What is the jury and what do they do?" Initially, we divided the responses into five categories, including *Don't know*; *Wrong/Unrelated*; *Talks to or helps the judge* (in a nonspecific way); *Listens to the case* (but only listening, not deciding); and *Makes a decision/Renders*

TABLE 8.4 "What is the jury and what do they do?" Percent of subjects answering by category.

Category	Age, in years										
	3	4	5	6	7	8	9	10	11	12	13
Don't know	91	68	67	65	65	49	47	33	19	30	0
"Jewelery"	9	21	23	13	0	3	0	0	0	0	0
Other wrong/unrelated	0	7	10	9	23	15	10	6	9	9	10
Talk to/help judge	0	4	0	4	0	3	3	1	4	2	0
Listen	0	0	0	0	8	10	19	15	13	6	40
Decide	0	0	0	9	4	20	21	45	55	53	50

a verdict. After closer examination, we found that a large number of young children mistook the word jury for "jewelery" ("Like if you're going to the dance you put some on," or "It sparkles on your finger"), even though they had already answered eight questions about the courtroom, including one designed to elicit the concept of jury. Thus, we added a separate category for this error. The results of this coding are shown in Table 8.4. In general, it was not until age ten that a significant number of children mentioned the jury's role in decision making. Even at age twelve, 30 percent of the children said they did not know what a jury does [$\chi^2(30, N = 563) = 686.3, p < .001$).

When asked "Why do people go to court?," the children most frequently gave the very vague but accurate answer "To settle arguments or solve problems." The only other categories of responses were *Don't know or Unrelated answer*; *Major crimes* (e.g., murder, larceny; only approximately 4 percent of all children's answers fell into this category); and *Other* (divorce, to sue someone, for a traffic violation; an average of 10 percent of all responses were of this type). Ninety-one percent of the three-year-olds could not provide any reasons, whereas the remaining 9 percent said to solve problems. For the four-, five-, six-, seven-, eight-, nine-, ten-, eleven-, twelve-, and thirteen-year-olds the percentages of *Don't know* responses were 75, 62, 43, 27, 23, 15, 8, 9, 13, and 0, respectively. Because these categories were not mutually exclusive (a single child could mention solving problems, murder, and divorce), separate one-way chi-square analyses were conducted on the two major response types. For the analysis of *Don't know* answers, $\chi^2(9, N = 553) = 218.6, p < .001$, and for *Solves problems*, $\chi^2(10, N = 563) = 123.1, p < .001$.

One of the most revealing questions to us was also the most simplistic. We asked, "Is court a good place or a bad place?." There may be a recency effect (bad was the word last mentioned), thus it is not terribly surprising that a large number of children responded "Bad" (e.g., 82 percent of the three-year-olds, 38 percent of all five- and seven-year-olds, 35 percent of the six-year-olds). However, Flin et al. (1987) also reported that children view court very negatively, perhaps because of their idea that only bad people go to court. In general, older children were more likely to say that court was "Neither good nor bad" or "Both good and bad" (approximately 22 percent age nine to twelve years old). Two anomalous age groups were quite optimistic; 80 percent of the thirteen-year-olds and 64 percent of the eight-year-olds thought court to be primarily good. The two-way chi-square, age by response type (don't know, good, bad, and both) was significant [$\chi^2(30, N = 563) = 470.0, p < .001$].

"Who sends people to jail?" was the next question we investigated. The possible response categories were *Judge, Police, Don't know*, and *Other*. Example of *Other* answers for the younger children were, "jail people," "God," and interestingly, "Their girlfriends, or their kids or moms." *Other* responses for older children were, "FBI," and "the jury." The majority of children eight and younger mentioned police, while 50 percent or more of the children nine and older mentioned both the police and the judge (both of which are accurate at different points in the legal system). Because one answer could contain multiple categories, one-way chi-square analyses were conducted. Both responses analyzed were significant ($p < .001$); for the response "Judge" $\chi^2(8, N = 552) = 66.4$, and for "Police", $\chi^2(10, N = 563) = 44.5$.

To begin with the social/cognition questions, we asked the children, "How can you tell or how can a judge or jury tell if someone is lying?" We divided the responses into eight categories as follows: (1) *Don't know*, (2) *By the consequences* (if they're lying they'll be in jail), (3) *Omniscient* (the judge just knows!), (4) *Nonverbal cues*, (5) *Verbal cues* (inconsistencies within story, stuttering), (6) *Lie detector*, (7) *By other evidence or testimony*, and (8) *You can't ever really tell, you have to guess*. A single child could potentially answer with more than one of these categories, so the percentages do not total 100. Ninety-one percent of the three-year-olds could not answer, but this figure steadily decreased with age (54 percent at age four, 48 percent at age six, 41 percent at age eight, 23 percent at age ten, 19 percent at age twelve). The chi-square analysis for this category revealed a significant age effect [$\chi^2(10, N = 563) = 102.7, p < .001$]. Children age ten and younger were the only ones to use the *consequences* category, and even they did so infrequently (9 percent or less). However, they often seemed to feel that people (themselves, parents, judges, and juries) are omnisicient (25 percent at age four, 10 percent at age five, 9 percent at six, then dropping to 3 percent at age eleven). The number of children mentioning nonverbal cues showed a significant linear progression with age ($\chi^2 = 86.69, p < .001$), increasing from 4 percent at age four to 50 percent at age thirteen (the figures for ages five to twelve years are 5, 9, 15, 21, 20, 28, 27, and 34 percent, respectively). Some of the nonverbal cues mentioned were quite amusing ("your eyes roam around in your head," "the area around your mouth turns blue"), whereas others were quite sophisiticated ("you hesitate because it takes time to think of a lie"). Verbal cues were less frequently mentioned overall, but showed a similar age trend [$\chi^2(9, N = 552) = 53.19, p < .001$], increasing from 7 percent at age four to 34 percent at age twelve (and back down to 30 percent at age thirteen). A few children (six- to eleven-year-olds) mentioned the use of a lie detector (although most did not know a technical or even approximate name, e.g., "the lie machine," "a Poligrary," and from a six-year-old, "they have ways to find out. Like those things you put on your heart to make you tell the truth. They're like brain helmets except you put them on your heart . . ."). Many more suggested that you could compare testimony with other testimony or physical evidence. This response increased with age, from 4 and 5 percent at ages four and five, to 25 and 28 percent at ages eleven and twelve [$\chi^2(9, N = 552) = 41.17, p < .001$]. Finally, a few (10 percent and less) of the older children (nine to thirteen years) said that there is simply no foolproof way to discern lying; you had to make your best guess.

In a primitive attempt to determine whether children can distinguish between accidental and intentional wrongdoing, we asked two questions, "What would happen to you if you did something bad by accident?" and "What would happen to you if you did something bad on purpose?" we then looked for differences between the answers to these questions, so the codes were *No answer at all*, *Same answer to both*, *Lesser punishment for accidents*, and *Greater punishment for accidents*. Most of the children who answered suggested a lesser punishment for accidents. A one-way chi-square for this category revealed a significant age difference as well [$\chi^2(11, N = 563) = 79.07, p < .001$], in that this response became more frequent with increasing age (18, 32, 46, 61, 46, 51, 59, 56, 63, 57, 60 percent at ages three to thirteen, respectively).

Finally, some of the children (see Table 8.1) were asked more personal questions about their own proclivity to tell the truth under stressful conditions, that is "If someone you knew broke the law (did something wrong), what would you do? and "If your mother or father did something bad and would be sent to jail if you told the judge they did it, would you still tell the truth?" These were forced-choice responses, with "Tell the truth no matter what," "Not say anything," and "Lie to keep that person out of trouble" as the alternatives to the first question. For this question, the majority of children suggested they would still tell the truth (except for the four-year-olds; only 27 percent responded in this fashion). When the question involved their own parents, children still insisted they would tell the truth (ranging from 33 percent at age three, 45 percent at age twelve, to 100 percent at ages four and six). There were no real age trends for either of these questions, except for the tendency of the older children to "hedge" on the second question ("I'm not sure what I would do. Maybe I would tell the truth."), which accounted for approximately 10 percent of the answers for ages eight to thirteen).

As stated previously, the responses of seventy-one children to additional questions surrounding a legal story were also analyzed. The story was based on Goodman's (1984) anecdote that a boy who was falsely accused of arson tried to convince the judge that the fire did not occur. It read as follows:

Joshua was standing next to the elementary school waiting for his mother to pick him up. A group of three older boys ran past him, and one of the boys ran into Joshua and dropped something. Joshua picked the thing up, and noticed it was a cigarette lighter. Suddenly, Joshua smelled smoke, and saw that the school was on fire. Joshua's mother had told him never to play with matches or cigarette lighters, so he was afraid of getting in trouble. A fireman saw Joshua standing there, and ran over to ask him if he knew who started the fire. When he got to Joshua, he saw that Joshua was holding a lighter in his hand. Joshua was scared and surprised when the fireman accused him of starting the fire. Joshua was questioned by the police, and had to go to court with his parents.

Following the story, the children were asked four questions. The first was "Why would the fireman, policeman and judge think Joshua started the fire?" Responses to this question were either "I don't know," "Because of the lighter," and "Other" (only two children's answers fit here, one younger who said "He did it," and one older who said "They had the evidence"). Eighty-six percent of the younger (ages 3 to 6;6), 96 percent of the middle (ages 7;6 to 9;5), and 92 percent of the older group (ages 11;1 to 12;10) realized that the lighter was the reason for suspicion. The chi-square analysis of these data was nonsignificant.

The next question was "How can Joshua show them he didn't start the fire?". Nineteen percent of the five-year-olds and 8 percent of the eight-year-olds did not know the answer. Many children suggested that Joshua should "just tell the truth, that he didn't do it" (52, 28, and 24 percent of the younger, middle, and older groups). The majority of the older groups (56 percent of the middle and 64 percent older) and 29 percent of the younger children suggested that Joshua could get the other boys or other people to testify, or produce some evidence (perhaps pictures, fingerprints) to exonerate him. Last, some of the older children indicated that there was no way for Joshua to prove his case, as there was too much evidence against him (middle = 8 percent, older = 12 percent). Analysis revealed a significant age difference in the frequencies of these responses $[\chi^2(6, N = 71) = 58.2, p < .001]$.

When asked "Do you think the judge or jury would believe Joshua?," 62 percent, 48 percent, and 64 percent of the five-, eight-, and eleven-year-olds said yes. Approximately a third of the younger (33 percent) and middle children (32 percent) and 20 percent of the older children said no, whereas a few answered with "maybe" (0, 12, and 8 percent, respectively). Finally, 5, 8, and 4 percent of the five-, eight-, and eleven-year-olds did not know. The chi-square analysis reflected a significant age difference $[\chi^2(6, N = 71) = 19.8, p < .003]$.

Finally, the children were asked "Do you think the judge or jury would believe a grown-up if the same thing had happened to them?" The pattern of answers was slightly different from that of the previous question. Younger children apparently saw adults as more believable (71 percent said yes), whereas the middle group was split (48 percent yes, 40 percent no, 8 percent maybe, and 4 percent I don't know). The older group seemed to see adults as somewhat less credible, with 44 percent answering yes, 52 percent no, and 4 percent maybe [$\chi^2(6, N = 71) = 30.7, p < .001$].

Discussion

In comparing our findings on children's knowledge of various legal personnel with those of Saywitz (this volume; Saywitz & Jaenicke, 1987) and Flin et al. (1987), we saw several commonalities. In general, we all found that children develop the concept of *Judge* before that of *Lawyer*, which is in turn developed prior to that of *Jury*. It is not surprising that *Judge* is the earliest achieved legal concept, given the fact that the judge is the most authoritative figure, may stand out from all other courtroom personnel because of his/her unusual dress, and is most often depicted on television. Similarly, Greenstein (1965) found that in developing ideas of our political system, children first understand the role of the president, whereas all other government personnel or branches were seen as "helpers." The children in our study were largely unaware of other courtroom personnel such as the court reporter and clerk, although many mentioned a "guard" or "policeman" (possibly the bailiff), and referred to "the judge's assistants and helpers" (in fact, several saw the jury as the "judge's helpers," a phenomenon also noted by Saywitz).

The fact that most children over five years of age *did* assign lesser punishments to accidental than purposeful wrongdoings suggests that Piaget (1932/1965) may have underestimated children's abilities to discriminate between these two, and their abilities to use information regarding intent. Our wording of the question may have helped, as Shultz (1980) reports that even three-year-olds use the terms "on purpose," "didn't mean to," and "not on purpose" appropriately in naturalistic settings. Perhaps these children have developed this distinction as a result of their own parents' differential punishments and explanations of such (Flavell, 1985). In any case, school-age children may understand our legal system's differential treatment of accidental and intentional actions better than we have previously supposed, which serves to highlight the danger in inferring children's legal knowledge from moral reasoning, rather than directly assessing the knowledge itself (Shultz, 1980).

Although the tendency to define lying by its consequences was uncommon, it illustrates nicely the early "objective reality" and "obedience orientation" stages of moral reasoning identified by Piaget and Kohlberg, wherein children have no internalized standards but rely on observable physical consequences for their judgments. This tendency was further reflected by the children's opinions about what happens in the courtroom and even the very nature of the court itself. "If bad people go to court, then court must be a punishment. If I have to go to court, and court is a punsihment, then I must have done something wrong." In fact, the children's answers to the questions on assigning punishment for accidental and intentional wrongdoing highlighted their assumption that court is a bad place or a punishment. Many children suggested that one would "have to go to court" if they had accidentally committed a violation, but would "go to jail" if they had done the same thing "on purpose." These responses also lead us to wonder what children understand of the concept "innocent until proven guilty." They seemed to believe that intentional violations result directly in jail sentences (no trial needed), whereas accidental violations would need to be sorted out in court. The fact that many young children reported that "police send you to jail" (and only older children saw this as the judge's responsibility) may also indicate that young children do not differentiate between the police, prison, and court process (see also Saywitz, this volume) Last, this point is underscored by children's understanding of a lawyer's role. A large proportion of the children seemed to think that lawyers are only for the defense of "criminals" (after all, only bad people go to court, and lawyers are only there to help these people stay out of jail). In fact, many children used the term "lawyer" exclusively for defense functions, and "attorney" for prosecution, so that several children when asked "Who is in a courtroom" listed both lawyers and attorneys.

This tendency to define actions by their consequences, combined with a form of cognitive egocentrism may have detrimental effects on children's testimony. Egocentrism was evidenced by the younger children's belief that adults are omniscient (adults just instinctively *know* not only what is true, but everything else that happens). In the legal knowledge story, a majority of children felt that all that Joshua needed to do to prove he did not start the fire was merely tell them he did not, and since it was the truth, he would automatically be believed. Children may have the egocentric view that if *they* know what happened, then all adults (or at least authority figures) know what happened too (e.g., Warren-Leubecker & Bohannon, 1983). In court, this could be a problem if children believe they are merely providing corroboration of what is already known, not realizing the implications of their testimony. Such beliefs may partially account for the child's well-known proclivity to provide only sketchy free recall accounts of events (e.g., Saywitz, 1987). An inability to *understand* the listener's role or perspective (e.g., not understanding the roles of attorneys, judges, and jury, as illustrated here) would necessarily translate into an inability to *take* the listener's perspective, in turn leading to deficits in forming or modifying messages (free recall accounts) accordingly (e.g., Warren-Leubecker & Bohannon, 1985). To complicate matters further, children are well described as limited information processors (Evans & Carr, 1984). Recalling information, setting that information in an appropriate form for a particular listener, and attending to the social/pragmatic cues all require cognitive capacity. Thus, even if children know the information desired by the court, have the capacity to relate this information appropriately to different listeners, and know the relevant social roles played by the legal actor, they may not be able to do all of them simultaneously. Thus children's behavior as witnesses may convey the impression of inaccuracy independent of the maturity of the component skills or even the validity of the child's story.

The older children were less likely to credit adults in general, and courtroom authority figures in particular, with omniscience or even special decision-making abilities. This was repeatedly reflected in their answers to various questions. For example, only older children questioned the judge or jury's abilities to discern lying. Also, 51 percent of the children knew that providing evidence of some kind (e.g., finding the older boys who actually did it) was one way for Joshua to prove he did not start the fire, but only the older children (and a very few of them) understood that there is no foolproof way to determine truth in the absence of physical evidence. Moreover, whereas the tendency to feel that Joshua would not be believed did not change substantially over age (33 percent for the youngest, and 20 percent for the oldest age group), the oldest children were much more likely to say that an adult under similar circumstances would not be believed (24 percent for the youngest compared to 52 percent for the oldest). When asked if they would still tell the truth (in court) if their parents would get in trouble as a result, the older children were less likely to respond affirmatively. These results may be indications of the higher levels of moral reasoning, which allow questioning of rules/laws (e.g., Kohlberg, 1963; Tapp & Kohlberg, 1971). The implications of these results for older children's testimony are unclear. Older children may be less suggestible because they have more confidence in their own memorial skills and they may question authority figures who might "lead" them into changing their stories (see Ceci et al., 1987). Older children have a greater understanding of the implications of their testimony and the roles of the attorneys, judge, and jury, factors that may enable them to provide more complete, "audience-adapted," and convincing accounts. However, this greater understanding may also induce greater fear and mistrust, thus perhaps young children's "ignorance is bliss." Whether the understanding that laws are changeable and questionable and violations occasionally acceptable is necessary for successfully witness performance is an important question for future child witness research.

Overall, the results of this study essentially replicate those of Saywitz (this volume) and Flin et al. (1987) using a much larger sample. For some of the legal concepts we assessed, fairly straightforward age trends were observed, in which older children simply possessed more knowledge than younger children or their knowledge included more detail or a greater number of basic features. Younger children suggested that lawyers "help" and "talk for" their clients (present the case), and older children often added the features of "asking questions" and "defending." On the other hand, some legal concepts appear to develop through several stages of misperceptions. For example, while three- to six-year-olds confused the term "jury" with "jewelry," several older children believed that the jury is another name for a judge or lawyer, or that the jury's role is to listen to testimony and take notes, which they then give to the judge. Thus, children do not always develop legal concepts in a logically ordered fashion, in that they may move from lack of knowledge to incorrect perceptions (for several years) and finally to accurate representations. Interestingly, many of the oldest children in our study had not achieved this level of accurate representations. Thus, we decided to focus on older children, to determine if and how legal concepts further develop in adolescence.

Study 2

Method

Subjects

Subjects for phase 1 of this study were 264 public school students (134 males, 130 females) ranging from nine to eighteen years of age. Most were eighth graders, between thirteen and fifteen years old (194 out of 264). We focused on three particular age groups for further analysis, the 14 children between 9;10 and 11;9, another 53 subjects ages 13;0 to 13;10, and the oldest 39 subjects ages 15;0 to 18;0. There were 62 subjects (25 males, 26 females, and 11 who did not identify their gender) obtained from schools and church groups for phase 2, ranging in age from fourteen years and 0 months to eighteen years and 3 months. Both samples were largely, though not exclusively, white and middle class.

Procedure

The first phase of the study used a multiple-choice test format questionnaire containing thirty questions about the legal system. Many of the distractor alternatives were developed from the answers previously given by the younger children in study 1. The questionnaire was group administered, with answers written on a separate sheet. For phase 2, we used an open-ended questionnaire similar to that from study 1. The questions from both questionnaires were selected for analysis using the same criteria used in study 1; these are discussed fully in the results section. For the open-ended questions, we developed a coding scheme similar to that derived for study 1. Again, 10 percent of the protocols were independently coded, and intercoder consistency was 98 percent.

Results and Discussion

The first question analyzed from the multiple-choice data was "Have you ever seen a courtroom?," and the answers included *on television*, *in a courthouse*, *in a newspaper*, *all of the above*, and *none of the above*. Only 9 percent of the overall sample reported that they seen the courtroom in the courthouse, but an additional 43 percent answered with *all of the above*, indicating that they had seen a courtroom in person as well as from other sources. Focusing on the three age subgroups, more of the older children (56 percent) than younger children (14 percent) answered with *all of the above*, whereas more of the younger (36 percent) than older (13 percent) children answered that they had only seen a courtroom in a courthouse. This surprising pattern perhaps suggests some confusion over the question, as it is actually more likely that younger children have seen a courtroom from other sources than in person.

Several of the subsequent questions concerned courtroom personnel. In response to the open-ended question "Who else is in a courtroom," jury was mentioned by 66 percent, lawyers 58 percent, court reporter 40 percent, defendant 39 percent, baliff 35 percent, plantiff 32 percent, audience 26 percent, witness 18 percent, court clerk 5 percent, and paralegal by 5 percent. Overall, 91 percent of the multiple-choice subjects indicated that they understood the role of the lawyer and were not distracted by alternatives such as "makes the laws" or "carries out the laws" (both common responses in study 1). Unlike in study 1, the majority of the open-ended responses were that lawyers either defend (47 percent) or defend and prosecute, or simply try to "win the case" (37 percent). Only 6 percent said they did not know what attorneys do. Sixty percent of the multiple-choice subjects also understood the concept of a public defender (although only 21 percent of the youngest subjects answered correctly, and most respondents simply suggested that "he defends the public"). In contrast, 77 percent of this sample fully understood the requirements for and of being a judge. Many of the younger subjects were distracted by the alternatives suggesting that judges were appointed by the sherriff (43 percent) or the governor (21 percent).

When asked, "What is the jury?," 75 percent of the subjects chose the correct alternative (14 percent of the youngest group, 81 percent of the middle, and 69 percent of the oldest). Of the subjects asked this same question in open-ended form, an overwhelming majority (82 percent) mentioned their decision-making capacity while only 10 percent indicated they did not know. The open-ended question "Who makes the final decision of guilt or innocence in court?" was answered with *the judge* by 68 percent of the respondents, while 18 percent said *jury*, and 13 percent said *jury or judge*. Of course the correct answer to this question depends on whether or not it is a jury trial; nevertheless, the low percentage of *jury* responses was remarkable.

To assess some of the more technical aspects of legal procedure, we asked "What is perjury?" and "What does it mean to take the fifth?" Only 60 percent of the subjects selected "lying under oath" as the answer to the first question. Many thought that perjury was what the jury decides or recommends. Twenty-eight percent of the respondents to open-ended questions said they did not know what perjury was, 52 percent answered correctly, and 20 percent were incorrect; the majority of these latter said that perjury is the term for the jury reviewing a case, or what happens "before the case goes to the jury," or even a replacement jury in case the "first jury couldn't make it." In reference to "taking the fifth," 67 percent of the subjects correctly chose *the witness does not answer so he won't get into trouble or be incriminated* as the appropriate answer, but 20 percent thought that taking the fifth means you don't have to answer after you have been asked a question five times. In fact, this alternative was chosen 57 percent of the time by the ten-year-olds. Two final open-ended questions were "What is the difference between first and second degree murder?" and "What is the difference between murder and manslaughter?" For the first question, only 23 percent correctly indicated the difference was premeditation, while 37 percent were incorrect (the most common misperception was that second degree murder was worse in some way), and a full 40 percent did not know. Concerning the distinction between murder and manslaughter, 44 percent knew the difference is based on the intent, 27 percent had no idea, and 29 percent held incorrect notions (e.g., manslaughter is with a knife, manslaughter is more cruel and inhumane, involving torture or decapitation and vivisection).

The next several questions were more concerned with personal opinions. When given the statement "Court trials are fair and impartial,' 15 percent strongly agreed, 65 percent agreed, 16 percent disagreed, and 4 percent strongly disagreed. Presented with the statement "Everyone is equal under the law (that is, everyone is treated the same in court)," 18 percent indicated they strongly agreed, 50 percent agreed, 25 percent disagreed, and 8 percent strongly disagreed. When asked, "If someone you knew broke the law, what would you do," the majority of the subjects indicated they would be honest and "tell the truth no matter what" (66 percent), 29 percent would not say anything, 2 percent admitted they would lie to keep the person out of trouble and 3 percent would take the blame themselves if accused. Finally, the question was asked, "If your mother or father did something illegal and would be sent to jail if you testified and told the truth, you would:" tell the truth (21 percent), not say anything (28%), lie (21%), undecided (30%). Thirty-four percent of the responses to the open-ended questions of this same type were negative (I would not tell the truth). Some of the subjects felt they needed to supply additional comments to tell us they would lie for one parent, but not the other, or other clarifying information such as, "I'd manipulate the words to her defense"; "I wouldn't tell the truth if I could help it"; "I would lie no matter what would happen to me"; "I would not testify against my friends or family"; "I wouldn't show up, and get contempt of court"; "I really can't answer that question because I love my family and I think that most of the time judges are wrong. . . how do they know if a person is lying or not and they may send an innocent person to prison or set a guilty person free"; "after taking an oath in the name of God you are sworn to tell the truth no matter what"; "yes, (I would tell the truth) because [my parents] are no different from ordinary people"; and "I plead the fifth."

In sum, the responses of the adolescents in study 2 provided stronger support for the idea that higher levels of moral reasoning and legal knowledge may coexist with increased mistrust and questioning of the authority of the legal system. Again, how this may affect their ability to participate in the legal system or testify in court is unknown. Although these adolescents appeared to possess accurate conceptions of most basic legal terms and functions (e.g., judge, jury, lawyer), their conceptions were still fairly nebulous, and their knowledge of more technical legal concepts and terms (e.g., perjury, manslaughter) was lacking.

General Discussion

The results of our studies suggest that most young children know very little about courtroom personnel and procedures. Moreover, both younger and older children expressed negative attitudes about court, apparently for different reasons. The younger children may have blind faith in the legal process and the adults involved in it, but see court as primarily a bad place where bad people are punished. Older children, on the other hand, may view court negatively as a result of their understanding that the judicial process is fallible.

Why do young children know so little about the legal system? One argument might be a maturational limit on their ability to process such information. For example, perhaps a certain level of moral reasoning is required for understanding certain legal concepts. But the question could be rephrased to reflect an environmental/learning point of view. Why do children know anything about the legal system at all, considering their limited exposure to it? It is hardly the topic of many parent–child conversations. However, as we discussed previously, children may gain an understanding of laws from rules at home and of the legal system in general from parental discipline and their justifications or explanations of punishments. School-age children have the additional opportunity of learning about justice through classroom rule and discipline systems (Macauley, 1987). They may even begin a formal curriculum concerning government, with the judicial system as a part (in fact, 40 percent of our older sample reported that they had actually visited a courtroom, most likely on school field trips).

Unfortunately, Macaulay (1987) noted that the few textbooks that include discussions of law provide only a simplified, formal picture of courts, trials, lawyers, and police. Theoretical or ideal descriptions of the legal systems are presented as if they are descriptions of how the systems actually operate in practice. This same criticism can be applied to depictions of the legal system on television, another likely source of legal knowledge for children.

As Saywitz (this volume) notes, six or seven daytimes shows are exclusively about court. Soap operas frequently feature trials (particularly murder trials, complete with all necessary courtroom personnel), and prime time television is heavily populated with police, detective, and court shows (e.g., in the 1986 season, *Matlock*, *L.A. Law*, *Hill Street Blues*, and *Night Court*). Macaulay (1987) argues that if television was children's sole source of legal knowledge, they would be badly misled, in that "entertainment programs misrepresent the nature and amount of crime . . . , the roles of actors in the legal system . . . and present important issues of civil liberties in distorted ways" (pp. 197–198). Moreover, punishment on television often comes from environmental circumstances (retribution delivered on the spot), bypassing the legal system. Even when the normal legal process is followed and court trials are presented, most TV court cases are resolved in "Perry Mason" fashion, wherein the "real" culprit breaks down under cross-examination and confesses. The job of a jury is certainly made easier under those circumstances. The daytime court shows rarely portray juries or lawyers (e.g., *People's Court*), which may help to explain why children seem to understand the concept of judge long before lawyer or jury. In fact, one child responded to the question "What does a lawyer do?" with "It (TV) didn't show it to me."

Considering that children know little about the legal system, and that what they learn from school and television may be misleading or incomplete, the assumption that child witnesses are largely unprepared for testifying is probably correct. In fact, Grisso and Lovinguth (1982) and Saywitz (this volume) suggest that even direct experience with the legal system may not enhance legal knowledge. Saywitz (this volume) argues further that television and school lesson depictions of court, though probably overly simplistic, may result in more coherent representations of legal knowledge than direct legal experience, which may present more complex information (various proceedings, more legal actors) but in a more confusing context (fraught with delays, continuances, and the like). How, then, can children be prepared to participate in legal processes? Emerging courtroom preparations are based on the assumption that children's credibility and competence to testify in court is neither more or less problematic than an adults' would be under similar circumstances, if potential knowledge gaps are addressed through pretrial education.

Berliner and Barbieri (1984) outlined what they believe are essential elements that should be included in preparing the child for court: familiarity with the physical setting and roles of participants, knowledge of legal procedures such as cross-examination, and the importance of telling the truth in the legal process. In one county in our state (Tennessee), a formal "court school" has been established (Davidson County Department of Human Services). This court school spans seven sessions (Third Annual Symposium on Child Abuse, 1987), which introduce the children to the technical names of the jobs of the court personnel, and allow the children to role-play a mock court scene involving a robbery. Each child is allowed to experience the roles of judge, witness, and either the prosecuting or defending attorney. Subsequent sessions include meeting the district attorney and emphasising the child's job of telling the truth, answering the questions they understand, and "taking care of themselves." Throughout the course of these sessions, as the roles of the different participants are introduced, it is explained that this person is either on your (the child's) team or the accused's team; that it is the child's responsibility to tell the truth; the judge's or jury's responsibility to decide who is telling the truth, and that their decision is the best they can make, though not always correct; and that it is the judge's responsibility to set the punishment. Since a further assumption of pretrial education is that it will reduce the amount of trauma experienced, the child is also told it is their responsibility to "take care" of themselves so they won't be upset.

Added benefits to such programs may include group support from being in "class" with other children in similar circumstances. Parents can also share their experiences while their children are in the school. The investigating team has a first-hand opportunity to observe the child's reactions and abilities to communicate in a mock courtroom setting, thus allowing time for additional preparation or for the decision that it would be in the child's best interest to avoid testifying entirely.

In spite of the face validity of such court preparation programs, we are still left with many unanswered questions. Since court school is optional, how do the children who participate differ, if at all, from those who do not? How much do these children know before they attend the court school and are they able to retain what they learn? Children attend these classes in groups, which may include a wide age span. Do the older children help the younger ones, as some staff members suggest, or would it be best for all children to attend class with children from their own cohort group (who may share the same misperceptions)? Do the children who graduate from these programs actually experience less trauma? Do they make more credible witnesses than children who do not receive such preparation? Finally, do they absorb more information than would a comparison group of nonabused children (or any children not currently involved in the legal system) because of its relevance to their impending participation in court, or are they so emotionally torn that much of the information is lost? These questions should provide an abundance of topics for future research.

References

Adelson, J., Green, B., & O'Neil, R. (1969). Growth of the idea of law in adolescence. *Developmental Psychology*, *1*, 327–332.

American Association for Protecting Children, Inc. (1983). *Highlights of Official Child Neglect and Abuse Reporting 1983*. Denver, CO: The American Humane Association.

Berliner, L., & Barbieri, M.K. (1984). The testimony of the child victim of sexual assault. *Journal of Social Issues*, *40(2)*, 9–31.

Ceci, S.J., Ross, D.F., & Toglia, M.P. (1987). Age differences in suggestibility of children's memory: Psycho-legal implications. *Journal of Experimental Psychology: General*, *116*, 38–49.

Chi, M.T.H. (Ed.). (1983). *Trends in memory development research*. Basel, Switzerland: Karger.

Chi, M.T.H., & Glaser, R. (1980). The measurement of expertise: Analysis of the development of knowledge and skill as a basis for assessing achievement. In E.L. Baker and E.S. Quellmalz, eds. *Educational testing and evaluation: Design, analysis and policy*. Beverly Hills, CA: Sage Publications.

Evans, M., & Carr, T. (1984). The ontogeny of description. In L. Feagans, C. Garvey, & R. Golinkoff, eds. *The origins and growth of communcation*. Norwood, NJ.: Ablex, 297–316.

Flavell, J.H. (1982). Structures, stages and sequences in cognitive development. In W.A. Collins, ed. *Minnesota symposia on child psychology* (Vol. 15). Hillsdale, NJ.: Lawrence Erlbaum Associates.

Flavell, J.H. (1985). *Cognitive development*, 2nd ed. Englewood Cliffs, NJ: Prentice-Hall.

Flin, R., Stevenson-Robb, Y., & Davies, G. (1987, May). Children's knowledge of the law. Paper presented at the Brittish Psychological Society Development Section Conference, Exeter, England.

Footlick, J.K. (1977). Children and the law. In T.J. Cottle, Ed. *Readings in adolescent psychology: Contemporary perspectives*. New York: Harper & Row, 279–281.

Goodman, G. (1984). The child witness: Conclusions and future. *Journal of Social Issues*, *40(2)*, 157–176.

Greenstein, F. (1965). *Children and politics*. New Haven: Yale University Press.

Grisso, T. (1981). *Juveniles' waiver of rights: Legal and psychological competence*. New York: Plenun Press.

Grisso, T., & Lovinguth, T. (1982). Lawyers and child clients: A call for research. In J.S. Henning, ed. *The rights of children: Legal and psychological perspectives*. Springfield, IL: Charles C Thomas, 215–232.

Hess, R.D., & Torney, J.V. (1967). *The development of political attitudes in children*. Chicago: Aldine.

Hogan, R., & Mills, C. (1976). Legal socialization. *Human Development*, *19*, 261–276.

Keniston, K. (1977). *All our children: The American family under pressure*. New York: Harcourt Brace Jovanovich.

Kohlberg, L. (1963). The development of children's orientations toward a moral order: I. Sequence in the development of moral thought. *Vita Humana*, *6*, 11–33.

Leming, J. (1978). Intrapersonal variation in stage of moral reasoning among adolescents as a function of situational context. *Journal of Youth and Adolescence*, *7*, 405–416.

Macaulay, S. (1987). Images of law in everyday life: The lessons of school, entertainment, and spectator sports. *Law and Society Review*, *21*, 185–218.

Melton, G.B. & Thompson, R.A. (1987). Getting out of a rut: Detours to less traveled paths in child-witness research. In S.J. Ceci, M.J. Toglia & D.F. Ross, eds. *Children's eyewitness memory*. New York: Springer-Verlag, 36–52.

Nelson, S.A. (1980). Factors influencing young children's use of motives and outcomes as moral criteria. *Child Development*, *51*, 823–829.

Pascual-Leone, J. (1970). A mathematical model for the transition rule in Piaget's development stages. *Acta Psychologica*, *32*, 301–345.

Piaget, J. (1965). *The moral judgement of the child*. New York: Free Press. (Original work published 1932).

Saywitz, K.J. (In this volume). Children's Conceptions of the legal system: "Court is a place to play basketball."

Saywitz, K.J. (1987). Children's testimony: Age-related patterns of memory errors. In S.J. Ceci, M.J. Toglia, & D.F. Ross, eds. *Children's eyewitness memory*. New York: Springer-Verlag, 36–52.

Saywitz, K.J., & Jaenicke, C. (1987, April). Children's understanding of legal terms: A preliminary report of grade-related trends. Paper presented at the Biennial meeting of the Society for Research on Child Development, Baltimore, MD.

Shultz, T.R. (1980). Development of the concept of intention. In W.A. Collins, ed. *Minnesota symposia on child psychology* (Vol. 13). Hillsdale, NJ: Lawrence Erlbaum Associates.

Tapp, J.L., & Kohlberg, L. (1971). Developing senses of law and legal justice. *Journal of Social Issues*, *27*, 65–91.

Tate, C.S., Hinton, I., Boyd, C., Tubbs, E., & Warren-Leubecker, A. (1987, March). Children's moral development and knowledge of the legal process. Paper presented at the Southeastern Psychological Convention, Atlanta, GA.

Third Annual Symposium on Child Abuse (1987, February), Huntsville, AL.

Torney, J.V. (1971). Socialization of attitudes toward the legal system. *Journal of Social Issues*, *27*, 137–154.

Uniform Crime Reports for the United States, 1975 (1980). Washington, DC: U.S. Government Printing Office.

Warren-Leubecker, A., & Bohannon, J.N. (1983). The effects of verbal feedback and listener type on the speech of preschool children. *Journal of Experimental Child Psychology*, *35*, 540–548.

Warren-Leubecker, A. & Bohannon, J.N. (1985). Language in society: Variation and adaptation. In J.B. Gleason, ed. *The development of language*. Columbus, OH: Charles E. Merrill, 331–367.

Warren-Leubecker, A., Tate, C., & Munday, G. (1986, November). "Jury is something you wear around your neck." Children's knowledge of the judicial process. Paper presented at the Tennessee Psychological Association Convention, Nashville, TN.

Westman, J.C. (1979). *Child advocacy: New professional roles for helping families*. New York: The Free Press.

Whitcomb, D., Shapiro, E.R., & Stellwagen, L.D., Esq. (1985). *When the victim is a child: Issues for judges and prosecutors*. Washington, DC: National Institute of Justice.

9
Problems in Evaluating Interviews of Children in Sexual Abuse Cases

DAVID C. RASKIN and JOHN C. YUILLE

In this chapter we explore the problems posed by rapidly increasing reports of sexual abuse of children and the need for effective methods to obtain reliable and valid information from children who may have been sexually abused. It begins with a description of the problematic nature of interviews of children as they are currently conducted and evaluated in cases of suspected child sexual abuse. Inadequacies in such methods frequently lead to lack of substantiation of valid allegations and may also reinforce false allegations of sexual abuse. The literature concerning the types and quality of evidence obtainable from children is then reviewed, other assessment methods are described and evaluated, and the need for systematic interviews and evaluations is demonstrated.

Escalating concerns about sexual abuse investigations and prosecutions have raised issues concerning statements and their testimony in court (see Graham, 1985). As a result, there has been a corresponding growth in research on children's abilities and performance as witnesses (see Goodman, 1984; Ceci, Toglia, & Ross, 1987). However, most of that research has focused on the problem of the *accuracy* of children's accounts and not the *validity* of their allegations of sexual abuse. The distinction between accuracy and validity is crucial when there is the possibility of motives to report falsely or to fabricate an allegation. Since the historical approach to child witnesses has generally ignored that distinction, the current situation requires a shift in emphasis to enable an assessment of the validity of allegations of sexual abuse.

The last section of the chapter provides a detailed description of a standardized interview technique and a procedure for assessing the content of the obtained statement (statement analysis). That method has been used for more than thirty years in Germany to overcome the problems inherent in other approaches. It is our hope that this exposition will encourage sci-

The authors wish to acknowledge the assistance of Dr. Max Steller in the preparation of this chapter.

entists to conduct research on the German techniques, in order to develop and validate methods that can be used by investigators and case workers in North America. Improved methods are urgently needed to cope effectively with substantial problems that are encountered in the investigation of reported cases of sexual abuse of children, which have been rapidly growing in number.

The Current Situation

The Association for Protecting Children (Suski, 1986) recently conducted a systematic national study to estimate the incidence of sexual abuse of children in the United States. They concluded that there were approximately 200,000 reports of child sexual abuse, of which 100,000 were investigated to the point of producing enough evidence to consider them seriously. Finkelhor and Hotaling (1984) have estimated that 150,000 to 200,000 new cases of sexual abuse occur each year.

In response to these alarming figures, many have called for programs to increase the reporting and prosecution of such cases. However, the former Director of the U.S. National Center on Child Abuse and Neglect (Besharov, 1985) has criticized the frequent and extensive media campaigns to expand child protective programs and the accompanying calls for hiring more caseworkers to investigate the increasing numbers of reports. Besharov stated that "more than sixty-five percent of all reports of suspected child maltreatment—involving over 750,000 children per year—turn out to be 'unfounded.' . . . the present level of overreporting is unreasonably high and is growing rapidly. There has been a steady increase in the number and percentage of 'unfounded' reports since 1976, when approximately only thirty-five percent of reports were 'unfounded'" (p. 556). He concluded that "The main result of these periodic flurries of activity is increased numbers of unfounded reports" (p. 554).

Reports from the 1970s indicated a rate of approximately 6 percent false allegations of sexual abuse among children brought to a hospital emergency room (Peters, 1976) and a child abuse agency (Goodwin, Sahd, & Rada, 1978). Recent reports are more disturbing. Benedek and Schetky (1985) were unable to confirm allegations of sexual abuse in 55 percent of a sample of cases involving custody and visitation disputes. Green (1986) reported a 36 percent rate of documented false allegations by children who reported they were sexually abused by the noncustodial parent in the context of child custody and visitation disputes.

Jones and McGraw (1987) studied two samples of reported incidents of sexual abuse. One consisted of the total of 576 reports of sexual abuse received by the Denver Department of Social Services during 1983, and the other was composed of 21 cases involving fictitious allegations of sexual abuse seen by Jones at the Kempe National Center from 1983–1985. Of the

Denver sample, 53 percent were considered by the social workers to be "founded," even though 8 percent of those involved subsequent recantation. The Kempe Center sample consisted of two cases in which the clinician considered the allegations to be "possibly" fictitious and nineteen cases that were considered to be "probably" or "definitely" fictitious. Fictitious accounts consisted of allegations generated by children, those produced by the coaching of an adult, or accusations improperly elicited by professional interviewers who "had not oriented themselves to the developmental status and language ability of the child, or they had used anatomically correct dolls in conjunction with a suggestive questioning style" (p.11).

Jones pointed to common features of fictitious reports, which include lack of appropriate expression of emotion, lack of detail, acrimonious custody or visitation disputes, and personality disturbance present in the adult who made fictitious allegations on behalf of the child. Such features are commonly reported by other investigators who have encountered fictitious allegations, and Raskin and Steller (in press) found similar characteristics in cases in which the accused had been exculpated by a polygraph examination and other evidence. Jones pointed out the need for professionals trained in child development and the dynamics of sexual abuse to be involved in the initial investigative process and the importance of keeping an open mind throughout the evaluation process. His approach and those of Raskin and Steller (in press) and Goodwin (1982) are consistent with an investigative attitude that contrasts strongly with the typical approaches of case workers.

According to the information presented here, in the United States approximately 8 percent or more of the investigated cases may be fictitious. That could result in 8,000 or more serious actions and false prosecutions each year. In cases involving disputed divorce, custody, and visitation issues, the rate of fictitious allegations may be as high as 50 percent. Since 1974, the first author has conducted polygraph examinations at the University of Utah on persons accused of sexual abuse of children. Test outcomes consistent with truthful denials of sexual abuse have increased from 50 percent in the 1974–82 period to 79 percent truthful outcomes in the 1983–87 period. A large proportion of those allegations arose in domestic relations disputes, further supporting the suspicion that the rate of fictitious allegations may be highest in such situations. In the present social and legal climate concerning sexual abuse, many of the formerly "unsubstantiated" cases may also proceed to formal actions, compounding the potential damage produced by inadequate training and performance of investigators and case workers.

A major cause of the problem is that case workers receive little training in conducting an investigative interview of children designed to gather information and assess the validity of accusations. It has become common practice for interviewers to assume that the allegations are true (Young,

1986), and the purpose of the assessment is to obtain information that can be used to arrive at that conclusion (Faller, 1984). A typical case-worker attitude was expressed in a recent book on sexual abuse of children (Conerly, 1986). She stated that "Very young children do not make up complex lies. . . . It is certainly true that children fantasize, but they do not fantasize about sexual relationships with adults" (p. 48).

A social worker recently wrote "we know that children do not make up stories asserting they have been sexually molested. It is not in their interests to do so. Young children do not have the sexual knowledge necessary to fabricate an allegation. Clinicians and researchers in the field of sexual abuse are in agreement that false allegations by children are extremely rare" (Faller, 1984, p. 475). Faller then proceeded to describe "strategies for corroborating the child's story" (p. 477). These included the use of statements to significant others, play, pictures, stories, anatomically explicit dolls, as well as assessment of the child's sexual knowledge, the sexual behavior of the child, and other behavioral indicators. This social worker concluded by stating that "the more supportive data the evaluator has, the more convinced he/she will be, and the more persuasive the evaluator's reported will be to others " (p. 480).

The foregoing represents a common approach to the assessment of allegations of sexual abuse of children. Many social workers, psychiatrists, and psychologists assume that certain behaviors of the child are definite indicators that abuse has occurred. Their goal is to provide an atmosphere of support and encouragement to assist the child in describing the abuse the therapist is certain has occurred. Almost anything the child says and does is interpreted as being consistent with the trauma associated with sexual abuse, including repeated and strong denials or recantations by the child (Summit, 1983). Building on that general premise, interviews are conducted in a therapeutic and suggestive manner instead of with an investigative and questioning approach. After one or more sessions with the child, the therapist almost always concludes that the allegations or suspicions are true.

Recent cases have underscored the problems that may result from poor techniques combined with zealous attempts on the part of case workers to prove that the allegations are correct. Those approaches produced considerable social and personal damage in Scott County, Minnesota, and Manhattan Beach, California. "In the Scott County cases, something clearly went awry" (Humphrey, 1985, p. 2). Cases were finally dismissed against twenty-one persons accused of child sexual abuse, even while investigations were in progress concerning allegations of homicides and sexual abuse made by some of the alleged child victims. The resulting extensive investigations by the FBI and the State of Minnesota concluded that there was no credible evidence of murders or justification for filing further charges of sexual abuse. Those allegations had been made by the children to their therapists.

The Scott County allegations arose after confirmed incidents of sexual abuse had occurred. However, problems of validity resulted from "repeated questioning, a lack of reports, and cross-germination of allegations" (Humphrey, 1985, p. 8). The child witnesses do not always appear to have been rehearsed, and testimony based on such procedures might cause investigators, prosecutors, and jurors to make errors of uncritically accepting the children's statements. A therapist reported that one child had already been interviewed by nine individuals, and a mother of another child indicated that her child had been interviewed between thirty and fifty times. Furthermore, interviews were frequently undocumented in any form, and there were instances of children being informed of what had been said by other witnesses and then being asked to report on abuse they had seen performed by those accused by the other witnesses. Children were interviewed together, housed in the same motels, given their meals together, and allowed to interact frequently. Parents were sometimes arrested and charged with abuse of their own children even though their children repeatedly denied the allegations over several weeks of interrogation after separation from their parents. The report concluded that "investigators, prosecutors, human service workers and therapists must all examine how they presently handle these cases in light of the Scott County experience " (p. 17).

The high incidence of sexual abuse of children combined with the growing number of unsubstantiated and fictitious reports are compelling arguments for minimizing the number of interviews of suspected child victims by using carefully structured interviews as early as possible in the investigative process. Interviews should be conducted by trained and skilled professionals who understand that their role is to obtain maximally reliable information to draw a conclusion concerning the validity of the allegations. Any therapy deemed necessary should be undertaken only after the investigation with the child has been substantially completed. Therapy should be conducted by a different professional, whose role is to treat the problems in the context of the incident, whether or not the allegations turn out to be true.

All interviews of the child should be based on a thorough acquaintance with the facts surrounding the allegations or suspicions, and they should be videotaped. A videotape is the only means whereby the procedures and data obtained during the interview can be fully documented. A typed transcript of the session is necessary for the systematic analysis of the content that is required to arrive at a conclusion regarding the validity of the statement the child gives. The videotape is made for the purposes of documentation and analysis by experts, and it should not be used as a substitute for live testimony by the child witness.

The nature and specific details of the interview process and the subsequent analysis of the obtained statement depend on a number of factors. These include the type and quality of evidence obtainable from child witnesses, the developmental level and specific language abilities of the child, the child's sexual knowledge and possible sources of that knowledge, the number of prior interviews and disclosures, the context of those events, and the roles and relationships of the interviewers and others to whom the child has provided information. Examples of each are given next.

The Quality of Children's Evidence

In this section we review the existing literature with a view to making an assessment of the quality of evidence children can provide. Employing the research literature to determine the quality of children's evidence presents a basic problem concerning ecological validity. In our experience, the most common type of case in which children provide evidence is that of sexual abuse. Less frequently, children are witnesses in cases of domestic violence (e.g., Pynoos & Eth, 1984) and automobile accidents (Davies, Flin, & Baxter, 1986). In cases of sexual abuse, the child is often the victim, is the only witness, and usually has been emotionally and sometimes physically traumatized by the events.

Providing testimony may have profound effects on the child's life. For example, a disclosure of sexual abuse may lead to the break up of the family, a change in its financial status, or placement of the child in a foster home. In contrast, research studies designed to investigate child witnessing abilities have none of these associated features. In research studies the children are usually unaffected by the events they are reporting, and their testimony has no consequences. These differences between the laboratory research context and those of actual crime situations place severe limitations on the conclusions that may be drawn from the published literature. Although experimental studies may be useful in answering some questions that arise in actual cases (see preface to Ceci, Toglia, & Ross, 1987), many issues can be adequately studied only within a field context (Undeutsch, 1982).

The difficulty in generalizing from research studies is exacerbated by the methodology researchers prefer. Typically, a researcher claims to have investigated children's eyewitness abilities by showing the child an event in a slide sequence (e.g., Parker, Haverfield, & Baker-Thomas, 1986), a film (e.g., Dale, Loftus, & Rathbun, 1978) or a video tape (e.g., List, 1986). Although children's memories for recorded events may be of interest to makers of television commercials and educators who use visual media, the relevance of this work to the eyewitness abilities of children remains to be demonstrated. There is little to suggest that a child's or an adult's memory for a recently seen movie is an indicator of capacity to report a sexual assault or robbery in which they were victimized.

King (1984) compared the recall of children for an event presented on slides to the recall of a live, staged event. The event was emotionally neutral, involving a man who entered the room to tend to some plants. She reported a variety of differences in both recognition and recall measures for the two types of events. For example, the slide presentation produced more accurate descriptions of the protagonist than did the live event, but much higher accuracy of facial recognition was obtained with the live event. King concluded that the patterns of memory performance for recorded and live events are distinct. It is our contention that anyone interested in studying the abilities of child witnesses should concentrate on a combination of staged live events and field research of actual witnesses in real crime situations. In our review of the literature that follows, we rarely refer to studies that employed recorded events (a review of these studies can be found in Cole & Loftus, 1987).

The Amount of Information Children Can Recall

When children are asked to recall complex events, the amount of information they recall tends to increase with age (see King & Yuille, 1987). Goodman, Aman, and Hirschman (1987) conducted three studies of children's memory for real-life events (e.g., receiving an immunization shot at a clinic). They reported only minor effects of age on recall, with three-year-olds showing poorer recall than older children. Marin, Holmes, Guth, and Kovac (1979) tested subjects ranging from five to twenty-two years old who interacted with a confederate. The younger children in their study provided less complete recall of the event. In contrast, Goetze (1980) staged a purse-snatching for each of seventy-two children from grades 3, 6, and 8, and they found little effect of age on free recall. Although the amount of detail may vary with age, the important point is that children from three years of age onward can supply details about a complex event that they observed, and the accuracy of children's testimony does not appear to vary with age (see King & Yuille, 1987). Jones and Krugman (1986) reported a case of a three-year-old child who was kidnapped and sexually assaulted by a stranger. Although the man left the girl for dead, she survived, provided a detailed account of the event, and selected a picture of the suspect. He later confessed and confirmed the details of the child's statement.

It is likely that attentional factors account for the finding that younger children provide less, but just as accurate, recall. We know that there is a developmental change in the amount or capacity of selective attention. Younger children have less ability than adults to deal simultaneously with the same variety of information. In this context, less attention means less processing capacity. It is likely that the younger the child, the less ability he or she has to attend to many aspects of an event. In short, the attentional limitations of children reduce the amount of information they encode about an event. However, there is evidence that very young children attend to more peripheral details than older children do (Ceci & Tishman, 1984).

In younger children there are retrieval problems coupled with the problem of an encoding deficit (e.g., Ceci & Howe, 1978). Skills and gimmicks to aid the retrieval of information are something that we develop with age and experience. The younger the child, the more limited the number and flexibility of his or her retrieval aids. When simply asked to provide a free recall about a complex event, the younger child has fewer memory aids to assist in the recall process. Thus, a more circumscribed storage of an event is compounded by less efficacious recall aids, leading the younger child to provide less recall.

Although the attentional deficits of younger children can be overcome only through growth and experience, the problems with retrieval aids may be amenable to interventions. It should be possible to provide younger children with explicit instructions in the use of memory aids. For example, in the cognitive interview developed by Geiselman and Fisher for use with adult witnesses (Geiselman, Fisher, MacKinnon, & Holland, 1985) the witness is asked to reinstate the context before recall, to recall the event from different perspectives, to recall the event in different orders, and to leave nothing out. Whether these instructions would be effective with children is unknown, but this is an area of research desperately in need of attention. It should be kept in mind, however, that the use of such memory aids may result in contamination of the criteria for statement analysis, since some of those criteria refer specifically to the spontaneous production of material that would be directly suggested by the methods of the cognitive interview.

The Problem of Suggestibility

The fact that children provide circumscribed versions of an event leads to a major problem associated with interviewing child witnesses. When a child provides only a limited version of an event that contains insufficient forensic information, the investigator will use specific questions to encourage the child to provide more information. The lack of information provided by the child for memory-related reasons may be compounded by a lack of the requisite verbal skills to provide a description of the event. The child may also be inhibited by the difficult dynamics of the adult–child interactions in the interview situation. In the case of sexual abuse, these problems may be compounded by an unwillingness of the child to discuss sexual or personal matters, as well as an awkwardness on the part of the adult interviewer in pursuing details about sexual events.

Encoding deficits, retrieval problems, limited verbal skills, and difficulty with adult–child interactions are more common in younger children. Therefore, the younger the child, the more likely it is that the interviewer will find it necessary to resort to specific questions when interviewing the child. This is a serious problem because, as detailed later, younger children are more susceptible to the effects of leading or suggestive questioning.

Thus, the very individuals who will be questioned in a specific manner are the ones who present the greatest problems when asked specific questions. A number of studies have shown that children are more susceptible to suggestions and leading questions (for a review, see King & Yuille, 1987). An example of the extent of this problem is found in a study of children's recognition memory for an actor they witnessed in an event. Yuille, Cutshall, and King (1986) had groups of children witness a confederate stealing a bicycle. The children were subsequently interviewed and presented with a group of photographs. For half of the children, the confederate's picture was included in the photo spread; for the other half it was not. In the confederate-absent condition, 60 percent of the children made an incorrect choice, rather than correctly rejecting the photo spread. The younger the child, the more likely that an incorrect choice was made. Presenting a child with a photo spread creates an implicit demand to pick out someone. Admonitions that the confederate's picture may not be present had no effect.

Children are generally oriented to please adults in an interview setting, and the younger they are the more this is true (Burkholder, 1986). All too often, they provide the interviewer with what they think the interviewer wants to hear. Therefore, it is essential in the interview situation to avoid presenting the child with either explicit or implicit demands. The interview must be conducted in a neutral fashion so that the information obtained depends on the memory of the child, not on the dynamics of the interview situation.

Ceci, Ross, and Toglia (1987) provided information concerning the effect of the adult–child interaction on the child's testimony. They tried to mislead three- to five-year-old children about aspects of a story read to them by a teacher or counselor at their nursury school or summer camp. Misleading information subsequently supplied by an adult interviewer was more effective at changing the child's testimony than the same misleading information supplied by an older child. Adults are a credible source of information, and a child may incorporate correct or incorrect information provided by an adult interviewer.

Interviewers should avoid specific questioning of children, particularly during the initial phase of the interview. Should further questioning be required, the interviewer must be sensitive to the potential for misunderstanding and the possibility that a child will treat a question as a demand for an answer, rather than an inquiry for information. Children respond to questions as best they can, even when a directive is unclear or ambiguous (e.g., Robinson & Whittaker, 1986). Hughes and Grieve (1980) demonstrated that children attempt to provide a plausible answer, no matter how bizarre the question. Any question has the potential to be suggestive to a child.

Repeated interviewing of children may also be suggestive. Moston

(1985) had a confederate appear before groups of children at their regular school assembly. The children were later individually questioned about the confederate. He found that repeated questioning about the same aspects of the event reduced the number of accurate responses provided by the children. This points to a special problem in the area of sexual abuse. Typically, a child victim of such abuse is repeatedly interviewed by concerned parents, the police, social workers, lawyers, and others. The younger the child, the more such repeated questioning may contaminate the child's testimony. The Scott County cases (Humphrey, 1985) provide clear examples of the negative effects of such repeated questioning.

Alternative Interviewing Techniques

When children lack verbal skills or are reticent to discuss sexual acts, interviewers frequently employ nonverbal techniques to assist the interview. One of these aids is the use of puppets. Young children will frequently tell a puppet things they will not reveal directly to an adult. At times, the child may use a puppet to disclose information. Puppets that are manipulated by the interviewer and the child can be useful to break through communication barriers between adult and child.

A doll house is another interview aid. A simple, furnished doll house, containing dolls to represent family members, may be helpful in assisting children who have descriptive or expressive problems. They can arrange the furniture to represent their house or the location where the alleged events occurred. If the interviewer has knowledge of this location, the validity of the child's "description" can be determined. The child can also use the dolls to act out the events of interest.

Other interview alternatives are most problematic. The use of anatomically detailed dolls has become commonplace, even mandated in some jurisdictions. The dolls have been greeted enthusiastically as a "nonthreatening" means to allow children to relate sexual experiences (e.g., Clausen, 1985). However, no standards have appeared concerning the correct manner of using the dolls (see White & Santilli, 1986), and almost no base rate data exist on how nonabused children interact with the dolls (White, Strom, & Santilli, 1986). Only two studies have attempted to examine children's spontaneous play with these dolls, and they provide conflicting evidence. White, Strom, Santilli, and Halpin (1986) compared twenty-five sexually abused and twenty-five nonabused children in their use of the dolls. In contrast to nonabused children, they found clear differences in the manner in which the abused children interacted with the dolls, which revealed the sexual experience of the abused children. However, Goranson (1986) studied fourteen young children who had not been abused and found that they interacted with the dolls in a fashion that an examiner would conclude was indicative of abuse. This is an area in need of immediate research, and interviewers must consider the problems concerning the proper and limited ways in which the anatomically detailed dolls should be used.

Another nonverbal alternative is the use of drawings. When used to check the child's labeling of body parts, showing the child drawings of nude figures can be a useful aid in the interview process. However, having the child produce drawings is problematic. Asking the child to sketch the layout of a room, or to draw the parts of a body, may assist in cases of linguistic problems. However, some interviewers have taken the use of drawings much further and claimed that the symbolism of drawings reveals the basic truth of a child's disclosure. For example, Goodwin (1982) claimed that child-generated drawings are useful to convey the "power of conflicts" and the presence of "unconscious perceptions." Such recourse to symbolism is a very dangerous business. Given our present state of knowledge, it should be avoided.

Aids and props, such as anatomically detailed dolls, puppets, and drawings, should be viewed as tools of last resort. They should be considered only if the interviewer has failed to elicit adequate information by means of the standard interview methods described in the next section. Since the use of such aids and props may actually create more problems than they solve, a systematic and properly conducted interview appears to be the best available procedure.

Systematic Interview and Assessments

To ensure that the child provides a maximum amount of uncontaminated information, it is necessary that the interviewer be properly trained in an investigative perspective. The training must include knowledge about the special problems associated with interviewing children and the nature of their cognitive, memory, and linguistic abilities. The interviewer must be sensitive to the suggestibility of children and possess the patience and ability to conduct an interview at a level appropriate for the child.

As noted earlier, the problem of false disclosures is real and growing. The rates of unfounded reports have increased, child abuse agencies have noted more instances of false allegations, and domestic relations disputes appear to produce alarming numbers of fictitious accusations. To collect as much information as possible, the interviewer should approach the interview with alternative hypotheses about the nature of the events. This can be done in a supportive manner, but with an orientation that ensures the child will provide a full description. After the information has been obtained from the child, a systematic procedure is needed to analyze the child's statements. This requires a set of criteria to differentiate a valid disclosure from a false one. Statement analysis holds real promise as the appropriate interview procedure and as a technique with which to assess the validity of the child's statement.

Statement Validity Assessment

Statement validity assessment is a comprehensive technique that uses various types of information and procedures to arrive at a conclusion regarding the validity of an allegation of sexual abuse of a child. A major component of that assessment is a criteria-based analysis of the statement obtained from a systematic investigative interview. The first approach to statement analysis was developed in Germany more than thirty years ago to cope with the problem of assessing the validity of allegations made by children (Undeutsch, 1982). It has been widely used by the courts in Germany since the Supreme Court of the Federal Republic of Germany made a landmark decision in 1954. It mandated that expert psychologists or psychiatrists must be employed to assess the truthfulness of children's testimony if that is the major evidence and is not corroborated by other evidence. Arntzen (1982) reported that such services are now provided mainly by forensic psychologists appointed by German courts to make validity assessments in 30,000 to 50,000 cases. Similar approaches are frequently employed in Sweden (Trankell, 1972).

Undeutsch (1982) reported that approximately 90 percent of children's allegations have been demonstrated by statement analysis to be valid, which has been very helpful in convicting the accused. The remaining 10 percent of the results raised questions about the validity of the statements and the advisability of pursuing the prosecutions. Also, statement analysis frequently produces additional high-quality evidence that butresses the case, but sometimes it yields information that strongly indicates the allegation is fictitious.

Statement analysis is based on the premise that descriptions of events that were actually experienced differ in content, quality, and expression from those that are invented. Those characteristics of the statement can be systematically assessed by means of a set of content criteria applied to the products of the interview. Therefore, it is necessary to obtain a carefully structured and fully documented interview of the child conducted by a qualified professional. The earlier the interview is performed in the handling of the case, the easier it is to obtain information on which to base the content analysis.

Interviewing the Child Witness

The child should be interviewed alone, at a neutral location, by a professional who may sometimes be assisted by another professional. Neither parent nor any other authority figure should be permitted to participate or be present in the interview room after the formal interview has begun. The entire proceeding must be videotaped, to document the interview. The content and style of questioning and the responses of the child must be preserved, including verbal and nonverbal expressions of emotion and reactions by the child. Notes and other partial reconstructions of the interview are not acceptable substitutes for a tape recording; they are subject to interpretation and distortion, and they do not provide adequate raw material for the formal analysis that must be conducted after the interview. This analysis may be performed independently from a typed transcript of the interview in conjunction with viewing of the videotape.

The interviewer must establish rapport with the child and explain the reason for the interview. The initial discussion also provides baseline information about the verbal and expressive abilities of the child. This information can be used in the subsequent evaluation of the child's statement. Early in the session there should be a discussion of the meaning of truth and deception, and the child should be motivated to be truthful. The interviewer should not increase the child's natural reluctance to discuss sexual matters by using aggressive or pressure tactics, and the interviewer should also avoid using questions or comments that imply criticism of the child or place a performance burden on the child. Crying and other disruptive behaviors should not be addressed directly, but the topic or focus of attention should be shifted to a less threatening or less emotional area until the disruptive behavior has subsided.

The interviewer should begin by encouraging a free narrative. That is accomplished by asking the child to describe the events from the beginning without interruptions, specific questions, corrections, or challenges. If the child stops the narrative, the interviewer should encourage a continuation by restating the child's last description or asking "and then what happened?" After the narrative is finished, open-ended questions should be asked to obtain necessary detail about important areas of the incident. These questions should not lead the child or suggest an answer, and the child should not be pressured to give a definite answer.

If open-ended questions do not provide the necessary details, various alternative answers to the question should be provided. However, specific questions should not incorporate information provided by another witness. For example, if the parent stated that the event occurred in the bedroom, the interviewer should ask "Did it happen in the kitchen, the living room, or the den?" Specific questions should be asked serially without the interviewer discussing the answers, commenting, or volunteering information. If the child does not provide an answer to a specific question, the interviewer should return to it later using a single alternative, which is contrary to a previous statement or other information.

To obtain more details or clarifications, the interviewer may pretend that a previous answer does not seem plausible. For example, if the child gave little detail after having said that touching of the genitals occurred, the interviewer might say "That seems strange because you had your pants on. How could that happen?" Sometimes ambiguous answers or responses of very young or relatively nonverbal children require clarification by the use of direct questions. The interviewer must guard against suggestion, but a cue may be used to reinstate the context, such as "Do you remember anything about a mirror?"

The child's susceptibility to suggestion may be assessed at the end of the interview by the use of suggestive questions unrelated to the incident or directly, but incorrectly, related to some aspect of the described incident. That should be done with caution so as not to upset the child or engender suspicion of the interviewer. However, if the child shows evidence of suggestibility, additional suggestions should be tested. Strong evidence of suggestibility causes concern about the accuracy of all of the information provided by the child.

Criteria-Based Statement Analysis

The assessment of the validity of the statement must be related to the verbal and intellectual abilities and sexual knowledge of the child, as well as to the nature of the reported event. Relatively simple events (e.g., a single, brief touching of the genital area outside the clothing in a commonplace situation) described by a child who has well-developed cognitive abilities and access to sexual information or experience produce less definitive results than do complex descriptions by a young child who has limited experience with such matters. Although it may not yield an assessment indicative of validity, an allegation concerning a simple event does not necessarily indicate deception by the child.

Analysis of the statement involves the systematic application of a set of content criteria to the transcript of the statement. Five major categories of criteria are subdivided as shown in Table 9.1. This classification system is adapted from Steller and Koehnken (in press), who integrated the criteria reported by other German investigators. It is based on a logical structure that permits relatively easy use in research and practical applications. The process begins with an assessment of the overall quality of the statement and proceeds to progressively more specific details and characteristics of the statement. A brief description of the criteria is presented here. A more detailed exposition of the conduct of the interview and application of the criteria can be found in Steller, Raskin, Yuille and Esplin (in preparation).

The *general characterisitics* of the statement are assessed without analysis of the details of its contents. "Logical structure" is fulfilled when the same course of events is described consistently by various details within the statement. Mention of unexpected complications (criterion 7) or unusual details (criterion 8) does not negate logical structure. "Unstructured production" refers to a manner of presentation that is not overly orgainzed and excessively chronological, as would be characteristic of a false and rehearsed account. As long as the fragments of the statement can be combined into a generally coherent account, this criterion is satisfied. A relatively large amount of detail, such as exact descriptions of places, detailed descriptions of persons from varying aspects, and sequential descrip-

TABLE 9.1 Content criteria for statement analysis.[a]

General characteristics
  1. Logical Structure
  2. Unstructured production
  3. Quantity of details
Specific contents
  4. Contexutal embedding
  5. Descriptions of interactions
  6. Reproduction of conversation
  7. Unexpected complications during the incident
Peculiarities of the content
  8. Unusual details
  9. Superfluous details
  10. Accurately reported details not understood
  11. Related external associations
  12. Accounts of subjective mental state
  13. Attribution of perpetrator's mental state
Motivation-related contents
  14. Spontaneous corrections
  15. Admitting lack of memory
  16. Raising doubts about one's own testimony
  17. Self-deprecation
  18. Pardoning the perpetrator
Offense-specific elements
  19. Details characteristic of the offense

[a] Adapted from Steller and Koehnken (in press).

tions of events, fulfills the "quantity of details" criterion. However, simple repetitions, as opposed to new facts or details, do not satisfy the criterion of quantity.

The *specific contents* of the statement constitutes the second major category. It focuses on individual parts of the statement in terms of the presence or extent of certain features. "Contextual embedding" refers to specific facts or events of peripheral interest that are anchored within the totality of the situation. Descriptions of everyday occurrences, family customs, and interactions with neighbors are examples of such inter-relationships.

"Descriptions of interactions" refers to a chain of mutual actions and reactions in the form of conversations or other behaviors. When such accounts contain misperceptions and misunderstandings on the part of the child, they are particularly consistent with validity. "Reproduction of conversation" lends support to validity when the child provides a virtual replication of a verbal interaction that differentiates the roles of the various speakers. An account is especially compelling when the child seems to re-experience the original verbal context of the conversation, the language repeated is not typical of that child's age, the arguments made by the accused are cited, and the conversation reveals the different attitudes of the participants. The intrusion of "unexpected complications"into the situation, such as a neighbor coming to the door, also reinforces validity.

Peculiarities of the content reflect the concreteness and vividness of the account and constitute the third major category of criteria. "Unusual details" refers to odd or unique details that are not obviously unrealistic. The presence of unusual or "superfluous details" that have a low probability of occurrence would not be expected in invented accounts or accusations. The same is true of descriptions of the "subjective mental state" of the child or "attributions of the perpetrator's mental state," such as expressions of fear or disgust, thoughts about how to escape from the situation, and the perpetrator's apparent nervousness.

"Accurately reported of details not understood" refers to accounts of behavior not understood by a child but easily understood by an adult. An example would be the child's misinterpretation that the perpetrator seemed to be in pain because of the groaning noises that he made during the sexual encounter. "Related external associations" describes references to overlapping relationships, as exemplified in a report by a girl who alleged incest by her father and also stated that her father had questioned her about her sexual experiences with other partners. This type of information is related to the general situation of the sexual incident and may occur within it, but it is not an integral part of it.

The *motivation-related contents* are the fourth category of criteria. In contrast to the two preceding categories for analyzing the cognitive characteristics of the account, this category focuses on motivational aspects regarding the ability of the child to fabricate an account that has certain qualities. "Spontaneous corrections" are unlikely in accounts that are fabricated or prompted by coaching because they tend to be perceived by the speaker as damaging the credibility of the account. Similar arguments apply to "admitting lack of memory" or "raising doubts about one's own testimony" by pointing out possible objections to its accuracy. In addition, expressions of "self-deprecation" and "pardoning the perpetrator," by providing explanations or rationalizations for the behavior in question, are consistent with validity.

The final category concerns *offense-specific elements*. However, they may not be present in many valid true statements. They refer to descriptions that are contrary to commonly held beliefs about sexual molestation by strangers or incestuous relationships. To evaluate this criterion, the expert must have specific knowledge about the typical ways in which such crimes are actually committed. Special value is attached to elements of a statement that includes correct descriptions that contradict common beliefs. For example, many incestuous relationships begin with a long period of relatively minor sexual behavior, which progressively develops into more serious acts that are accompanied by a substantial change in the victim's attitude toward the perpetrator (Sgroi, 1982). This criterion is based on empirical findings concerning such acts, the characteristics of which are contrary to the beliefs held by nonprofessionals.

Validity Checks

After the statement has been analyzed according to the content criteria, it is necessary to examine other factors and information, to determine the validity of the results. In addition to the more formal and specific characteristics of the statement, other aspects must be evaluated in making an overall assessment of the validity of the allegations. The evaluation may produce results that strengthen or weaken the conclusions obtained from the criteria-based statement analysis. This is accomplished by considering the presence or absence of certain information or characteristics in the statement or obtained from other sources. A validity checklist is provided in Table 9.2.

Some of the validity checks are closely related to the interview technique and the obtained statement (statement-related factors). Therefore, they are the domain of the psychological expert who is uniquely qualified to evaluate them by virtue of specialized training and experience. Other areas of inquiry may be suggested by the contents of the obtained statement but are more appropriately pursued by other experts and investigators (investigative questions). Although they may arise from the interview conducted by the psychologist, their resolution depends on information

---

TABLE 9.2 Validity checklist.

I. Statement-related factors
    A.   Psychological characteristics
          1. Appropriateness of language
          2. Appropriateness of knowledge
          3. Presence of affect
          4. Appropriateness of affect
          5. Spontaneous gestures
          6. Susceptibility to suggestion
    B.   Interview characteristics
          7. Adequacy of the interview
          8. Suggestive or leading questions
          9. Pressure or coercion
    C.   Motivation
          10. Context of the original report
          11. Motives to report
          12. Pressures to report
II. Investigative questions
    D.   Medical evidence
    E.   Consistency with the laws of nature
    F.   Consistency with other statements
    G.   Consistency with other evidence

---

gathered by other experts who use different methods and techniques derived from their special training and experience.

Statement-related factors constitute a category of information derived directly from the statement. Some of them are "psychological characteristics" regarding the behavior of the witness during the interview. It is important to determine if the language and knowledge displayed in the interview were appropriate to the developmental knowledge and experience of the witness. Their evaluation may require a psychometric assessment of the child and interviews with teachers and parents to determine the extent to which the child may have been exposed to the type of sexual information described by the witness during the interview.

Other psychological characteristics concern the presence or absence of affect that would be expected at certain times during the interview. For example, if a child is describing a painful penetration, one would expect that description to be accompanied by some nonverbal expression of negative affect. A timely display of appropriate affect reinforces validity, but the absence of affect or a display of inappropriate affect detracts from validity. Also, spontaneous and timely occurrences of appropriate gestures add to the validity of descriptions of actions or events, such as raising the arms above the head while describing being held down by the perpetrator. However, if the child laughs or acts silly while describing an embarrassing or painful event, questions about validity arise.

The resistance or susceptibility of the witness to suggestion should be evaluated. The child may have rejected incorrect alternatives proposed by the interviewer, or corrected erroneous suggestions proposed by the interviewer, or contradicted information known to be incorrect. Such a demonstration of lack of suggestibility reinforces the validity of the statement. On the other hand, definite indications of suggestibility raise questions about the validity of the child's statement.

"Interview characteristics" refers to the manner in which the interviewer conducts the interview and elicits information from the witness. An interview that elicited adequate information and avoided suggestions, leading questions, pressure, and coercion lends weight to the validity of its contents. However, the lack of an adequate interview and the presence of those factors raise substantial questions about the validity of the statement.

"Motivation" refers to psychological factors surrounding the initial disclosures and the report obtained by the interview. If the original report was spontaneously provided in a typical context, such as telling a teacher, pediatrician, nonadversarial parent, friend, or playmate, then validity is reinforced. However, if the allegations had been initiated by a parent involved in a divorce or custody dispute with the alleged perpetrator, or there are indications of motives to report an incident to achieve an end, such as a conduct-disordered juvenile wishing to move out of a restrictive home environment or have a disliked parent removed from the home, validity may be questioned. Any indications of pressures to report a fictitious allegation must also be considered.

Investigative questions refers to issues that may arise or be derived from the interview that should be pursued and evaluated by other experts or professionals. If the witness described a sexual act that is likely to have caused physical damage or physiological change, then a medical examination may provide confirmation or disconfirmation of the alleged event. If the descriptions of actions and events are consistent with the laws of nature, other statements by the witness, and other evidence, the validity of the statement is strengthened. However, if one or more major element in the statement is contrary to the laws of nature or inconsistent with previous statements or other evidence, questions about validity of the allegations must be raised. For example, the description of red and blue semen or sexual acts performed in physically impossible ways raise cautions regarding the validity of the statement. Although such questions may be raised by the psychologist who conducted the interview or evaluated the contents of the statements, it not the role of the psychologist to seek the additional investigative information or provide the resolution of the discrepancies. These are the reponsibilities of other professionals, investigators, and legal officials.

The Overall Assessment

The ultimate decisions concerning the validity of the allegations and how best to proceed with the investigation and other formal actions must be based on a composite judgment that considers the quality of the statement, the adequacy of the interview, and the extent to which the content criteria were fulfilled. That judgment is tempered by the degree to which the validity checks are satisfied, as well as the diagnostic evaluation and general competence of the child, and the probable suitability and effectiveness of the child as a witness. The latter considerations involve the use of additional information obtained by other psychologists, investigators, case workers, and legal professionals. They are therefore independent of the interview and beyond the scope of this chapter.

At this time no specific rules exist concerning the number of criteria that must be fulfilled to conclude a statement is valid. That depends on the nature of the incident and the age, developmental level, and expressive abilities of the child. However, logical structure and unstructured production (criteria 1 and 2) are usually necessary for one to arrive at a conclusion of validity of the statement. Fulfillment of larger numbers of other criteria will lead to stronger conclusions regarding validity, and the presence of specific criteria might provide a particularly strong case. It must be kept in mind that contraindications arising from the presence of one or more indicators of invalidity can prevent a conclusion of validity about a statement that is otherwise of high quality.

It is also important to consider the possibility that the basic allegations are true but the child has named the wrong perpetrator. Many cases occur in which the child has been abused but is afraid to name the actual perpetrator. An example is a situation in which the child is living with her mother and stepfather. The stepfather is abusing the child, but the child names her biological father, whom she does not fear. Under those circumstances, the statement may be rated high in validity because all of the descriptions of acts and events are true except the identity of the perpetrator. If such a situation seems possible or likely, the interviewer must be careful to explore this possibility by asking questions that would provide enough critical details to allow a clear determination regarding that issue. The presence of contextual embedding (criterion 4) might resolve the question.

A similar problem can arise when some of the allegations made by the child are true but there has been embellishment or outright fabrication concerning other acts, events, and perpetrators. In such situations, the interviewer must be very careful to assess the validity of each of the alleged acts and perpetrators separately. Appropriate information should be sought by the interviewer, and the presence or absence of criteria must be considered separately for the various components of the allegations. The final conclusions would also require a separate validity check for each of those components.

A Case Study

A recent case in the Midwest involved the application of statement reality analysis and demonstrated the value of the technique in differentiating between valid and fictitious contents of the statement. Four eight-year-old boys became involved in a series of accusations against the parents of one of the children. The accusations included touching the genitals of the boys, taking pictures of them in the nude, and fellatio. The central figure of those accusations was interviewed using the statement analysis procedure. The analysis of his statements indicated that the accusation concerning the touching of his genitals was valid. Many of the criteria of statement reality analysis were found in this aspect of his statement. In contrast, the boy's description of the picture-taking incident and fellatio raised a number of doubts about the validity of these disclosures. Between sessions, the interviewer visited the locations of the alleged events and discovered that many of the details the boy had provided were incorrect. When confronted with this fact, the boy recanted the allegations concerning the pictures and the fellatio incident and provided a credible explanation for his fabrications.

Statement analysis differentiated between the apparently valid and the fabricated parts of the child's statement. This differentiation proved to be consistent with the forensic evidence in the case and the results of polygraph testing of the accused parents. It is important to note that the boy had been interviewed several times before the statement analysis interview, and no differentiation of the various contents of his statement had been made.

Conclusions

The assessment of validity of the statement is both quantitative and qualitative, and it provides information about the probable accuracy of the accusation. However, no specific rules have been developed for quantifying and combining the data to arrive at a decision for which a margin of error and an accuracy rate can be defined. Considerable research is needed to determine if that type of information can be developed and used effectively. Fundamental research is needed to validate the content criteria using statements sampled from cases in which the allegations were subsequently proven to be true or false. The authors are beginning such research in North America, and Steller and Koehnken are undertaking similar studies in Germany. It is our hope that this brief exposition will stimulate other researchers to join in those efforts.

It is clear that procedures currently employed in the United States for conducting interviews and assessing allegations of sexual abuse are considerably less well documented and less systematic than those employed for decades in Germany, and not as scientifically credible. There are many inadequacies in the training and beliefs of American professionals who work on sexual abuse cases. The availability of systematic interview and assessment techniques based on theoretically plausible assumptions and apparent utility argues for their use in North America. Standardization of the interviews and their evaluation would necessarily improve the quality of investigations and the processing of cases involving allegations of sexual abuse of children. More rapid and efficient prosecutions of bona fide cases would greatly benefit the children and society. Better methods would also reduce the number of fictitious allegations and the attendant damage to those who are falsely accused, the judicial process, and social programs.

References

Arntzen, F. (1982). Die Situation der Forensischen Aussagepsychologie in der Bundesrepublik Deutschland. In A. Trankell, ed. *Reconstructing the past: The role of psychologists in criminal trials.* Stockholm: Norstedt & Soners, 107–120.

Benedek, E.P., & Schetky, D.H. (1985). Allegations of sexual abuse in child custody and visitation disputes. In D.H. Schetky & E.P. Benedek, eds. *Emerging issues in child psychiatry and the law.* New York: Brunner Mazel.

Besharov, D.J. (1985). "Doing something" about child abuse: The need to narrow the grounds for state intervention. *Harvard Journal of Law and Public Policy, 8,* 539–589.

Burkholder, R. (1986). "The use of videotaping in the interviewing of child abuse victims." Unpublished manuscript.

Ceci, S., & Howe, M.J.A. (1978). Age-related differences in recall as a function of retrieval flexibility. *Journal of Experimental Child Psychology, 26,* 432–442.

Ceci, S.J., Ross, D.F. & Toglia, M.P. (1987). Age differences in suggestibility:

Narrowing the uncertainties. In S.J. Ceci, M.P. Toglia, & D.F. Ross, eds. *Children's eyewitness memory*. New York: Springer-Verlag.

Ceci, S.J., & Tishman, J. (1984). Hyperactivity and incidental memory: Evidence for attentional diffusion. *Child Development*, *55*, 2192–2203.

Ceci, S.J., Toglia, M.P., & Ross, D.F., eds. (1987) *Children's eyewitness memory*. New York: Springer-Verlag.

Clausen, J.M. (1985). Using anatomically correct dolls. *Law and Order*, March, 40–44.

Cole, C.B., & Loftus, E.F. (1987). The memory of children. In S.J. Ceci, M.P. Toglia, & D.F. Ross, eds. *Children's eyewitness memory*. New York: Springer-Verlag.

Conerly, S. (1986). Assessment of suspected child sexual abuse. In K. MacFarlane, J. Waterman, S. Conerly, L. Damon, M. Durfee, & S. Long, eds. *Sexual abuse of young children: Evaluation and treatment*. New York: Guilford, 30–51.

Dale, P.S., Loftus, E.F., & Rathbun, L. (1978). The influence of the form of the question on the eyewitness testimony of preschool children. *Journal of Psycholinguistic Research*, *74*, 269–277.

Davies, G.M., Flin, R., & Baxter, J. (1986). The child witness. *The Howard Journal*, *25*, 81–99.

Faller, K.C. (1984). Is the child victim of sexual abuse telling the truth? *Child Abuse & Neglect*, *8*, 471–481.

Finkelhor, D., & Hotaling, G.T. (1984) Sexual abuse in the national incidence study of child abuse and neglect: An appraisal. *Child Abuse & Neglect*, *8*, 23–33.

Geiselman, R.E., Fisher, R.P., MacKinnon, D.P., & Holland, H.L. (1985). Eyewitness memory enhancement in the police interview: Cognitive retrieval mnemonics versus hypnosis. *Journal of Applied Psychology*, *70*, 401–412.

Goetze, H.J. (1980). "The effect of age and method of interview on the accuracy and completeness of eyewitness accounts." Unpublished doctoral dissertation. Hofstra University, New York.

Goodman, G.S. (1984). Children's testimony in historical perspective. *Journal of Social Issues*, *40(2)*, 9–32.

Goodman, G.S., Aman, C., & Hirschman, J. (1987). Child sexual and physical abuse: Children's testimony. In S.J. Ceci, M.P. Toglia, & D.F. Ross, eds. *Children's eyewitness memory*. New York: Springer-Verlag.

Goodwin, J. (1982). The use of drawings in incest cases. In J. Goodwin, ed. *Sexual abuse: Incest victims and their families*. London: John Wright, 47–57.

Goodwin, J., Sahd, D., & Rada, R. (1978). Incest hoax: False accusations, false denials. *Bulletin of the American Academy of Psychiatry and Law*, *6*, 269–276.

Goranson, S.E. (1986). "Young child interview responses to anatomically detailed dolls: Implications for practice and research in child sexual abuse." Unpublished master's thesis, University of British Columbia, Vancouver, Canada.

Graham, M.H. (1985). Child sexual abuse prosecution: The state of the art. *University of Miami Law Review*, *40*, 1–4.

Green, A.H. (1986). True and false allegations of sexual abuse in child custody disputes. *Journal of the American Academy of Child Psychiatry*, *25*, 449–456.

Hughes, M., & Grieve, R. (1980). On asking children bizarre questions. In M. Donaldson, R. Grieve, & C. Pratt, eds. *Early childhood development and education*. Oxford: Basil Blackwell, 104–114.

Humphrey, H.H. (1985). *Report on Scott County investigations*. Office of the Attorney General of Minnesota.

Jones, D.P.H., & Krugman, R.D. (1986). Case report: Can a three-year-old child bear witness to her sexaul assault and attempted murder? *Child Abuse and Neglect, 10*, 253–258.

Jones, D.P.H., & McGraw, J. M. (1987). Reliable and fictitious accounts of sexual abuse in children. *Journal of Interpersonal Violence, 2*, 27–45.

King, M.A. (1984). "An investigation of the eyewitness abilities of children." Unpublished doctoral dissertation, University of British Columbia, Vancouver, Canada.

King, M.A., & Yuille, J.C. (1987). Suggestibility and the child witness. In S.J. Ceci, M.P. Toglia, & D.F. Ross, eds. *Children's eyewitness memory*. New York: Springer-Verlag.

List, J.A. (1986). Age and schematic differences in the reliability of eyewitness testimony. *Developmental Psychology, 22(1)*, 50–57.

Marin, B.V., Holmes, D.L., Guth, M., & Kovac, P. (1979). The potential of children as eyewitnesses: A comparison of children and adults on eyewitness tasks. *Law and Human Behavior, 3*, 295–306.

Moston, S. (1985). "An experimental study of the suggestibility of children in an eyewitness memory task." Unpublished master's thesis, University of Manchester, England.

Parker, J.F., Haverfield, E., & Basker-Thomas, S. (1986). Eyewitness testimony of children. *Journal of Applied Social Psychology, 16*, 287–302.

Peters, J. (1976). Children who are victims of sexual assault and the psychology of offenders. *American Journal of Psychotherapy, 30*, 398–421.

Pynoos, R.S., & Eth, S. (1984). The child as a witness to homicide. *Journal of Social Issues, 40(2)*, 87–108.

Raskin, D.C., & Steller, M. (in press). Assessing credibility of allegations of child sexual abuse: Polygraph examinations and statement analysis. In H. Wegener, F. Loesel, & J. Haisch, eds. *Criminal behavior and the justice system: Psychological perspectives*. New York: Springer-Verlag.

Robinson, E.J., & Whittaker, S.J. (1986). Children's conceptions of meaning-message relationships. *Cognition, 22*, 41–60.

Sgroi, S.M., ed. (1982). *Handbook of clinical intervention in child sexual abuse*. Lexington, MA: Lexington.

Steller, M., & Koehnken, G. (in press). Statement analysis: Credibility assessment of children's testimonies in sexual abuse cases. In D.C. Raskin, ed. *Psychological methods for criminal investigation and evidence*. New York: Springer-Verlag.

Steller, M., Raskin, D.C., Yuille, J.C. & Esplin, P.W. (in preparation). *Child sexual abuse: Forensic interviews and assessments*. New York: Springer-Verlag.

Summit, R.C. (1983). The child sexual abuse accommodation syndrome. *Child Abuse and Neglect, 7*, 177–193.

Suski, L.B. (1986). Child sexual abuse: An increasingly important part of child protective service practice. *Protecting Children, 3*, 3–7.

Trankell, A. (1972). *Reliability of evidence*. Stockholm: Beckmans.

Undeutsch, U. (1982). In A. Trankell, ed. *Reconstructing the past: The role of pyschologists in criminal trials*. Stockholm: Norstedt & Soners, 27–56.

White, S., & Santilli, G.S. (1986). *Uses and abuses of sexually anatomically detailed dolls*. Cleveland, OH: Cleveland Metropolitan General Hospital, Department of Psychiatry.

White, S., Strom, G.A., and Santilli, G.S. (1986) Clinical protocol for interviewing preschoolers with sexually anatomically detailed dolls. Unpublished paper, Case Western Reserve University, Cleveland, OH.

White, S., Strom, G.A., Santilli, G., & Halpin, O.M. (1986). Interviewing young sexual abuse victims with anatomically correct dolls. *Child Abuse and Neglect*, *10*, 519–529.

Young, M. de (1986). A conceptual model for judging the truthfulness of a young child's allegation of sexual abuse. *American Journal of Orthopsychiatry*, *56*, 550–559.

Yuille, J.C., Cutshall, J.L., & King, M.A. (1986). *Age related changes in eyewitness accounts and photo-identification*. Unpublished manuscript, University of British Columbia, Vancouver, Canada.

10
The Impact of New Child Witness Research on Sexual Abuse Prosecutions

JOSEPHINE A. BULKLEY, J.D.

From 1975 to 1985, sexual abuse of children, once believed rare, became nationally recognized as a serious and significant social problem. Reports of all forms of child abuse and neglect also skyrocketed during this period. In 1976, 669,000 reports of child maltreatment were made to reporting agencies, and 1.9 million similar reports were made in 1985.[1] Although there also has been a significant rise in unsubstantiated reports during this time, most experts agree that child abuse remains significantly under-reported.[2] For example, although sexual abuse reports rose to 200,000 in 1985, it is believed that this figure still represents a small portion of the actual number of incidents of child sexual abuse. Based on retro-spective surveys of adult women, researchers estimate that 12 to 38 per-cent of women in some way have been sexually molested as children.[3]

As might be expected, the greater awareness and reporting of sexual abuse has led to growing public, government, and professional support for criminal prosecution of child sex offenders.[4] Criminal prosecution of child abuse and neglect traditionally has been rare, and generally initiated only

---

[1] American Association for Protecting Children (1987). Highlights of official child neglect and abuse reporting 1985, 3.

[2] Besharov (1985). Doing something about abuse: The need to narrow the grounds for state intervention, *Harvard Journal of Law & Public Policy, 8(3)*, 539, 550; Peters, Wyatt, & Finkelhor (1986). Prevalence, in *A sourcebook on child sexual abuse*. D. Finkelhor, ed.

[3] Peters et al., *supra* note 2, at 18.

[4] Attorney General's Task Force on Family Violence, *Final report* (1984); Berliner and Stevens, Advocating for sexually abused children in the criminal justice system, in *Sexual abuse of children: Selected readings*, U.S. Dept. Health & Hum. Serv. B. Jones & K. MacFarlance, eds. (1980); Berliner & Barbieri (1984). The testimony of child victims of sexual assault, *40(2) Journal of Social Issues* 125, 128 (G. Goodman, ed.); Besharov, Child abuse: Arrest and prosecution decision-making, 24 *Amer. Crim. L. Rev.* 315, 317–19 (1986); Harshbarger, Prosecution is an appropriate response in child sexual abuse cases, *2(1)* J. Interpersonal Violence 108 (1987).

in egregious cases involving major media attention, severe physical injury or death, and recently, in sexual abuse cases. The lack of criminal justice system involvement partly can be attributed to the predominant use of the juvenile court system, which was considered to be the best means of dealing with parental abuse and neglect.[5] Indeed, the reporting and juvenile court laws were designed to protect children abused by caretakers and to provide services to families to preserve the family unit. Reporting laws grew out of recognition of the "battered child syndrome," a type of severe physical abuse generally committed by parents or parent substitutes, and they were intended to address the lack of reporting of such abuse by physicians.[6]

Until recently, child maltreatment by unrelated adults or in out-of-home care was largely unreported. Based on recent reports and research, however, it is now believed that a significant amount of sexual abuse is committed by unrelated adults children know and trust.[7] In these cases, prosecution is more common, since the juvenile court system deals only with parental abuse and neglect. Moreover, many have argued that incest cases, as well as cases involving nonparent perpetrators, should be prosecuted, and that all child molestation should be treated as a serious criminal offense.[8] Indeed, prosecutors reports major increases in their child sexual abuse caseloads.[9]

Another factor that seems to have influenced the increase in criminal prosecution of child sexual abuse is that prosecutors, police officers, judges, and others in the legal system have more confidence that such cases are "prosecutable." This increased confidence may be explained in part by the legal system's improved handling of sexual abuse cases in the past few years. In the late 1970s, as cases began to enter the criminal justice system, child advocates raised serious problems in prosecuting these cases.[10] One major concern was the emotional trauma that child victims often suffered because of insensitive legal procedures and testifying in court. Another major problem was the extreme difficulty in proving cases of child sexual abuse. For example, these cases frequently lack medical evidence, since the abuse often involves only fondling or there is a long delay in reporting.

---

[5] Bulkley & Davidson, *Child sexual abuse—legal issues and approaches*, American Bar Association (1981).

[6] Davidson & Horowitz (1984). Protection of children from family maltreatment. In *Legal rights of children* R. Horowitz & H. Davidson, eds., 262.

[7] Russell (1983). Incidence and prevalence of intrafamilial and extrafamilial sexual abuse of female children, 7 *Child Abuse & Neglect* 133; Finkelhor (1979). *Sexually victimized children.*

[8] *Final report, supra* note 4, at 4.

[9] Donnelly (Sept. 18, 1987). Child sexual abuse, Editorial Research Reports, *Congressional Quarterly, 4(11).*

[10] Berliner & Stevens, *supra* note 4; DeFrancis, *Protecting the child victim of sex crimes*, American Humane Association (1969).

Further, the key witness, and often the only witness, is a child, who may be found or believed to be incompetent to testify, or whose credibility may be questioned because of beliefs about a child's limited cognitive and verbal abilities, suggestibility, or inability to distinguish between fact and fantasy. Finally, the higher burden of proof and constitutional protections for the defendant make criminal cases more difficult to prove than civil cases.

Beginning in the early 1980s, many began to recommend reforms to make the legal system more sensitive to child victims and to eliminate evidence barriers to prosecuting cases of child sexual abuse. Numerous state legislatures and local jurisdictions have adopted innovative approaches to reduce trauma to children and to improve prosecutions.[11] Reforms for reducing trauma to children include (1) reducing multiple interviews with children by different professionals through joint interviewing, using one-way mirrors, or videotaping interviews; (2) establishing interdisciplinary teams; (3) coordinating criminal and juvenile court proceedings; (4) providing a victim advocate for the child in criminal court; (5) establishing special child abuse prosecution units and assigning the same prosecutor to all stages of a case (vertical prosecution); (6) expediting cases set for trial; and (7) closing the courtroom to the public and permitting alternatives to a child's testimony in open court (e.g., closed-circuit television, videotaped depositions, use of one-way mirrors or screens to hide the defendant from the child).

Reforms for improving prosecutions include (1) eliminating competency requirements for children; (2) admitting psychological expert testimony; (3) extending statutes of limitations; and (4) abolishing corroboration requirements. During the past five years, all jurisdictions have abolished corroboration requirements for serious sex offenses against children, which was a major impediment to prosecution of these cases. Many prosecutions are still not initiated, however, because children are disqualified from testifying.

Today, more than half the states have adopted Rule 601 of the Federal Rules of Evidence, which establishes a rebuttable presumption of competency for children, providing "Every person in competent to be a witness, except as otherwise provided in these rules." Rule 601 reflects the modern trend toward eliminating rules that disqualify witnesses from testifying simply because they belong to a particular group (e.g., children, the insane, or convicted persons).[12] Under Rule 601, any deficiencies in a child's testimony relating to memory or narration abilities no longer are

---

[11] Bulkley (1985). Evidentiary and procedural trends in state legislation and other emerging legal issues in child sexual abuse cases, 89 *Dickinson Law Review*, 645; Eatman & Bulkley (1986). Protecting child victim/witnesses: Sample laws and materials, American Bar Association.
[12] 3 Weinstein on Evidence, Section 601–17 (Supp. 1985).

part of the determination of a child's competency, but as with adults, are left to the jury to decide the weight and credibility of the testimony.

Many states, however, retain competency requirements, providing that a child below a certain age, usually ten or fourteen years, must be subjected to *voir dire* or questioning to determine his or her competency. The tests for assessing competency are whether the child knows the difference between truth and falsity, and appreciates the obligation to tell the truth, and whether the child is able to observe, remember, and communicate what happened and answer simple questions about the event.

For many years, legal commentators have recommended abolishing competency requirements for children.[13] Even Professor Wigmore, who has been severely criticized for his negative views regarding the credibility of rape victims, long has advocated that children be allowed to testify without prior qualification:

A rational view of the peculiarities of child nature, and of the daily course of justice in our courts, must lead to the conclusion that the effort to measure *a priori* the degree of trustworthiness in children's statements, and to distinguish the point at which they cease to be totally incredible and acquire some degree of credibility, is futile and unprofitable. . . . Recognizing on the one hand the childish disposition to weave romances and to treat imagination for verity and on the other the rooted ingenuousness of children and their tendency to speak straightforwardly what is in their minds, it must be concluded that the sensible way is to put the child upon the stand and let the story come out for what it may be worth.[14]

Though this was written nearly half a century ago, it is interesting to note that Wigmore's belief about children's "ingenuousness," honesty, or sincerity is apparently a common view, as research findings in this volume indicate, and that it tends to enhance a child's credibility.[15] On the other hand, Wigmore's view that children "treat imagination for verity" has not found support in current research on children's ability to distinguish imagined for real events.[16] Nevertheless, he recommends that children be allowed to testify and the jury decide the child's credibility.

It should be noted that even in states that have abolished special competency requirements, the practice of qualifying at least young children in advance is likely to continue. Rule 601 merely establishes a presumption of

---

[13] 2 Wigmore, Evidence in Trials at Common Law, Section 509 (1940); McCormick on Evidence, Section 62 (1972); Bulkley (1982). *Recommendations for improving legal intervention in child sexual abuse cases*, American Bar Association; Eatman & Bulkley, *supra* note 11.

[14] 2 Wigmore, Section 509.

[15] See also Leippe & Romanczyk, (1987). Children on the witness stand: A communication/persuasion analysis of jurors' reactions to child witnesses. In *Children's eyewitnesses memory*, S. Ceci, M. Toglia, & D. Ross, eds., 155.

[16] Johnson & Foley (1984). Differentiating fact from fantasy: The reliability of children's memory, *40(2) Journal of Social Issues, 33* (G. Goodman ed.).

competency, which means that the judge retains discretion to exclude any person's testimony if a reasonable juror could believe that "the witness is so bereft of his powers of observation, recordation, recollection, and recount as to be so untrustworthy as a witness as to make his testimony lack relevance."[17] Although theoretically a test of competency, it has been characterized as requiring "minimum credibility."[18]

Thus, although the trend is to allow the jury to decide the credibility of the witness, the court must still satisfy itself that a witness meets the minimum credibility standard.[19] Moreover, the defendant can always object to a witness' competency. It may be that somewhat older school-age children, such as children over eight years of age, may no longer be subject to *voir dire* on the theory that these children would be assumed to satisfy the "minimum credibility" standard. This is supported by some of the research in this volume and in *Children's Eyewitness Memory*, as well as the position that children eight years or older are perceived as having more accurate memories than younger children.[20] With more cases being reported involving children under eight years, however, this younger age group is more likely to be subjected to competency tests even in states that have abolished such requirements.

Most legal reforms have not enjoyed the growing empirical support from psychological research that has supported abolishment of competency requirements for children.[21] With respect to other legislative innovations, one researcher has stated that "The most basic problem with the statutory reforms is that neither need nor efficacy has been demonstrated."[22] For example, in the area of reducing trauma to children from testifying at trial, Melton states: "Both the vacuum in relevant data and the infrequency of open testimony by child victims suggest that attempts at procedural reform are premature. . . . Moreover, the assumption that open, confrontational testimony is traumatic for child victims of

---

[17] Graham (1981). *Handbook of federal evidence*, Section 602.2; Weinstein, Section 601–10.

[18] Id.

[19] Weinstein, Section 601–9–10.

[20] Ross, Miller & Moran, The child in the eyes of the jury: Assessing mock jurors' perceptions of the child witness. In *Children's eyewitness memory*, *supra* note 15, at 142.

[21] See, e.g., The child witness, *40(2) Journal of Social Issues*, *supra* note 1; *Children's eyewitness memory*, *supra* note 15; Melton (1981). Children's competency to testify, 5 *Law & Human Behavior*, *73*, Goodman & Helgeson, (1985). Child sexual assault: Children's memory and the law, *University of Miami Law Review* 181, 40; Loftus & Cole, The memory of children, in *Children's eyewitness memory*, *supra* note 15, at 178.

[22] Melton (1987). Children's testimony in cases of alleged sexual abuse. In *Advances in developmental and behavioral pediatrics* M. Wolraich & D.K. Routh, eds.; Goodman, The child witness: Conclusions and future directions for research and legal practice, *40(2) Journal of Social Issues*, *157*, 167–169.

sexual offenses has yet to be validated."[23] It is only in the past couple of years that studies have begun to look at the effects of legal intervention on children and whether legal reforms are effective in reducing emotional trauma or in improving the outcome of criminal prosecutions.[24]

Another reform for which adequate empirical data are lacking is the use of psychological expert testimony on typical characteristics of victims or cases to prove a child has been sexually abused. As discussed elsewhere, although studies indicate that there are emotional effects common to many victims of child sexual abuse, there is no clinically or scientifically accepted typical child victim.[25] For this reason, as discussed later, courts generally have not allowed experts to give opinions about whether a child has been abused because he or she shows characteristics of sexually abused children. Nevertheless, courts often allow experts to provide general testimony about common reactions of child sexual abuse victims without giving an opinion about a particular child.

Beginning in the early 1980s, renewed interest in child witness research resulted in many new studies dealing with children's memory, suggestibility, ability to distinguish fact from fantasy, and more recently, jurors' perceptions of children's credibility. Much of the new research supports the reform to abolish competency requirements by challenging commonly held myths or assumptions regarding children's poorer memories, greater suggestibility, and intermingling of imagination and reality. Such research has been received with great enthusiasm by the legal community, particularly prosecutors, legislators, and other child advocates eager for support to permit children to testify in the ever-increasing number of child abuse cases. Some researchers have stated specifically that most children can satisfy minimum competency requirements and provide reliable testimony.[26]

The current interest in and availability of research on children as witnesses comes at a time when more and more children, including younger children, may be called on to testify in sexual abuse prosecutions or whose credibility may be the major factor in plea negotiations. Turtle and Wells have noted recently that it would be a mistake to believe current psy-

---

[23] *Id.*

[24] See, e.g., Office of Juvenile Justice and Delinquency Prevention grant to Educational Development Corporation, Principal Investigator, Debra Whitcomb; National Institute of Justice grant to University of Denver, Principal Investigator, Gail Goodman.

[25] Berliner (1988). Deciding whether a child has been sexually abused, In *Sexual abuse allegations in custody and visitation cases*, American Bar Association, 48. B. Nicholson, ed.

[26] See, e.g., Melton, *supra* note 21; Marin, Holmes, Guth, & Kovac (1979). *The potential of children as eyewitnesses*, *Law & Human Behavior 3(4)*, 295; Goodman, Children's testimony in historical perspective, *Journal of Social Issues, 40(2)*, 9.

chological research on child eyewitnesses will not have an impact on judicial policy. In fact, a much stronger statement can be made: current research has already influenced state legislatures and courts.[27] Moreover, such research is beginning to have an effect on methods of interviewing children and on decisions to prosecute cases. Legal commentators increasingly cite psychological research in their recommendations relating to legal reforms and children as witnesses.[28] Finally, some researchers have been directly involved in supporting or cautioning against legal reforms and have worked closely with national legal organizations, served as witnesses before Congress and state legislatures, and testified in court regarding their views about the abilities of child witnesses.[29]

In light of the impact on legislative and judicial policies, the potential misuse of this new research must be considered. In other areas, social science research has been used erroneously, even in U.S. Supreme Court decisions. A recent article by Turtle and Wells provides an excellent discussion of some of the problems involved in the use of research to support legal policies.[30] They caution that researchers should not reflect a level of certainty that exceeds actual knowledge, because policymakers are not equipped to evaluate research findings. Turtle and Wells also state that research can be used selectively to support a particular side in the judicial system, in part because of the adversarial nature of the legal system. They further note that, "With respect to children's testimony, the failure to qualify many of the conclusions that one might be tempted to draw, on the basis of the existing literature, would be a failure to represent accurately the state of the art."[31] For example, researchers should indicate that, because

---

[27] See, e.g., Eatman & Bulkley, *supra* note 11. See, e.g., *People v. Grady*, 506 N.Y.S.2d 922, 933 (S.Ct. 1986) (citing Goodman & Helgeson, Child sexual assault: Children's memory and the law, 40 *University of Miami Law Review*, *181* (1985); The child witness, *40, Journal of Social Issues* (G. Goodman, ed. 1984); *State v. Jarzbek*, 529 A.2d 1245 (Conn. 1987) (Court noted that recent studies indicate some minors may benefit from legal proceedings and that there was no empirical data that all victims will suffer from testifying in front of the defendant, citing Melton, *Sexually Abused Children in the Legal System, infra* note 29.)

[28] Eatman & Bulkley, *supra* note 11; Whitcomb et al. (1985). *When the victim is a child: Issues for judges and prosecutors*, National Inst. of Justice, U.S. Dept. of Justice; The competency requirement for the child victim of sexual abuse: Must we abandon it? *University of Miami Law Review*, *40*, 245 (1985).

[29] See, e.g., Goodman & Helgeson, *supra* note 21; Melton, *supra* note 22; Turtle & Wells, Setting the stage for psychological research on the child eyewitness. In *Children's eyewitness memory*, 230, *supra* note 15; Goodman, Aman, & Hirschman, Child sexual and physical abuse: Children's testimony, In *Children's eyewitness memory*, *supra* note 15; Melton & Thompson, Getting out of a rut: Detours to less-traveled paths in child-witness research. In *Children's eyewitness memory*, *supra* note 15; Melton (1985). Sexually abused children and the legal system: Some policy recommendations, *American Journal of Family Therapy*, *13*, 61.

[30] Turtle & Wells, *supra* note 29.

[31] *Id.*, at 244.

the experimental methods they use may not be like real-life events, their conclusions may not be generalizable to actual cases.

For these reasons, one overriding concern about the outpouring of studies, articles, and books is the need to communicate the information in a way that synthesizes the issues in nontechnical terms for nonresearchers but does not distort them. As Turtle and Wells stated, authors should indicate clearly when the applicability of findings is limited, when they are preliminary or inconsistent, or that certain caveats should be kept in mind (e.g., mock jurors are college students and thus not representative of the general population). Moreover, although several recent books including this one make a major contribution to the field and will inform future research, the likelihood of most legal practitioners, legislators, or judges reading these materials is slight.

First, the amount of new research in the past five years on child witnesses is so overwhelming that it is difficult for researchers, not to mention others, to be aware of all the available studies and to draw conclusions from them about children's eyewitness abilities. Many of the articles in this book and others have been written primarily for other researchers, who understand the terminology, concepts, and statistical data and its limitations. A few excellent articles have been written by researchers attempting to summarize the issues or discuss their relevance to the legal process, some of which have appeared in psychological or legal journals.[32] More of these types of articles, particularly in law reviews, would be read by attorneys. For the public, who ultimately become jurors, it is even more important to communicate the information in an understandable way in publications, such as newspapers or magazines, that laypersons are more likely to read. Indeed, some journalists have written articles on these issues, although more of them are needed.

Although selective use of research findings is also a concern, it probably cannot be entirely avoided, not just because of the adversary nature of the legal system, but because there always will be two legitimate sides to an issue, including child abuse. Over the past few years, there has been a growing advocacy movement on behalf of individuals falsely accused of child sexual abuse. A number of articles have been written on the topic,[33]

---

[32] See, e.g., Goodman & Helgeson, *supra* note 21; Loftus & Cole, *supra* note 21; Melton, *supra* notes 21 and 22.

[33] See, e.g., Green (1986). True and false allegations of sexual abuse in custody disputes, *Journal of the American Academy of Child Psychiatry*, 25, 449; Coleman (1985). False allegations of child sexual abuse: Have the experts been caught with their pants down? Unpublished paper; Schuman (1986). False allegations of physical and sexual abuse, *Bulletin of the American Academy of Psychiatry & Law*, 14, 5; Underwager et al. (1986, Aug.). The role of the psychologist in the assessment of cases of alleged sexual abuse of children. Paper presented at the 94th Annual Convention of the American Psychological Association, Washington, DC; Renshaw (Jan./Feb. 1986). When sex abuse is falsely charged, *The Champion, 10(1)*; Slicker (1986). Child sex abuse: The innocent accused, *Case & Comment, 12*.

and mental health professionals now regularly provide expert testimony for the defense in child sexual abuse cases. It appears, however, that some have gone beyond merely being advocates for a particular side, and have distorted or exaggerated research findings in articles or testimony regarding children as witnesses or false allegations of child sexual abuse, particularly in custody cases.[34] Indeed, several noted researchers and clinicians have recently criticized the increasing frequency of unsupported or exaggerated claims relating to false accusations of child sexual abuse.[35]

Raskin and Yuille (this volume) suggest an approach for interviewing children and assessing the validity of children's statements of sexual abuse based on a procedure that originated in Germany. Unfortunately, in justifying the need for such an approach, they make a number of assertions that are not supported by current research. For example, there have only been a handful of studies regarding false reports of child sexual abuse, all of which have serious methodological flaws.[36] Most agree that the results of these studies cannot be used to generalize about a rate of false reports in this country.[37] Yet Raskin and Yuille state that " . . . in the United States, 8 percent or more of the investigated cases may be fictitious. That could result in 8000 or more serious actions and false prosecutions each year. In cases involving disputed divorce, custody, and visitation issues, the rate of fictitious allegations may be as high as 50 percent."

These authors further state that "domestic relations disputes appear to produce alarming numbers of fictitious accusations." However, the available data regarding custody cases comes from clinical reports involving extremely small, nonrandom samples, and as many have noted, these data cannot be used to make statistical probability projections about the overall rate of false reports in divorce proceedings.[38] Indeed, a major new study of sexual abuse allegations in custody cases indicates that such allegations are a very small percentage of contested cases and that, although deliberately false allegations occur, they are exceedingly rare.[39]

Another study in this book by Leippe, Brigham, Cousins, and Romanczyk examines attorneys' beliefs about child witnesses, finding that attorneys lack awareness of or even disregard new research regarding children's abilities. They found that both prosecuting and defense attorneys perceived

---

[34] See Green, *supra* note 33; Renshaw, *supra* note 33; Slicker, *supra* note 33; Underwager et al. *supra* note 33.

[35] Sink, Studies of true and false allegations: A critical review. In *Sexual abuse allegations in custody and visitation cases* 37, *supra* note 25; Berliner, *supra* note 25.

[36] Corwin, Berliner, Goodman, Goodwin, & White (1986). Child sexual abuse and custody disputes: No easy answers, *Journal of Interpersonal Violence*, *2(1)*, 91; Sink, *supra* note 35; Berliner, *supra* note 25.

[37] *Id.*

[38] Thoennes & Pearson, Summary of findings from the sexual abuse allegations project. In *Sexual abuse allegations in custody and visitation cases*, *1*, *supra* note 25.

[39] *Id.*

five- to nine-year-olds as having poorer memories and greater suggestibility than adults, and that defense attorneys were even more skeptical about children's abilities as witnesses. The situation however, may be much worse than the survey indicates. Not only may defense attorneys be more likely to view children with greater skepticism, but some are disseminating erroneous information despite awareness of current research. For example, in a legal magazine for defense attorneys, a major part of a recent issue was devoted to false allegations of child sexual abuse. In one article written by a doctor, she states:

Facts to consider about a child's testimony:
Children are not born knowing right from wrong, truth from untruth. . . .
Children are suggestible and compliant, especially with parents and those adults they seek to please and protect. . . .
Children can be rehearsed or taught to say things. . . .[40]

In another article, an attorney recently stated that "even some sociologists are beginning to admit that children can make false reports,"[41] quoting an excerpt from an article by Goodman in *The Journal of Social Issues*. Of course, not only was the author wrong about Goodman's profession, but he quoted her totally out of context. The author further stated that "suggestibility of children is a matter of great concern in cases where child sex abuse is alleged, because the child is questioned by a social worker who believes all such allegations are true. . . . In such a setting, the social worker is able to lead a child into making a response that the social worker wants."[42]

The belief that children are highly suggestible coupled with a concern that false allegations of sexual abuse are increasing has led to criticism of interviewing techniques by investigators in child sexual abuse cases. Some have advised against the use of "coercive techniques," defined to include demands or enticements for the truth; providing food, drink, or other tangibles; repetitive questions and multiple interviews; refusal to accept a child's answers; and correcting "wrong" answers.[43] "Behavioral influences" have been cautioned against as well; these include being overly solicitous, being too harsh or cold, offering "inappropriate rewards," or physical caressing.[44] An interviewer who confuses his or her role of investi-

---

[40] Renshaw, *supra* note 33, at 9.
[41] Slicker, *supra* note 33, at 16.
[42] *Id.*
[43] Santilli & White (1987). Guidelines for a structured interviewing approach with child abuse victims: Advantages and disadvantages. Presentation at conference In Search of the Truth: the Child Sexual Abuse Expert in the courtroom, Annenberg Center for Health Sciences at Eisenhower, Rancho Mirage, CA, Oct. 29–31, 1987; Underwager et al., *supra* note 33.
[44] Santilli & White, *supra* note 43.

gator with that of a therapist and the use of leading or suggestive questions are also considered inappropriate.[45]

Although concern about methods of interviewing is legitimate, its effects have been distorted or exaggerated beyond the true scope of the problem. In one court decision, a judge disqualified two children from testifying based on a psychologists's testimony that "each child had been subjected to layers and layers of interviews, questions, examinations, etc., which were fraught with textbook examples of poor interviewing techniques. . . ."[46] The expert in this case is one of a number of professionals in the social science or mental health professions to testify regularly for the defense in child sexual abuse cases. Moreover, this psychologist's recent writings also include dubious assertions, such as the following:

Few children indeed are likely to have either the competence or balefulness to . . . [intentionally lie], although some adolescents may do so. Rather, given the plastic and malleable nature of children, the question is what degree, kind and type of influence has been exerted upon them.[47]

In the Raskin and Yuille chapter, the authors also make statements regarding current investigative techniques for which no evidence is cited. For example, they state that improved methods "are urgently needed to cope effectively with substantial problems that are encountered in the investigation of reported cases of sexual abuse of children. . . ." However, they cite no research showing that there are substantial problems in investigating these cases. The authors mention the dismissal of two highly publicized cases in Minnesota and California as examples of "the problems that may result from poor techniques combined with zealous attempts on the part of caseworkers to prove that the allegations are correct." Yet these are considered to be highly unusual cases and should not be used to generalize about the typical handling of the average child sexual abuse case. These two cases may well be unrepresentative of most cases of child sexual abuse.

Most important, as one journalist has pointed out, although both of these prosecutions were unsuccessful, it does not mean that the children had not been sexually abused.[48] Although these cases have been used to decry what's being done to innocent people, their outcome clearly does not stand for that proposition. As most legal professionals know, criminal pro-

---

[45] Id.; Raskin, D.C., & Yuille, J.C. (in this volume). *Problems in evaluating interviews of children in sexual abuse cases.*

[46] *State v. McKellar*, No. 85-0553 (Haw. Cir. Ct. Jan. 15, 1983).

[47] Underwager et al., *supra* note 33.

[48] Crewdson (1988). *By silence betrayed: Sexual abuse of children in America*; See also Turkle (1988). Dangerous relations, *New York Times Book Review*, Feb. 7, 1988.

secutions may be dismissed for many reasons, and dismissal does not mean the defendant committed no crime. Finally, in the McMartin cases in California, it was not a caseworker, but rather a nationally recognized child sexual abuse expert who interviewed many of the children, and videotaped the interviews.[49] When considered in retrospect, the techniques employed may have been unduly suggestive, but her approach was based on the need to obtain information from young children terrified to disclose what had happened to them. In a recent article, she states:

In the best of all possible worlds, it would be advisable not to ask children leading questions in order to avoid the concern that children are responding to suggestions that certain things occurred or that they are being compliant and acquiescent to an adult authority figure. But, in the best of all possible worlds, children are not sexually assaulted in secrecy, and then bribed, threatened or intimidated not to talk about it. In the real world, leading questions may sometimes be necessary to enable frightened young children to respond and talk about particular subjects.[50]

Moreover, little research has been done to demonstrate that so-called improper interviewing techniques actually lead to false reports of sexual abuse or more importantly, that procedures such as "statement validity assessment" produce accurate and reliable accounts. As one researcher notes, "There are few empirical studies of total fabrication of events, false reports, or the development of the ability to distinguish fact from fantasy. . . . We know of no substantial evidence to support the notion that children frequently fabricate such events."[51] Indeed, Raskin and Yuille indicate that their concern is that most research has focused on the accuracy of children's accounts rather than on their validity. Although few disagree that the number of false reports may be growing, at present there is insufficient evidence that children make more false reports about sexual assault than adults do. One researcher has noted that there is little correlation between age and honesty.[52] Moreover, research in this book and elsewhere indicates that jurors perceive children as equally or more sincere or honest than adults.[53]

Two types of cases that may present special difficulty in terms of assessing their validity, or in which children may be considered less credible, are contested custody cases and cases involving teenagers—the latter described in the study by Duggan, Aubrey, Doherty, Isquith, Levine, and

---

[49] Kee MacFarlane, Director, Child Sexual Abuse Diagnostic Center, Children's Institute International, Los Angeles, California.
[50] MacFarlane (1985). Diagnostic evaluations and the use of videotapes in child sexual abuse cases, *Miami Law Review*, 40, 135, 155.
[51] Loftus & Cole, *supra* note 21, at 180.
[52] Melton, *supra* note 21.
[53] Ross et al. (in this volume). *Age stereotypes, communication modality, and mock jurors' perceptions of the child witness*; Leippe et al., *supra* note 15.

Scheiner presented in this book, as well as in other studies.[54] In all cases, however, child sexual abuse is uniquely difficult to prove; as one researcher has stated, the problem of false reports of child sexual abuse "is particularly difficult to study in the case of child molestation because often the child and offender are the only witnesses, and there may be no other corroborating evidence."[55] Many seem to be searching for some kind of test, like a polygraph, that can establish the veracity or validity of children's statements of sexual abuse. Yet, as one expert notes, there is no known reliable psychological or physiological test or method for determining whether a person has been sexually abused or whether someone has committed an act of sexual abuse.[56] Although clinicians may form professional judgments about whether or not abuse has taken place, most believe they cannot and should not perform a fact-finding role and that their concern is with the effects of sexual abuse on a child or offender.[57] It is the judicial system that makes a legal determination that a child has or has not been abused. Indeed, many clinicians believe that a legal finding should not necessarily affect their professional conclusion that a child was sexually abused.

This author and others are also concerned about the prosecution's growing use of psychological experts who not only provide testimony about typical characteristics of child victims, but also give opinon as to a child's credibility or state that a child was victim of abuse or fits the "child sexual abuse accommodation syndrome."[58] Indeed, a majority of courts do not permit this type of testimony, because it is the trier-of-fact's responsibility to determine the credibility of witnesses and to decide the outcome of the case—whether or not a child was abused.[59] Moreover, a number of California appeals courts recently have applied the *Frye* test when a psychological expert testifies that a child fits the child sexual abuse accommodation syndrome, gives an opinion that a child has been sexually abused, or di-

---

[54] See Goodwin et al. (1982). False allegations and false denials of incest: Clinical myths and chinical realities. In *Sexual abuse: Incest victims and their families*, J. Goodwin, ed. 17; Jones (1987). Reliable and fictitious accounts of sexual abuse to children, *Journal of Interpersonal Violence, 2(1)*, 27. See also articles cited in note 33; Benedek & Schetky (1985). Allegations of sexual abuse in child custody and visitation disputes. In *Emerging issues in child psychiatry and the law*, D. Schetky & E. Benedek, eds.

[55] Loftus & Cole, *supra* note 21.

[56] Berliner, *supra* note 25.

[57] MacFarlane, *supra* note 50, at 156; Berliner, presentation at Conference In Search of the Truth, *supra* note 43; MacFarlane & Bulkley (1982). Treating child sexual abuse: An overview of current program models, *Jorunal of Human Sexuality & Social Work*, 1/2, 69.

[58] Bulkley (1988). Psychological expert testimony in child sexual abuse cases. In *Sexual abuse allegations in custody and visitation cases*, 191, *supra* note 25; Melton (1988). Psychologists' involvement in cases of child maltreatment: Limits of role and expertise, *American Psychologist, 43*.

[59] *Id.*

agnoses that a child has been sexually abused based on the child's behavior with anatomically correct dolls.[60] Many courts apply the *Frye* doctrine when expert testimony is based on a new scientific principle, requiring that it have "gained general acceptance in the particular field to which it belongs."[61]

However, courts disagree over whether psychological expert evidence is a type of scientific evidence or simply expert testimony. In 1984, the California Supreme Court did not apply *Frye* to a psychologist's testimony regarding the accuracy of eyewitness testimony,[62] although the same court earlier held that *Frye* applies to hypnosis,[63] which it called "a new scientific process operating on purely psychological principles." In the eyewitness accuracy decision, the court indicated that *Frye* had never been applied to expert medical testimony, including testimony by psychiatrists, and that it applies only to proof from scientific instruments, procedures, or mechanisms. Indeed, *Frye* typically has been applied to physical tests such as polygraphs, truth serum, bloodtyping, and breathalyzers.

The California Supreme Court also held, however, that rape trauma syndrome expert testimony does not meet the *Frye* test.[64] Moreover, two of the recent child sexual abuse cases in which the *Frye* test was applied found that the child sexual abuse accommodation syndrome had not gained general acceptance in the field as a reliable means of proof that a child had been sexually abused.[65] Like rape trauma syndrome, one court indicated, this syndrome had been developed as a therapeutic tool, not as a method of determining the truth of whether a child had been abused.[66] Another decision also stated that a diagnosis of sexual abuse based on a child's behavior with anatomical dolls and statements of the child constituted a new scien-

---

[60] *In re Amber B.*, 236 Cal. Rptr. 623 (Cal. Ct. App. 1987); *In re Christine C.*, 236 Cal. Rptr. 630 (Cal. Ct. App. 1987); *Seering* v. *Dept. Soc. Serv.*, 239 Cal. Rptr. 422 (Cal. Ct. App. 1987); *In re Sara M.*, No. 68005 (Cal. Ct. App. Aug. 28, 1987). *See also State* v. *Black*, 537 A.2d 1154 (Me. 1988) ("Whether described in terms of indicators, syndromes, patterns, or clinical features, the objective of such evidence is to establish on the basis of present conduct that in the past someone has been subject to a specific trauma. We conclude that the present record fails to demonstrate the scientific reliability of such evidence." (cf. *State* v. *Lawrence*, 541 A.2d 1291 (Me. 1988) (both cases citing the state's decision establishing the *Frye* test, *State* v. *Philbrick*, 436 A.2d 844 (Me. 1981). But see *In re Rinesmith*, 376 N.W.2d 139 (Mich. 1985). (Court said *Frye* does not apply to the use of dolls since it is a tool to permit a child to communicate what she is unable to express verbally. Expert testimony was upheld that violent reaction of dolls indicated *potential* sexual abuse, but not *conclusive* of sexual abuse.)

[61] *Frye v. United States*, 293 F. 1013 (D.C. Cir. 1923).

[62] *People v. McDonald*, 690 P.2d 709 (Ca. 1984).

[63] *People v. Shirley*, 723 P.2d 1354 (Ca. 1982).

[64] *People v. Bledsoe*, 681 P.2d 291 (Ca. 1984).

[65] *In re Sara M.*; *Seering* v. *Dept. of Soc. Serv.*

[66] *In re Sara M.*

tific principle opertating on purely psychological principles, following the hypnosis decision.[67]

Few other courts have applied the *Frye* test to this type of expert testimony. One might argue that the *Frye* test is a convenient vehicle for keeping out this type of psychological expert testimony; the purpose of the *Frye* rule is to ensure the reliability of novel scientific evidence that might unduly impress the trier-of-fact or whose legitimacy the trier-of-fact may not be able to assess independently. Without invoking the *Frye* test, however, courts have easily excluded psychological opinions regarding a child's credibility or that a child has been sexually abused, indicating that such testimony bolsters the witness' credibility, that it invades the province of the jury, or that the testimony's prejudicial effect outweighs its probative value.

Similarly, the method proposed by Raskin and Yuille for evaluating statements of alleged child sexual victims, called "statement validity assessment," should not be used by psychological experts to give an opinion at trial that a child is or is not telling the truth. In Germany, whose legal system differs substantially from ours, the country's highest court held in a 1954 decision that psychological experts must be called to testify at trial as to the truthfulness of the alleged victim, primarily in sex offense cases, when the victim is a child or when no other corroborative evidence exists.[68] Their testimony is generally based on use of the statement validity assessment described by Raskin and Yuille. Additionally, the German statute requires psychologists to be called in to assist the prosecutor in deciding whether or not to file charges in cases involving a child when there is any doubt as to the child's credibility.

In the United States, however, courts would be unlikely to admit an expert's opinion as to a child's truthfulness based on statement validity assessment, either because it fails to meet the *Frye* test since it is a new scientific method of proof that has not gained general acceptance in the scientific community, or because it usurps the trier-of-fact's decision-making authority. As Raskin and Yuille themselves note, research is needed to determine the accuracy rate of this method and the validity of the content criteria by using samples from real cases. Until such time, the proposed statement validity assessment procedure may be valuable to investigators or prosecutors as an investigative tool to assist them in determining if probable cause exists to file charges, but even more than the polygraph, it lacks sufficient

---

[67] *In re Amber B.* See also *People v. Bowker*, No. D004675 (Ca. Ct. App. 4th D. Jul. 29, 1988), which held that general testimony re "child sexual abuse accommodation syndrome" without an opinion whether the child was sexually abused does not meet the *Frye* test, since it was offered to prove the child had been abused, and the syndrome may not be used to determine the truth of a past event.
[68] Undeutsch, Courtroom evaluation of eyewitness testimony, *33 International Review of Applied Psychology*, *51*, 61 (1984).

scientific reliability to be used as evidence in court that a child has or has not been sexually abused.

One means of ensuring that jurors are accurately informed of current research regarding children's abilities as witnesses is through use of experts at trial. Few reported child sexual abuse cases, however, have involved the prosecution's use of psychological experts relating to children's eyewitness abilities or competency to testify. One court permitted an expert to testify as to the victim's ability to distinguish fact from fantasy, indicating that the expert was not giving an opinion about the child's credibility, while another court came to the opposite conclusion.[69] With the burgeoning studies in the area of adult eyewitness accuracy, courts have increasingly considered the admissibility of expert testimony on adult eyewitness research. Although most courts in the past did not admit such testimony, in recent years, some appellate courts have reversed a lower court's failure to admit such evidence.[70]

For example, in a 1984 California Supreme Court decision, *People v. McDonald*, the court held that expert testimony by the defense on psychological factors affecting adult eyewitness accuracy should have been admitted.[71] The court justified its holding on a number of grounds. It indicated that the witness did not give an opinion about the truthfulness of any particular witness, but rather informed the jury of factors that may affect general powers of observation and memory in the typical eyewitness. The expert therefore did not usurp the jury's role of deciding credibility.

The court also noted that an expert opinion may be admitted if it will assist the jury, even if the jury has some knowledge of the subject matter. The court stated that the literature or research indicates that certain issues relating to eyewitness accuracy may be known only to some jurors, and that jurors actually possess misinformation. The court also held that the *Frye* standard does not apply to this type of expert evidence, indicating that *Frye* is more often applied to scientific procedures, mechanisms, or instruments, but not to medical or psychiatric testimony.

The preceding decision, as well as several others, seem to argue for greater use of psychological experts regarding children's eyewitness abili-

---

[69] *State* v. *Pettit*. 675P, ad 183 (or. Ct. App. 1984) (expert opinion allowed as to victim's ability to distinguish fact and fantasy); *U.S. v. Binder* 769F. ad 595 (9th Cir. 1985) (expert opinion not allowed as to victim's ability to distinguish truth and falsehood improper bolstering of victim's credibility and usurps jury's function. Dissent said expert should be allowed as to *ability* to tell the truth not whether witness *is* truthful.)

[70] See, e.g., *State v. Chapple*, 660 P.2d 1208 (Ariz. 1983); *People v. McDonald*, 690 P.2d 709 (Ca. 1984). See also Leippe et al. (in this volume). *The opinions and practices of criminal attorneys regarding child eyewitnesses: A survey*; McCord (1985). The admissibility of expert testimony regarding rape trauma sysndrome in rape prosecutions, *B.C. Law Review*, 26, 1143, 1183.

[71] 690 P.2d 709.

ties in child sexual abuse cases or other cases involving child witnesses. However, if an expert is offered by the prosecution, the testimony would deal with research that supports the premise that children's abilities are better than were once believed. In the adult eyewitness cases, it is usually the defense that seeks to use experts, to show that adult eyewitness abilities are worse than is believed. Unfortunately, because of the adversarial nature of the legal system, if more prosecution experts are permitted to testify, it is likely to open the door for defense experts to testify that children are more suggestible or have less accurate memories than adults.

There have already been several reported court decisions involving defense experts offered to testify on the credibility or competency of a child, and the decisions have gone both ways. In a case in Iowa,[72] the defense was not permitted to obtain a psychological evaluation of the child because "substituting an expert's testimony on the victim's credibility for the jury's own determination of that matter" invades the province of the jury. The court indicated that the majority rule today is that mental health examinations of sex offense complainants may not be ordered unless the defense presents a compelling reason. This decision is similar to those involving prosecution experts who were not permitted to testify as to the child's credibility.

In an Arizona decision,[73] however, a court held that a psychologist offered by the defense was permitted to testify about the victim's credibility, including her truthfulness and reliability, as well as her competency, in a case in which psychological tests indicated the child had an organically based learning disability and showed unusual preoccupation with fantasies of hostility and violence. In this case, the court was dealing with an exception to the general rule disallowing expert opinions regarding a witness' credibility, which permits an expert to testify about a witness' serious mental or physical disorder if it affects his or her competency to testify.

A case in Hawaii discussed earlier best illustrates the problem with using psychological experts relating to children's abilities as witnesses. The court found two children to be incompetent to testify based on the testimony of a psychological expert called by the defense, who testified that because of highly suggestive, repeated, and coercive questioning, the children's memory had been so distorted they were unable to independently recall what had happened. This case once again highlights the distinction often made between adults and children. As two researchers note:

When adults provide eyewitness testimony, we may question their ability to accurately report what they have seen and the extent to which their memories may have been distorted, but we do not routinely suggest that they are fabricating entire incidents, such as a rape, robbery, or accidents. More often, it is suggested that an adult misperceived or misremembered some detail or mistakenly identified the

---

[72] *State* v. *Tharp*, 372 N.W.2d 280 (Iowa Ct. App. 1985).
[73] *State* v. *Roberts*, 677 P.2d 280 (Ariz. Ct. App. 1983).

wrong perpetrator. When a child is involved, however, his or her entire story is sometimes considered suspect, as it was in the Hawaii case.[74]

An interesting feature of the German legal system is that experts are not presented by either side, but are appointed by the court.[75] Indeed, much has been written criticizing the inherent bias of experts who testify for a particular side in our judicial system. Perhaps a solution to the problem would be to provide for court-appointment of experts, at least in cases in which young children are witnesses. Furthermore, if the use of psychological experts by both sides is limited to general testimony about research relating to children's eyewitness abilities, and courts do not permit experts for the prosecution or the defense to give opinions about the credibility of specific witnesses, the dangers of this type of testimony may be reduced.

Another idea for providing accurate information to jurors about children's abilities might be to develop a set of model jury instructions. As the court in the *McDonald* decision indicated, however, typical jury instructions are inadequate to provide the amount of information necessary to explain the issues.[76] Moreover, jury instructions are generally designed to explain issues relating to the law, not to the facts, and therefore are probably inappropriate for communicating this type of data.

The remainder of this discussion focuses on the two major areas covered by this book, jurors' perceptions of child witnesses and children's understanding of the legal system. The research reported here regarding adults' perceptions of children's credibility explores issues missing in previous research. Some researchers previously had recommended that new studies should examine not just the source but also the quality of a child's account, noting that "individual differences in the quality of the accounts provided by young children may be more important that the age of the eyewitness per se."[77] As many of the authors of this volume note, although previous studies have been mixed, most indicated that jurors have a generally negative view of children's eyewitness abilities. Perhaps the single most important finding to emerge from the new studies in this book is that a child's age indeed may be less important than the quality of a particular child's testimony at trial, especially when it violates a juror's negative stereotype or expectations of children. The negative effect of age, this research shows, may be mitigated by other positive qualities or characteristics of a child witness.

The other interesting issue explored in this book is that other variables, in addition to characteristics of the child, may affect perceptions of a child's

---

[74] Loftus & Cole, *supra* note 21, at 180.
[75] Undeutsch, *Statement reality analysis*, in *Reconstructing the past—The role of psychologists in criminal trials* (A. Trankell ed. 1982).
[76] 690 P.2d at 733.
[77] Melton, *supra* note 29, at 214.

credibility, including the type or nature of case, the nature of the evidence, characteristics of jurors (e.g., sex, socioeconomic status), communication modality, or the real-life effect of the child's testimony on the child or the offender.

The finding that certain qualities of a child's testimony may be better predictors of a child's credibility than age corresponds with a similar emerging belief that explains the accuracy of memory or suggestibility of witnesses. As one researcher recently noted:

> . . . we believe that age is not a special variable for purposes of predicting or explaining variance in eyewitness memory accuracy. There are numerous other variables alone or in combination that may account for as much or more of the variance in accuracy or eyewitness memory than does age.[78]

Some of these variables have been mentioned by a number of researchers, including the following (1) an event may be brief or a one-time occurrence; (2) the delay between or event and questioning may be short; (3) an event may be neutral, without personal significance or interest; (4) a witness may be a bystander, not an active participant or victim; (5) questions may be about peripheral information; and (6) an event may be stressful.[79]

In this book, several factors were shown to have a significant mediating effect on age in terms of jurors' perceptions of a child's credibility. First, Ross et al. (this volume) found that adults perceive children as equally honest or more honest than adults, a finding consistent with past research.[80] More importantly, two studies—one by Ross and one by Goodman—indicate that the nature of the case may affect whether honesty or cognitive abilities is the more important issue in deciding a child's credibility. In some cases, as illustrated by one of Goodman's studies, when accuracy of memory is considered critical, a young child's lack of cognitive abilities may reduce his or her credibility. According to Goodman, however, in cases in which honesty is more important, such as sexual assault cases involving a younger child and a perpetrator known to the child, the child's lack of cognitive abilities may enhance his or her credibility. In the other study by Goodman in this volume, which involved a written description of a child sexual assault case, a six-year-old witness was perceived as more credible than a twenty-two-year-old. In the Duggan study involving a mock child sexual abuse trial, both the nine- and five-year-olds were perceived as more credible than the thirteen-year-old. These studies indicate that in many cases of child sexual abuse, younger children's honesty combined with lack of cognitive abilities may make them more credible witnesses.

---

[78] Turtle & Wells, *supra* note 29, at 235.
[79] See Goodman et al., *supra* note 29; Loftus & Cole, *supra* note 21; Turtle & Wells, *supra* note 29; Melton, *supra* note 29.
[80] See *supra* note 53.

Many researchers hav begun to raise the issue that most experimental techniques used to test child witnesses lack "real-world applicability" or "ecological validity."[81] Turtle and Wells note that many laboratory tests use recognition tasks and test recognition and identification accuracy, which are not crucial issues in many cases of child sexual abuse.[82] The authors further note that questioning of child victims in a trial or an interview normally requires greater free recall ability on the part of the child, an area in which young children are weaker than adults. As these authors point out, research that explores methods of interviewing or questioning children that enhance the completeness of their recall would be valuable.

In general, one recommendation for future research is to "develop acceptable retrieval techniques that maximize the accuracy and usefulness of children's testimony, while at the same time, ensuring the defendant's right to due process."[83] Indeed, in the Goodman and Wells studies in this book, the authors found that jurors are not always able to distinguish between accurate and inaccurate testimony of children, a finding that has surfaced in jurors' perceptions of adult as well. These studies underscore the need to find methods for improving the accuracy as much as the credibility of younger children's accounts. Goodman found that older children, in this case six-year-olds as opposed to three-year-olds, were perceived as more accurate than they in fact were. Wells also found that eight-year-olds, compared with twelve-year-olds and college students, were perceived as having greater accuracy than they actually had. In both studies, the children's confidence enhanced their credibility, as well as their perceived accuracy, although their actual accuracy was much lower.

The Wells and Nigro studies found that two characteristics of child witnesses or qualities of a child's actual testimony—confidence and powerfulness of speech style—may be more important factors than age in predicting their credibility. Wells and Duggan were especially interested in the effect of a child providing actual testimony in a courtroomlike setting, unlike previous research in which the same scripted testimony is given by both an adult and a child and the testimony is written rather than oral. In the Wells study, eight-year-olds were found to be more credible "real witnesses"; that is, they provide better testimony than the negative stereotype of an eight-year-old's abilities. They found that both child and adult witnesses who were perceived as more confident were also perceived as more credible and accurate.

In one of the only studies to date to simulate a child sexual abuse trial,

---

[81] Goodman et al. (in this volume). Determinants of the child victim's perceived credibility; Turtle & Wells, *supra* note 29, at 236; Melton, *supra* note 29; Ceci, Ross, & Toglia, *Suggestibility of children's memory: Psycho-legal implications*, *supra* note 29.

[82] Turtle & Wells, *supra* note 29, at 237.

[83] *Id.*, at 238. See also Cole & Loftus, *supra* note 21, at 207.

the Duggan et al. experiment illustrates the type of research that will be most applicable to real cases. In this and the Goodman study of a child sexual assault case, the authors were interested in reactions of jurors to child victims. Little research exists on jurors' perceptions of child sexual abuse victims, who represent the majority of witnesses who will testify in criminal prosecutions. Duggan et al. found that a higher percentage of jurors handed down guilty verdicts with nine-year-olds (81 percent) and five-year-olds (75 percent) than with thirteen-year-olds (65 percent). This study did not, however, have an adult comparison group. The study's most interesting finding was that teenagers were viewed with greater skepticism than the younger children; the teenagers' credibility was perceived as more like that of adult rape victims. As noted earlier, the Goodman study found that younger child sex offense victims may be perceived as more credible because they lack certain cognitive abilities, particularly knowledge of sexual acts and ability to act revengeful.

The Saywitz and Warren-Leubecker et al. studies provide some of the first data on children's understanding of the legal system, an area that many have argued needs studying.[84] Their findings are not especially surprising, but they seem to provide fairly strong evidence that older children generally possess more knowledge of the legal process, that certain essential concepts of our legal system such as attorneys, courts, and judges are not accurately understood by children under eight, and that concepts such as jury are not understood before the age of twelve years.

The studies on juror's perceptions of children's credibility provide new evidence that children can be credible and effective witnesses, particularly when they are under ten years old in cases of sexual abuse or when they provide testimony in a confident or forceful manner. Moreover, two studies confirm empirically that children lack an understanding of basic aspects of the legal system, which is likely to negatively affect their performance as witnesses as well as their credibility. These results seem to provide much-needed preliminary empirical support for the legal system's adoption of special approaches to dealing with child victim-witnesses. As noted earlier, a number of jurisdictions in the past five to ten years have reformed their legal procedures for dealing with child victims in a number of ways. Many jurisdictions prepare child witnesses for trial, explain the legal process to them, or provide a victim advocate or guardian *ad litem* for the child.[85] Many have trained investigators and prosecutors who are sensitive to a child's needs and developmental levels, and attempt to minimize the number of interviews of the child with different professionals.[86]

---

[84] Melton, *supra* note 29, 219–221; Goodman. The child witness: Conclusions and future directions for research and legal practice, *Journal of Issues, 40(2)*, 157, 166.
[85] See Bulkley et al. (1981). Innovations in the prosecution of child sexual abuse cases, American Bar Association.
[86] *Id.*

Still, much research is needed. Although the new research indicates that, for example, young children do not understand basic features of the legal system, the authors point out that research is needed to determine whether pretrial preparation and education of young children can improve a child's understanding of the legal system or whether children simply have not reached a level of maturity to have the moral reasoning necessary to understand legal concepts. Further research is needed to determine whether improving a child's understanding through pretrial preparation actually results in less trauma to the child and improves performance and accuracy as a witness.[87] As noted earlier, several studies are underway to evaluate the impact of various aspects of legal intervention and reforms on a child's emotional well-being and on the outcome of cases.

As noted previously, research regarding methods of enhancing children's accuracy or of reducing inaccuracies would also be valuable. For example, repeated interviews are considered traumatic for children, but little research has been done on their effect on the accuracy of later accounts given by a child. In this book Raskin and Yuille note one study that indicates greater inaccuracies after repeated interviews.

Research that explores techniques for maximizing accuracy and increasing completeness of a child's recall would be most helpful, and perhaps a better focus of efforts than studying the rate of false reports or testing the validity of children's statements of sexual abuse. This is particularly true for younger children. Indeed, research presented in this book indicates that jurors perceive older children, for example six-year-olds or eight-year-olds compared to three-year-olds, as more credible. Wells specifically notes that the finding that confident eight-year-olds may be better witnesses than the negative stereotype of this age may not apply to younger children. Research with preschool-age children indicates their somewhat greater suggestibility, especially with adults. Moreover, as noted earlier in this discussion, although judges may have relatively little difficulty in permitting eight-year-olds to testify, preschoolers or early-school-age children are likely to cause greater problems. Additional research with children from ages three to seven years would be beneficial, since this is the age group that jurors perceive as less credible, whose memory, accuracy, and suggestibility may be more problematic, and who attorneys and judges are most likely to consider incompetent or subject to *voir dire.*

---

[87] See Saywitz (in this volume), "Children's Conceptions of the Legal System: 'Court Is a Place to Play Basketball'"; Warren-Leubecker et al. (in this volume), "What Do Children Know about the Legal System and When Do They Know It? First Steps Down a Less Traveled Path in Child Witness Research."

11
Research on Children's Eyewitness Testimony: Perspectives on Its Past and Future

DAVID DUNNING

The previous authors have well chronicled the impressive growth of legal cases involving the child eyewitness occurring from the 1970s through the 1980s. Equally impressive is the explosion of psychological research on the child witness. The stereotype of social science, held by some in the legal community and by some psychologists themselves, is of a field that moves slowly from definition of the issues to experimentation to reanalysis and theoretical refinement—often reaching its conclusions far after the legal community has finished dealing with the matter. On the topic of the child eyewitness, however, we have seen numerous studies on a variety of child eyewitness concerns. Social scientists have observed and documented the course of child witness suggestibility (Ceci, Ross, & Toglia, 1987; see also Ceci, Toglia, & Ross, 1987). They have also completed several studies, including a wide range of stimuli and circumstances, on juror perceptions of the child witness (Duggan et al.; Goodman et al.; Leippe et al.; Nigro et al.; Ross et al.; Wells et al., all in this volume; see also Goodman et al., 1987; Leippe & Romanczyk, 1987). In this volume, we see work on how well children understand the legal process (Saywitz; Warren-Leubecker et al., both this volume). We have also seen in this volume a first attempt at assessing whether child witnesses are offering accurate or fallacious accounts of their experiences (Raskin & Yuille, this volume).

This chapter attempts to pull together some themes and conclusions suggested by the work of the previous authors in this volume. It then proposes that this past work reveals the task of the social scientist interested in child eyewitness testimony is hardly complete; kernels of observations present in the previous chapters suggest new issues that social scientists must address if they wish to give a complete picture of the child as witness in the criminal justice system. In short, although the work chronicled in the previous chapters settles many issues, it also reveals many more challenges left for both the social science and legal communities.

Juror Perceptions and Child Eyewitness Performance

Many of the chapters in this volume focus on perceptions of the child witness. Most frame this question in terms of whether jurors (and legal professionals, for that manner) perceive the testimony of a child as less credible than comparable testimony proffered by an adult. Before specifically reviewing the research presented in this volume, it is appropriate to summarize past work on children's actual performance when faced with eyewitness tasks. In the past, three sources of potential difficulty have been investigated.

Completeness and Accuracy of Child Eyewitness Testimony

The most relevant question one could ask about child eyewitness testimony is whether children provide accounts that are both accurate and complete. In a typical study, Saywitz (1987) asked third, sixth, and ninth graders to read a story about a crime (e.g., a burglary) and then to recount the story both in free recall and recognition formats. Relative to older children, third graders (about seven to eight years old) provided less complete reports and added more embellishments to their accounts. The proportion of accurate to inaccurate statements, however, was not reliably different across age groups, nor were there any differences in performance on recognition questions. Wells et al. (this volume) also indirectly studied the performance of eight-, ten-, and twelve-year-old children called to testify about an alleged kidnapping they had seen on videotape. Under direct examination, the age groups performed comparably. But under cross-examination, the accuracy of the eight-year-olds suffered. In sum, it appears that younger children do provide less complete and accurate testimony, although the deficit is small and depends on the type of questions confronted.

Susceptibility to Misleading Information

A greater volume of research has concentrated on whether child eyewitness testimony can be misled. Here the evidence is more compelling. A series of studies by Ceci, Ross, & Toglia (1987) exposed children to misleading information after they had been presented with a story to be recalled later. As the age of the children decreased—from twelve to three years—their susceptibility to misleading information rose dramatically. Other research has reached similar conclusions (King & Yuille, 1987; though see Zaragoza, 1987, for a failure to find this decrement).

Ability to Tell Reality from Fantasy

A third area of research has concentrated on *reality monitoring*, that is, the ability to tell actual events from ones merely imagined (see Johnson & Raye, 1981). Research focused on children has indicated that children of age eight years have a rather fully developed (though imperfect) ability to distinguish what they have experienced from what they have imagined (Johnson, Raye, Hasher, & Chromiak, 1979). But below age eight, deficits in this ability begin to show. For example, in some experiments children have been asked either to say a word or simply to imagine saying it (Foley, Johnson, & Raye, 1983). Six-year-olds have relatively greater difficulty than older children in distinguishing between what was said and what was imagined (see also Foley & Johnson, 1985).

In sum, age is associated with some deficits of memory ability. Younger children remember less in free recall, are more easily misled, and are more likely to fail to distinguish reality from imagination than older children and adults. It should be noted, however, that these age differences are not dramatic. Indeed, at any particular age level there exist wide variations in memory performance (see Wells et al., this volume).

The Perceptions of Jurors

But are jurors cognizant of these age trends and their relative strength (or lack thereof)? And, given the wide variation in accuracy for witnesses in the same age group, are jurors able to pick out who in the age group is accurate and who is mistaken? This was the focus of the major portion of this book.

A casual reading of the work presented here presents a muddled picture of juror perceptions of the child witness. First, there is the work of Goodman et al. (this volume). In the first study they report, children who had received a shot at a clinic were asked to testify about and identify the nurse who had given them a shot. When videotapes of the various children's testimony were shown to college students, these mock jurors perceived the older children be to more accurate and credible—in line both with patterns of actual performance, as reviewed here, and our intuitions and stereotypes of how jurors should react to children. This finding is also consistent with those of Goodman et al. (1987), who discovered that child witnesses were perceived as less credible than adults in a case involving a hit-and-run car accident.

But other research in this volume finds the exact opposite result—the younger the witness the more credible. Ross et al. (this volume) presented college students with a case (either videotaped or written) in which a child, young adult, or elderly witness testified that he or she had seen illegal drugs in a neighbor's house. Subject-jurors viewed the child witness as the *most* truthful and honest, the elderly as next credible, and the young adult as least. Nigro et al. (this volume) also reported the same, at first counterintuitive, finding. The eight-year-old witness in their mock trial was seen as more credible that the twenty-five-year old one, although only when witnesses used "powerful" speech—that is, they spoke confidently and without hesitation. Duggan et al. (this volume) discovered the same pattern of responses in their elaborate study of child witness credibility. In a case involving possible child sexual abuse, subject jurors held the five- and nine-year-old witnesses as more credible than the thirteen-year-old. Finally, Goodman et al. (this volume), after conducting a study in which younger children are seen as less credible, conducted an experiment in which a young child was seen as more credible than those older. This case, like that of Duggan et al., involved a suspected sexual assault.

But before discussing these findings, it is important to note that Wells et al. (this volume) conducted a study, employing children who were allowed to use their own words, in which younger children (eight years old) were seen as *equally* credible to older ones (twelve years old). In some sense, this is a null finding; but Wells et al. propose that their study is best understood as one containing some situations in which younger children are seen as less credible and others in which younger children are seen as more so. In sum, their study can be understood as one in which both findings of other studies were found at the same time, canceling each other out.

The only predictable finding on this topic presented in this volume concerns the perceptions of defense attorneys and prosecutors, who each seem to adhere to a "party line". Both attorney groups reported that five- to nine-year-olds were likely to remember fewer details about a crime, be unable to identify a perpetrator, and be more susceptible to suggestion. However, defense attorneys were much more likely to report that children possessed these deficiencies than prosecutors, who portrayed the child as only slightly less able than the adult. Defense attorneys also viewed the child witness as just as likely to be dishonest as an adult, whereas prosecutors saw the child as particularly sincere.

Reconciling the Contradictory Findings

Without a careful reading of this book, a social scientists could not help but fear the following scenario: A lawyer assigned to a case involving a child witness calls the researcher to have lunch to discuss the issue. At lunch, the lawyer asks the psychologist a question of straightforward interest: "Would jurors believe a child as much as an adult?" The social scientist, armed with the rich array of data presented here and elsewhere, would be forced to answer clearly and concisely with the following: "Well, you see, it all depends. Sometimes jurors disbelieve the child. Sometimes they believe the testimony of a child more than an adult offering comparable testimony.

And there is a third possibility—sometimes they believe each equally." It is easy to imagine the lawyer, on hearing this "it all depends" conclusion, rolling his or her eyes to the high heavens and wishing that social scientists would just once provide a clear and usable bottom line.

But although they furnish contradictory data, each chapter provides, either directly or indirectly, a single coherent analysis that states when children will be seen as more or less credible than adults. That is, if the lawyer in the preceding lunch allowed the social scientist to expound a little longer, he or she would learn that the field already knows a great deal about what child credibility "depends on." The analysis rests on two observations.

Cognitive Competence versus Honesty

Several of the researchers in the present volume have noted that credibility rests on two components: the cognitive competence of the witness and the witness' sincerity.

On the matter of cognitive competence, the credibility of the child witness suffers. And if the credibility of the child witness depends more on his or her ability to remember, jurors will likely not perceive the child as believable. Such a case might be one in which the child is a mere bystander to events that latter may be recalled (e.g., witnessing a car accident). In cases involving these circumstances (see, e.g., Goodman et al., 1987), research has shown that the child witness is less credible.

But children are seen as more honest than adults or, rather, likely not to harbor ulterior motives when providing testimony. For some types of cases, such as sexual abuse cases, jurors might consider the issue of ulterior motives. If that is the case, then jurors have a potential reason to discount the testimony of the adult but not the child witness—and then view the child as more credible. This analysis inspired the design and supports the results of Goodman et al. reported in this volume. In a sexual abuse case involving a teacher and student, subject-jurors viewed the eight-year-old as unlikely to make up an abuse story (as an eigtheen-year-old might) for purposes of vengeance. The results of Duggan et al. (this volume) reconfirm this analysis. In their study of alleged sexual assault, thirteen-year-old witnesses were seen as potentially responsible for the events they experienced, and also were seen as being less credible than their younger counterparts.

But it should be noted that there are some instances in which children might be seen as more likely to provide dishonest testimony. Consider an incident in which a child has been injured on a swing set. In any liability case, a paramount issue would be whether the child used the swing set inappropriately. It is easy to imagine a child lying in this case to avoid punishment. If that is the case, jurors might give less credence to the testimony of a child that to testimony proferred by an adult—a finding already described in current research focusing on an incident much like this example (Jones & Lee, 1988).

The Competence of the Child

The second component of analysis involves the specific behavior of the child witness. Does the witness act like a kid, as jurors would expect? Or does the child violate every tenant of the juror's stereotype? Several authors have suggested that if the child acts in accordance with the juror's stereotype (e.g., is confused on the stand, unconfident, inarticulate), then jurors will assume their expectations about accuracy will hold. If the child violates those expectations (e.g., by appearing confident, alert, maybe even correcting an attorney's grammar), then the child will be seen as peculiarly precocious and credible. Indeed, Nigro et al. (this volume) give particular credence to this analysis. In their experiment, it was only when the child witness employed "powerful" speech (i.e., no hesitations or hedges) that jurors viewed him or her as more credible than an adult.

This reasoning is consistent with classic and recent research on the influence of stereotypes on social judgment (see Jussim, Coleman, & Lerch, 1987; Manis, Nelson, & Shedler, 1988). Judgments of the child will *assimilate* toward the stereotype of the child when the actual behavior of the child is close to the stereotype. Conversely, judgments will *contrast* away from the stereotype when the observed performance lies beyond that allowed by the stereotype.

Usefulness of This Analysis for Real-World Contexts

Armed with this analysis and the specific characteristics of any case, it is clear that a legal professional can glean quite a bit of "useful" information from this book. If the relevant case involves sexual abuse, a child is likely to be seen as particularly credible. If the child is rather unconfident, then the jury might be prone to discount the testimony offered. Indeed, the research in this book could be well used by an attorney to add to or take away from the credibility of the child witness. If one wishes the child to appear credible, highlight the child's capacity for honesty. If one wishes to impugn the credibility of the child, focus on a lack of ability to remember. It appears from Leippe et al.'s research (this volume) that a number of these tactics are already employed by practicing attorneys dealing with child witnesses on a day-to-day basis. For example, if the child witness is presenting testimony favorable to an attorney's side, the attorney emphasizes the positive aspects of our stereotypes about children (i.e., their honesty). If the child is a witness from the opposing side, attorneys report pointing out negative aspects of the stereotype (e.g., inability to remember) and may even attempt to fluster or confuse the child witness on the stand.

The Issue of Calibration

But in a sense, the research reported here on the credibility of the child witness has been "framed" in a slightly irrelevant way. That is, perceptions of the child witness have been framed against, or rather compared to, perceptions of adult witnesses. This does confirm the negative stereotype that laypeople, and potential jurors, have of the child witness. It also highlights the dimensions (e.g., honesty) that jurors consider important in judgments about child witnesses. However, the question of whether or not jurors discount the testimony of children over that of adults is, perhaps, not as important as the question of whether jurors discount the testimony of children (and adults) when need be—that is, when the witness is inaccurate.

In short, future research could profit by framing jurors' perceptions against the "truth." Are expectations about the fallibility of childhood memory reflected in comparisons of actual memory performance of children to adults? Are children more honest than adults, as juror-subjects believe? Most important, do jurors hold the witness (either adult or child) as credible when they should—that is, when the witness is accurate?

To date, we have little research comparing the perceptions of jurors to the actual performance of child and adult witnesses. Thus, the question of "calibration" between juror expectations and actual performance could be a useful avenue for future research. Indeed, the work of Wells et al. in this volume serves as a good start. In that research children, acting as witnesses, viewed a videotape of a rather ecologically valid playground scene. In the tape, a child entered a car driven by an adult and was taken away. Later, when asked to testify about this staged "kidnapping," the testimony of eight-year-old witnesses, relative to those of ten- and twelve-year-olds, suffered during cross-examination. College students, serving as mock jurors, who viewed the testimony of the children tended to overbelieve these eight-year-old witnesses.

It should be noted that the special "wrinkle" of this research is not only that it documents when children are more fallible than adults (as has been done in previous research; see Ceci, Ross, & Toglia, 1987), but also that it assesses whether juror perceptions are in line with actual performance. If juror perceptions do accurately reflect the abilities of children in general or of a particular child witness, we can rest assurred that the legal system is functioning properly. But if the perceptions of jurors are miscalibrated, the fact must be brought out and ameliorated.

In a sense, the results of any research calibrating juror judgments with actual performance can be presaged. The Wells et al. research here, as well as that of Goodman et al. (this volume), suggests that jurors are hopelessly miscalibrated. When assessing credibility, jurors give great weight to the level of confidence exhibited by the witness, as well as to other irrelevant indicators such as memory for peripheral details (see Lindsay, Wells, &

Rumpel, 1981; Wells, Lindsay, & Ferguson, 1979). Unfortunately, time and again, it has been shown that indicators such as witness confidence correlate only weakly with accuracy, if at all (for reviews, see Loftus, 1979; Wells & Loftus, 1984). If this is the state of affairs in the legal system, then the question of calibration, for all intents and purposes, is already settled and the most useful approach for future research (discussed later) would be to find ways to *improve* the association between perception and actual reliability of testimony.

Children's Perceptions of the Court and Legal Process

Other chapters in this volume focused on children's understanding of trial procedure and the court (Saywitz; Warren-Leubecker et al., both this volume). In a fascinating series of surveys, these researchers consistently found that children have, at best, only a skeletal comprehension of what a trial is all about. As some of the researchers observed, a few children believe a *court* is a place to play basketball and others thought that *jury* was something worn around the neck. Other consistencies arose from these surveys. For example, children come to understand the concept of *judge* and *police* before they comprehended the role of the *jury*. Some legal terms, such as *arraign*, were never understood (not surprising, since these terms would trip up many adults as well).

Given this pandemic lack of understanding, the course of future research becomes clear: To what degree can children be *educated* about the role of the court and the particular role of the witness in the legal process? Can children be taught about the role of the jury, and at what age? When can misperceptions about the judge's role be cleared up? The answers to these sorts of questions have obvious importance to any practitioner dealing with child witnesses in the courts.

The answers would also be theoretically significant. As mentioned in one of the chapters, an understanding the roles of the judge, jury, and trial would depend to an important degree on moral understanding in general and comprehension of punishment in particular (see Tapp & Kohlberg, 1971). If children believe that any bad act, whether intentional or not, will be punished, then they would never understand the role of the trial in punishment and its goal of determining intention. To the extent that children to understand the importance of intention in punishment, the reasoning behind the trial process can be made clear to them.

In some sense, the reports published in the preceding chapters give us contradictory evidence about the "trainability" of children on legal matters. Recall that in Saywitz, chapter (this volume), the researchers compared the understanding of "experienced" children (e.g., those who had made contact with the legal system) to that of children who had never encountered a court or a trial. Experienced children had no more knowledge about the legal system than did inexperienced ones. The researchers noted the difficulty of interpreting this finding, since most experienced children in their sample came from disadvantaged and less intact homes.

But when Saywitz (this volume) explored the role of television viewing on understanding of the legal system, she found that children who watched a lot of TV understood more about the role of trial and judge than those who did not. Indeed, part of the increase in comprehension from five- to fourteen-year-olds was explained by an increase in television watching. This finding suggests that children are educable about the legal system— indeed, the networks and television producers are already carrying out an informal training program in our living rooms. But as Saywitz was wise to point out, this informal training might convey as many falsehoods (e.g., the role of the lawyer is to find the real perpetrator, like Perry Mason does) as truths.

Future research might also focus more specifically on children's understanding of their specific role as *witness*. Do they believe that the judge or jury actually punishes the defendant? Do children believe that they can be punished for what they say or do on the stand? Do children believe that the witness has the power to punish? The research reported in the chapters here began to address these issues, but they remain largely unexplored.

Future Research: On the Social Aspects of Eyewitness Testimony

The notion of education and trainability, as well as the surveys of attorney's impressions of the child witness, brings up a fundamental issue at the heart of research on the child witness. Specifically, though the recall of a memory is inherently an act of cognition, this act occurs in a complex and often confusing social context. Getting involved in the legal system is complex drama involving many roles, actors, directors, and scripts. Children are sensitive not only to what they remember, but also to their understanding of their role, the potential wants and needs of the people around them, and the goals they believe the legal community possesses. Providing eyewitness testimony is, thus, also an inherent social task—and that aspect must not be forgotten in any future research.

Indeed, past research on eyewitness suggestibility has already implicated the importance of social factors. For example, when Ceci, Ross, & Toglia (1987) investigated whether the testimony of child witnesses could be altered by misleading information, they found that children's reports were swayed more by misleading information given by an adult than by that of child. That is, children were sensitive to the authority of the individual questioning them. Other research focusing on the authority of the questioner has found the same effect for adults as well (Dodd & Bradshaw, 1980; Smith & Ellsworth, 1987).

What social factors might we need to investigate? Some are suggested by the common stereotype held of the child witness, who is seen as eager to please any interrogator. Is that the case? Do child witnesses pick up on the hypotheses or wishes of the criminal justice officer or attorney questioning them? Do they shape their testimony to please those individuals? And what is the developmental course of this eagerness to please—if it exists? Do older children resist it or succumb to it to a greater degree? Assessing the developmental course of this "eagerness" to please is an important issue, especially given the finding of Hughes and Grieve (1980) that children will strive to provide answers to blatantly bizarre questions.

It should be noted that adults show tendencies to please their interrogators as well. It is well known in attitude survey research, for example, that survey respondents offer an opinion (e.g., "what is your leaning on the Monetary Control Bill, or the Metallic Metals Act?") even when the issue is completely fictitious (for a review, see Schuman & Presser, 1981). Also, in court proceedings, adults are sensitive to the desires and wishes of "our side" versus "their side." The extent of this tendency was illustrated by Vidmar and Laird (1983). In their experiment, subject-witnesses saw a slide show of a fight at a bar and were later called to testify. Some of these witnesses, randomly determined, were subpoenaed by the plaintiff in the case, some by the defendant. Witnesses tended to provide testimony that was perceived as favorable to the side that had called on them, even though witnesses had received no special preparation of their testimony in either group.

The issue that children may strive to please their interrogators suggests other specific avenues of research. Recall in the survey of practicing defense and prosecuting attorneys that the bulk of cases involving child witnesses centered on domestic abuse and violence. If that is the case, then the dynamics of social influence in the family becomes a paramount issue (Belsky, 1981; Zilbach, 1968). Are children reluctant to provide testimony about family members? Or, if family members conflict over what they want the child to do, to whom, if anyone, does the child defer? How eager are children to please strangers in this context? In a sense, researchers addressing these issues may wish to avoid studying the "normal" or happy family, since a disproportionately large share of the cases being brought before the courts involve families in strife, or in conflict, or in which violence and abuse has become the norm. In a sense, whether or not a child renders accurate testimony may not depend on his or her cognitive abilities as much as on the social dynamics of the abusive family syndrome.

Beyond the issue of whether children pick up on the interrogator's motives (whether or not any actually exist), little research has focused on the efficacy of any particular questioning technique for child witnesses. Indeed, only one study has explicitly addressed the issue on the adult side. In that study, Lipton (1977) compared the usefulness of four types of questioning procedures to elicit testimony that was both accurate and complete: free recall (e.g., just tell what happened), open-ended queries (e.g., asking witnesses to describe various aspects of the crime in their own words), leading questions (e.g., queries about specific aspects of the crime, e.g., did the perpetrator have a gun), and multiple-choice questions. The technique of leading questions was by far the best in ensuring accurate and complete testimony. But it is this type of questioning (e.g., "Did the thief wear a hat?" "Did he hit Mary?") that many fear as too suggestive for the child witness. The prospect of using more nondirective questioning (e.g., free recall), however, does not appear, from Lipton's data, to be useful—even adults tend to provide incomplete testimony when faced with such vague queries.

Other issues become prominent when questioning techniques are considered. In past research on suggestibility, children have been asked questions that are rather unambiguous (e.g., "Did Johnny take the toy rabbit or the paint set?"), and are asked those questions only once. In the legal system, the questions asked children are not that clear-cut (e.g., "Did he touch you?") and children are asked to give their testimony repeatedly. This repetition opens up the potential for two problems: First, children might begin to confabulate when asked to repeat their testimony more than once. Second, and more troubling, testimony might be "shaped." That is, in first interview, the child might be led to give information that is only slightly inaccurate. On the second interview, when that information is followed up on, more inaccuracies might be built around the first. Slowly, but surely, the inaccuracies might become more and more prevalent. In the end, what might at one time have been a small error could become a large, though unintentional, error. Given the ambiguous nature of the questions asked children, and the repetitious quality of questioning, the issue of shaping should be addressed.

The questioning process, from the perspective of the child, is also somewhat more complex than was traditionally considered. Namely, the child not only must report what he or she has seen and experienced, but must be able to tell when the questionner has an accurate understanding. This last step is not automatic. Classic studies of egocentrism (see Piaget & Inhelder, 1956), although discredited in many of their specific claims, and new work on conceptual perspective taking (e.g., Taylor, 1988) reveal that children often believe that other people know as much as they do—almost automatically—about a stimulus. In studies conducted by Taylor, for example, children are shown a picture of a boat, which is then almost completely covered up. When children are asked what they see, they respond that they see a boat. When asked what another person walking into the room would see if they viewed the almost completely obscured (indeed, unrecognizable) boat, the child respond that that other individual would also see a boat.

This pattern of responses is reminiscent of those found in the present volume by Warren-Leubecker et al. In their study, children were presented with a scenario in which a young child, Joshua, was caught looking at a burning school building with a cigarette lighter in his hand (which had been put there by the actual arsonist). When asked what Joshua should do when caught, a majority of five-year-olds suggested that Joshua simply explain that he did not set the fire, and this statement would be sufficient. According to the authors, this sort of response reveals that children cannot understand how someone else "might see it differently." In sum, children have little appreciation of the other person's level of understanding in a conversation. Indeed, they often believe that the other person understands "everything" completely. This belief prompts two problems: (1) children will tend to give incomplete reports and (2) not be able to recognize misconceptions on the part of their interrogator.

Notes on the Approach to Future Research

Before ending this commentary, it would be appropriate to consider a few notes about the difficulties of translating eyewitness research, whether on adults or children, into knowledge that can be easily applied by the legal system. In a sense, psychological research on eyewitness testimony takes on a descriptive or *passive* cast. By that, I mean that researchers in their laboratories and field studies merely act as observers on the legal process, passively attempting to discovering which variables (e.g., age, stress, crime seriousness) affect eyewitness accuracy in the natural course of the legal process. There is, in contrast, little work in which researchers cast themselves as *active* participants in the legal system, attempting to find ways that the accuracy of the eyewitness can be influenced and hopefully enhanced.

The passive role that researchers take for themselves limits the applicability of their research in the legal community. Indeed, this passive observational role limits the actual participation of social scientists in the legal system to that of the expert witness. That is, without research on ways to enhance the accuracy of eyewitness testimony directly, the only manner in which the social scientist can contribute to a legal determination of witness accuracy is to testify a trial, attempting to educate jurors about the role (or lack thereof) of naturally occurring variables on the testimony of the relevant eyewitness.

Limiting the contribution of the social scientist to expert testimony has serious drawbacks; not the least of which is the fact, documented by the survey of practicing attorneys presented in this volume (Leippe et al.), that lawyers are reticent about employing expert witnesses. Not only that, but in some legal jurisdictions (e.g., Florida) the courts themselves share that reluctance. In some sense, this lack of enthusiasm for expert testimony is not unfounded. It is quite difficult for an attorney, who must present the evidence in the light most favorable to his or her side, to deal with a scientist committed to offering data in all its muddling complexity. In addition, the use of social scientists as witnesses always generates the possibility of a "battle of experts."

If lawyers are relunctant to employ social science data in the form of expert testimony, is there a way to modify our methods to make the legal community more enthusiastic "consumers," without losing hold of the basic theoretical concerns that originally attract researchers to the legal domain?

What Do Lawyers Really Want?

Talking to a practicing attorney is a useful way to determine how the legal community could become more enthusiastic supporters of social science research. The attorney is invariably disinterested in the goals of current social science research, in which the general association of variables to accuracy is determined. Instead, the practicing attorney is supremely interested in whether *the specific eyewitness he or she interviewed today* is accurate. In short, lawyers want reliable tests that separate accurate witnesses from mistaken ones, and often find themselves baffled by social scientists because they refuse to devise these obviously useful instruments.

The social scientist, however, knows well that such tests cannot be created, for decades of research has found that few traits or characteristics mark who will be accurate and who will be mistaken. Research focused on memory has documented that cognitive performance depends more on the particular circumstances of the task than on any general ability or trait on the part of the individaul (Ceci & Bronfenbrenner, 1985; Gardner, 1983; Neisser, 1982). Also, the psychological literature has yet to produce a personological marker that reliably indicates who is most likely to fall prey to suggestive information. Indeed, in this volume Wells et al. have shown that the memory abilities of children of the same age is much more variable than any reliable difference across ages. It is this lack of personological markers that has forced psychologists to turn to analyses of the witness's circumstance (e.g., was the witness under stress, how long did the witness see the perpetrator) to determine whether or not a witness is accurate.

But recent research has opened the possibility of methods for providing the attorney with the "test" that he or she desires. What is evaluated, however, is not the characteristics of the individual, but rather the *nature of the testimony itself*. For example, research described earlier on "reality monitoring" shows that accurate recollections of experienced events differs reliably from memories of imagined incidents (Johnson & Raye, 1981). Namely, externally derived memories (i.e., those of experienced events) have more sensory, spatial, and temporal information than those derived internally (i.e., from imagination).

This sort of finding has implications for eyewitness testimony that has fortunately already received experimental attention. For example, Schooler, Gerhard, & Loftus (1986) showed college students a slide show of a car accident in which one of the vehicles went through a yield sign. Subsequently, some students were given misleading information that indicated that the car had run a stop sign. These subjects in later testimony indicated that the sign had, indeed, been a stop sign. When the accounts of these misled subjects were compared with those given by accurate witnesses, it was found that the testimony differed in reliable ways. Specifically, misled subjects used more hedges when describing the sign and were more likely to describe the cognitive processes that had led them to their particular answer. They were less likely than accurate subject-witnesses to include sensory information in their description. Indeed, the differences between accurate and misled subjects were so dramatic that a separate group of students examining these "eyewitness" reports could distinguish accurate from inaccurate testimony. When they were given information of the characteristics that did reliably distinguish the two groups, they were able to sort examples of accurate and inaccurate testimony rather reliably.

These sort of "tests" could be extended in many ways to testimony proferred by children. Indeed, Raskin and Yuille (this volume) describe such a system, the "statement validity assessment" (SVA), used widely in Germany (see also Undeutsch, 1982), and they recount its usefulness in a recent case. Further work on assessments like these seems most exciting.

"Tests" of this sort may also prove useful in dealing with child witnesses when they are reticent about providing testimony. A case in point is the current work of Peters (1988), who videotaped the faces of children as they attempted to make eyewitness identifications of a thief they had seen earlier in a stressful and confusing incident. These children witnesses proved to be reluctant to identify any of the people they saw in the lineup. However, adults who observed the children's faces on videotape were surprisingly accurate in determining when the child was looking at the correct lineup choice. Indeed, these adults were more accurate in their identification judgments than the children themselves!

It should be noted, however, that the cautions of Bulkley (this volume) about this sort of technology seem appropriate. According to Bulkley, assessments such as SVA should be confined to use in the investigative phase, as an aid to police in determining the nature of the crime and the identity of the criminal. Opinions based on these techniques should not yet be allowed in court. These assessments are still relatively novel, have yet to be replicated widely in studies using rigorous methodological controls, and have been applied in America primarily to lab settings. They thus do not meet the *Frye* standard—that is, general acceptance by the scientific community—that courts consider when allowing such technology in the court. As an aid to investigation, however, the usefulness of such techniques remains intriguing.

Active Interventions to Enhance Accuracy

If this type of research suggests anything, it suggests that psychologists have been too passive in their investigations of eyewitness testimony. That is, instead of standing on the sidelines, looking into the game, trying to estimate the variables that influence accuracy and error, psychologists might profitably jump into the game and become agents that influence accuracy itself. Specifically, psychologists could focus on developing methods that prompt accuracy on the part of witnesses, whether adult or child, or at least prevent the memory of the witness from decaying and being distorted.

The literature on adult eyewitness testimony already contains many examples of interventions that increase the accuracy of eyewitnesses. One such technique is the *cognitive interview* (Geiselman, Fisher, MacKinnon, & Holland, 1985). In this method, interrogators are taught many techniques used in cognitive psychology to enhance memory reports (e.g., recalling the story in reverse). This arsenal of techniques, though requiring only fifteen minutes of training to learn, raises the accuracy and completeness of eyewitness reports as much as the more intrusive and troublesome technique of hypnosis.

Other researchers have focused on enhancing the accuracy of lineup or photospread indentifications. Malpass and Devine (1981), for example, led subject-witnesses through a "guided interview" in which they asked mock witnesses to create a mental picture of a classroom incident happening five months before in which a student destroyed some electronic equipment on the classroom stage. After the guided interview, subjects were much more accurate in their identifications of the student who had instigated the vandalism. Krafka and Penrod (1985), as well, demonstrated that reinstating the context of an incident enhanced the accuracy of witnesses in a ecologically valid domain (i.e., convenience stores).

These sorts of techniques could profitably be extended to the child witness, who might require more basic memory aids to recreate the experiences he or she had confronted. Can the interviewer, for example, teach the child some techniques for better memory?

It should be noted that including attempts to improve eyewitness accuracy does not require a major "retooling" for social science researchers, but rather only an extra step in the research process. Before constructing techniques to enhance eyewitness accuracy, researchers (as they do today) would still be obliged to identify particularly important biases and difficulties relevant to the eyewitness. But the social science researcher would then be impelled not to stop there but to create a technique that "undoes" the difficulty in question. In some sense, the social scientist should be conducting this step anyway, since undoing a phenomenon has always been the hallmark of achieving a theoretical understanding of it.

In addition, attempts to improve accuracy directly would truly be a contribution to the legal system. Social science today has focused, whether passively or actively, on distinguishing inaccurate from accurate witnesses. Helping the legal system make those distinctions would be an important step. But the benefit of those distinctions pales in comparison to the advantages of simply reducing the number of mistaken witnesses providing erroneous testimony in a thousand different police stations and courtrooms.

References

Belsky, J. (1981) Early human experience: A family perspective. *Developmental Psychology, 17*, 3–23.

Bulkely, J.A. (In this volume). The impact of new child witness research on sexual abuse prosecutions.

Ceci, S.J., & Bronfenbrenner, U. (1985). Don't forget to take the cupcakes out of the oven: Prospective memory, strategic time-monitoring, and context. *Child Development, 56*, 152–164.

Ceci, S.J., Ross, D.F., & Toglia, M.P. (1987). Suggestibility of children's memory: Psycholegal implications. *Journal of Experimental Psychology: General, 116*, 38–49.

Ceci, S.J., Toglia, M.P., & Ross, D.F., eds. (1987). *Children's eyewitness testimony*. New York: Springer-Verlag.

Dodd, D.H., & Bradshaw, J.M. (1980). Leading questions and memory: Pragmatic constraints. *Journal of Verbal Learning and Verbal Behavior, 21*, 207–219.

Duggan, L.M., Aubrey, M., Doherty, E., Isquith, P., Levine, M., & Scheiner, J. (In this volume). The credibility of children as witnesses in a simulated child sex abuse trial.

Foley, M.A., & Johnson, M.K. (1985). Confusions between memories for performed and imagined actions: A developmental comparison. *Child Development, 56*, 1145–1155.

Foley, M.A., Johnson, M.K., & Raye, C.L. (1983). Age-related changes in confusions between memories for thoughts and memories for speech. *Child Development, 54*, 51–60.

Gardner, H. (1983). *Frames of mind: The theory of multiple intelligences*. New York: Cambridge University Press.

Geiselman, E.R., Fisher, R.P., MacKinnon, D.P., & Holland, H.L. (1985). Eyewitness memory enhancement in the police interview: Cognitive retrieval mneumonics versus hyponosis. *Journal of Applied Psychology, 70*, 401–420.

Goodman, G.S., Bottoms, B.L., Herscovici, B.B., & Shaver, P. (In this volume). Determinants of the child victim's perceived credibility.

Goodman, G.S., Goldin, J.M., Helgeson, V., Haith, M., & Michelli, J. (1987). When a child takes the stand: Jurors' perceptions of children's eyewitness testimony. *Law and Human Behavior, 11*, 27–40.

Hughes, M., & Grieve, R. (1980). On asking children bizarre questions. In M. Donaldson, R. Grieve, & C. Pratt. eds. *Early childhood development and education*. Oxford: Basil Blackwell, 104–114.

Johnson, M.K., & Raye, C.L. (1981). Reality monitoring. *Psychological Review, 88*, 67–85.

Johnson, M.K., Raye, C.L., Hasher, L., & Chromiak, W. (1979). Are there developmental differences in reality monitoring? *Journal of Experimental Child Psychology*, *27*, 120–128.

Jones, L.M., & Lee, K.G. (1988, August). *Effect of child versus adults witnesses on jurors' verdicts*. Paper presented at the Annual Convention of the American Psychological Association, Atlanta, GA.

Jussim, L., Coleman, L., & Lerch, L. (1987). The nature of stereotypes: A comparison and integration of three theories. *Journal of Personality and Social Psychology*, *52*, 536–546.

King, M.A., & Yuille, J.C. (1987). Suggestibility and the child witness. In S.J. Ceci, M.P. Toglia, & D.F. Ross, eds. *Children's eyewitness testimony*. New York: Springer-Verlag, 24–35.

Krafka, C., & Penrod, S. (1985). Reinstatement of context in a field experiment on eyewitness identification. *Journal of Personality and Social Psychology*, *49*, 58–69.

Leippe, M.R., Brigham, J.C., Cousins, C., & Romanczyk, A. (In this volume). The opinions and practices of criminal attorneys regarding child eyewitnesses: A survey.

Leippe, M.R., & Romaczyk, A. (1987). Children on the witness stand: A communication/persuasion analysis of jurors' reactions to child witnesses. In S.J. Ceci, M.P. Toglia, & D.F. Ross, eds. *Children's eyewitness testimony*. New York: Springer-Verlag, 155–177.

Lindsay, R.C.L., Wells, G.L., & Rumpel, C.M. (1981). Can people detect eyewitness identification accuracy within and across situations? *Journal of Applied Psychology*, *66*, 79–89.

Lipton, J.P. (1977). On the psychology of eyewitness testimony. *Journal of Applied Psychology*, *62*, 90–95.

Loftus, E.F. (1979). *Eyewitness testimony*. Cambridge, MA: Harvard University Press.

Malpass, R.S., & Devine, P.G. (1981). Guided memory in eyewitness identifications. *Journal of Applied Psychology*, *66*, 343–350.

Manis, M., Nelson, T.E., & Shedler, J. (1988). Stereotypes and social judgment: Extremity, assimilation and contrast. *Journal of Personality and Social Psychology*, *55*, 28–36.

Neisser, U. (1982). *Remembering in natural context*. San Francisco: W.H. Freeman.

Nigro, G.N., & Buckley, M.A. (In this volume). When juries "hear" children testify: The effects of eyewitness age and speech style on jurors' perceptions of testimony.

Peters, D.P. (1988, August). *Influence of stress and arousal on the child witness*. Paper presented at the Annual Convention of the American Psychological Association, Atlanta, GA.

Piaget, J., & Inhelder, B. (1956). *The child's conception of space*. London: Routlege & Kegan Paul.

Raskin, D.C., & Yuille, J.C. (In this volume). Problems in evaluating interviews of children in sexual abuse cases.

Ross, D.L., Dunning, D., Toglia, M.P., & Ceci, S.J. (In this volume). Age stereotypes, communication modality, and mock jurors' perceptions of the child witness.

Saywitz, K.J. (1987). Children's testimony: Age-related patterns of memory errors. In S.J. Ceci, M.P. Toglia, & D.F. Ross, eds. *Children's eyewitness testimony*. New York: Springer-Verlag, 36–52.

Saywitz, K.J. (In this volume). Children's conceptions of the legal system: Court is a place to play basketball.

Schooler, J.W., Gerhard, D., & Loftus, E.F. (1986). Qualities of the unreal. *Journal of Experimental Psychology: Learning, Memory and Cognition, 12*, 141–181.

Schuman, J., & Presser, S. (1981). *Questions and answers in attitude surveys: Experiments in question form, wording, and context.* New York: Academic Press.

Smith, V.L., & Ellsworth, P.C. (1987). The social psychology of eyewitness testimony: Misleading questions and communicator expertise. *Journal of Applied Psychology, 72*, 294–300.

Taylor, M. (1988). Conceptual perspective taking: Children's ability to distinguish what they know from what they see. *Child Development, 59*, 703–718.

Tapp, J.L., & Kohlberg, L. (1971). Developing senses of law and legal justice. *Journal of Social Issues, 27*, 65–91.

Undeutsch, U. (1982). Statement Validity Assessment. In A. Trankell, ed. *Reconstructing the past: The role of psychologists in criminal trials.* Stockholm: Norstedt & Soners, 27–56.

Vidmar, N., & Laird, N.M. (1983). Adversary social roles: Their effects on witneses' communication of evidence and the assessments of adjudicators. *Journal of Personality and Social Psychology, 44*, 888–898.

Warren-Leubecker, A., Tate, C.S., Hinton, I.D., Ozbek, I.N. (In this volume). What do children know about the legal system and when do they know it? First steps down a less-traveled path in child witness research.

Wells, G.L., Lindsay, R.C.L., & Ferguson, T.J. (1979). Accuracy, confidence, and juror perceptions in eyewitness identifications. *Journal of Applied Psychology, 64*, 440–448.

Wells, G.L., & Loftus, E.F., eds. (1984). *Eyewitness testimony: Psychological perspectives.* New York: Cambridge University Press.

Wells, G.L., Turtle, J.W., & Luus, C.A. (In volume). The perceived credibility of child eyewitnesses: What happens when they use their own words?

Zaragoza, M.S. (1987). Memory, suggestibility, and eyewitness testimony in children and adults. In S.J. Ceci, M.P. Toglia, & D.F. Ross, eds. *Children's eyewitness testimony*. New York: Springer-Verlag, 53–78.

Zibach, J.I. (1968). Family development. In J. Marmor, ed. *Modern psychoanalysis*. New York: Basic Books.

Author Index

Subject Index